Darren Goodsir has been a police his fifteen years in the media. He advisor to the NSW commissione ended, purely by chance, only m the Wood Royal Commission. His first book, *Line of Fire*, formed the basis of 'Blue Murder', the acclaimed ABC TV mini-series on the Sydney underworld wars in the 1980s. Darren Goodsir is now a journalist with the *Sydney Morning Herald*.

DEATH at BONDI

Cops, cocaine, corruption and the killing of Roni Levi

Darren Goodsir

MACMILLAN
Pan Macmillan Australia

First published 2001 in Macmillan by Pan Macmillan Australia Pty Limited
St Martins Tower, 31 Market Street, Sydney

National Library of Australia
Cataloguing-in-Publication Data:

Goodsir, Darren.
Death at Bondi.

ISBN 0 7329 1091 9.

1. Levi, Roni, 1964–1997. 2. Podesta, Rodney.
3. Dilorenzo, Tony. 4. Police shootings – New South Wales – Bondi Beach.
5. Police corruption – New South Wales. 6. Police in mass media. I. Title.

363.232

Typeset in 12/15.5 pt Galliard by Post Pre-press Group
Printed in Australia by McPherson's Printing Group
Text design by Deborah Parry Graphics

For Louise, my soul mate and
companion

'The trigger gave, I felt the underside of the polished butt and it was there, in that sharp but deafening noise, that it all started. I shook off the sweat and the sun. I realised that I'd destroyed the balance of the day and the perfect silence of the beach where I'd been happy. And I fired four more times at a lifeless body and the bullets sank in without leaving a mark. And it was like giving four sharp knocks at the door of unhappiness.'

Albert Camus, *The Outsider* (quote used by the Newcastle Legal Centre in the foreword to its submission to the Police Integrity Commission, *A Very Public Death*, in 1998, for public hearings on the circumstances surrounding the police killing of Roni Levi on Bondi Beach)

CONTENTS

ACKNOWLEDGMENTS

This book, like all of my endeavours, would not have been possible without the support of my wife Louise. For many tiring months, she juggled the demands of a young family and her own career with my need for isolation. Her love sustained me during this difficult journey. Many other individuals, some of whom wish to remain anonymous, assisted in the preparation of this manuscript: police, lawyers, Internal Affairs operatives, journalists and drug users. But it was a barman, Mark, a cocaine user, whose revelatory letter, and subsequent discussions, encouraged me to gaze into the life and times of the Bondi shooters.

Thanks are also due, in no particular order, to Tim Sage and Julie Wynn at the Police Integrity Commission (PIC), for allowing me access to public exhibits tendered during their Saigon hearings. It is significant that the PIC was, of course, unable to supply a considerable quantity of confidential exhibits – or reveal the names of some of their witnesses; for legal reasons, the full picture may never be shown. During my self-imposed exile in the garden shed, Nick Leys and Clare Stanford attended to important housekeeping matters at crucial times, allowing my fingers to stay at the keyboard. I would like to thank Melinda Dundas, the widow of the man at the centre of this story, Roni Levi, for agreeing to the release of material from her solicitor, John Boersig; intellectual property that her barrister, Robert Cavanagh, had helped compile. I am grateful to the photographers at Fairfax who have allowed their work to be used – and to Daniel Adams, in particular, who helped compile the images. However, my greatest supporter was Associate Professor Ray Watterson, from the University of Newcastle Legal Centre. Simply put, without his encouragement and extraordinary devotion to detail, this book would never have been written.

CAST OF CHARACTERS

The victim

Roni Levi

The shooters

Senior Constable Anthony Dilorenzo
Constable Rodney Podesta

The other police officers on the beach

Constable Christopher Goodman
Senior Constable John Jones
Senior Constable Grant Seddon
Constable Geoffrey Smith

The witnesses

Karen Allison jogger on the beach
Deborah Bogle watches the shooting through
binoculars from her apartment opposite the beach
Peter Bourke on the promenade
Jean Pierre Bratanoff-Firgoff photographer who
captures shooting
Roger Cubitt on the promenade

Pascal Czerwenka newspaper deliverer who sees Levi at his flat before he raced to the beach

John Durack, SC witness to the shooting

Leo Hamlin council cleaner who witnesses the shooting

Lani Jensen on his way to work, sees Levi

David Michael writes letter to the police commissioner, tendered in evidence at the coronial inquest, deploring the shooting

Arnold Payment sees Levi and Brunner racing through streets of Bondi

Craig Payne ambulance paramedic at the beach

Lieutenant Commander Noel Pont witnesses Brunner trying to persuade Levi to drop the knife

Gregory Sikkens ambulance paramedic at the beach

Danny Weidler newspaper journalist who sees lead-up to shooting

The coronial investigation team

Deputy Coroner John Abernethy

Detective Robert Allison observer in interview with Dilorenzo

Detective Comans observer in interview with Podesta

David Cowan independent counsel assisting the coroner; in charge of directing police investigation on behalf of coroner

Detective Senior Constable Michael Fitzgerald policeman second in charge of Levi shooting investigation; conducts interview with Podesta

Coroner Derrick Hand

Detective Senior Sergeant Robert McDougall policeman in charge of Levi shooting investigation; conducts interview with Dilorenzo

Detective Sergeant Adam Purcell Bondi officer drafted in to assist in shooting investigation

Stuart Robinson instructing solicitor to Cowan

Detective Senior Constable Michael Sinadinovic seconded by McDougall on eve of inquest to chase leads and find witnesses

Detective Senior Constable Murray Wilson Bondi officer drafted in to assist in shooting investigation

The Police Integrity Commission

Ernest (Tim) Sage assistant commissioner in charge of operations and investigations

Judge Paul Urquhart, QC commissioner who presides over all three hearings in Operation Saigon

The director of public prosecutions

Nicholas Cowdery, QC declines to prosecute Podesta and Dilorenzo over the killing after the police case was referred to him by the coroner

Savva Persinidis solicitor appointed to manage the Levi case

The New South Wales Police Force

Chief Inspector Richard Baker commander of Bondi police station at time of shooting

Constable Paul Begbie member of the Living Dangerously Club

Constable Patrick Brown member of the Living Dangerously Club

Senior Constable Christian Bruce police helicopter surveillance officer and friend of Podesta

Senior Constable Michael Cooper Bondi station education officer

Sergeant Terry Dalton police negotiator called to attend beach

Constable Peter Forsyth officer stabbed to death in Ultimo during Levi coronial inquest

Senior Constable Mark Hargraves interviewed by journalist about Levi's behaviour on beach

Deputy Commissioner Jeffrey Jarratt comments on Levi shooting in Ryan's absence on holidays

Inspector John Kent duty operations inspector on day of the shooting

Superintendent Robert May commander of Bondi police station after shooting

Constable Brian Neville officer with Forsyth on night of stabbing

Senior Constable Dave Rose police media officer who facilitates Baker's press conference

Commissioner Peter Ryan

Probationary Constable Jason Semple wounded by knife during fatal attack on Forsyth

Constable Ted Shea member of the Living Dangerously Club

Assistant Commissioner Clive Small endorses official complaint over Internal Affairs' handling of Levi case

Sergeant Graham Taylor sets up command post at Bondi promenade and watches Levi stand-off

Chief Superintendent Robert Waites eastern suburbs district commander

Internal Affairs

Assistant Commissioner Malcolm Brammer commander in charge of Levi investigation

Detective Inspector Peter Fitzpatrick reviewing officer sent to ensure police officers adhere to Commissioner's

Instructions in investigation into shooting

Detective Inspector Paul Jones officer investigating claims Podesta is involved in drug use and supply

Detective Sergeant Christopher Keen runs several operations targeting Podesta

Inspector Robert Martin legal officer who gives counsel to Detectives Jones and Keen at crucial times in Levi investigation

Chief Inspector Bernard McSorley appointed by Brammer as liaison with shooting investigation

Detective Senior Constable David Minarik leads investigation targeting Dilorenzo

Gary Richmond second-in-charge of Levi investigation

Detective Senior Constable Duncan Tchakalian conducts interviews at Soho Bar nightclub

Detective Sergeant Wayne Thorn interviews informants regarding behaviour of Dilorenzo and Podesta prior to shooting

The Newcastle Legal Centre

John Boersig solicitor appointed by Melinda Dundas to represent her at coronial inquest

Robert Cavanagh barrister given leave to appear for Melinda Dundas at coronial inquest

Associate Professor Ray Watterson leads the research, conducted by law students, into the police investigation of Levi's shooting

The lawyers

Patrick Barrett counsel assisting PIC at first hearing in Operation Saigon

'Jock' Dailly barrister representing Bondi shooters at coronial inquest

Ken Horler, QC barrister representing Levi family at coronial inquest

Peter Johnson, SC counsel assisting PIC in second and third hearings in Operation Saigon

Kenneth Madden solicitor representing Podesta and Dilorenzo at coronial inquest and at all three hearings in Operation Saigon

Michael Marx solicitor who gives counsel to Melinda Dundas and the Levi family

Chester Porter, QC barrister representing Podesta in cocaine supply charge in 1999

Alison Stenmark counsel representing police commissioner at all three hearings in Operation Saigon

Greg Willis in-house solicitor representing police at coronial inquest

The Informants

Amanda codenamed informant of Internal Affairs who says a man, Robert, was with shooters late in the night before the shooting

Robert Bromwich barrister who writes up statement for coroner after hearing rumour regarding behaviour of Podesta and Dilorenzo on night before shooting

Murray Dowling (not his real name) rings police customer assistance line in middle of inquest with information about behaviour of shooters before Levi killing

Simon Duncan (not his real name) security guard at Soho Bar nightclub

Katrina Rafferty hairdresser who tells Bromwich about rumours

Samantha codenamed informant who claims she was Podesta's girlfriend before the shooting

Susan police administrative officer who supplies hearsay information about behaviour of shooters before Levi killing

Levi's friends and family

Dr Caroline Atlani observes Levi at dinner at Hagege and Dalton's home

Dr Freddy Atlani escorts Levi to St Vincent's Hospital

Stefan Bialoguski friend of Levi; gathers information on case; writes newspaper article on legal implications

Warren Brunner Levi's flatmate

Fiona Christopher sister of Melinda Dundas

Jane Cole friend of Melinda Dundas

Tina Dalton notices Levi speaking strangely at coffee shop on morning before the shooting

Melinda Dundas Levi's wife

Daniel Hagege hosts dinner at which Levi is present on night before shooting

Ilan Levi Levi's brother

Rebecca Levi Levi's mother

Richard Levi Levi's father

The shooters' friends and family

Angelo 'Chill' Astudillo friend of Dilorenzo

Annabelle Dilorenzo Dilorenzo's wife

David Hitchens (not his real name) schoolfriend of Podesta

Kylie Kummings (not her real name) girlfriend of Podesta

John Lorenzo Dilorenzo's brother

Mark Lorenzo Dilorenzo's brother

Charmaine Podesta Podesta's mother

The Liberty Lunch crowd

Damien Bell one of the restaurant managers

Joanne Diamond (not her real name) Langton's girlfriend

Stanley Dowse becomes co-owner of restaurant

Susan Dowse co-owner with husband Stan

Craig Field manager of Sejuiced cafe at Bondi

Robert Gould (not his real name) restaurant regular and drug user

Allan Graney (not his real name) one of the restaurant's barmen

Easton Barrington 'TC' James night manager of restaurant

Stephen Langton (not his real name) one of the restaurant's managers

David Lucas owner of Sejuiced cafe at Bronte after the shooting

Kieran O'Connor original owner of the Liberty Lunch and Sydney property developer; close friend of Bondi shooters

Ronald Quin sees Podesta on night before shooting; first person Podesta calls after killing Levi

Peter Richardson (not his real name) one of the Liberty Lunch's barmen

Renee Robertshaw waitress at restaurant and Quin's girlfriend

Andrew Ruwald owner of Sejuiced cafe at Bondi; sells Bronte premises to Lucas in days after shooting

Terry Voto Quin's flatmate

The drugs

Jim Bond drug user

Lenin Lambert TC's supplier

Zac MacKenzie (not his real name) drug supplier from Marrickville; close friend of Podesta

Madison Mander (not her real name) close friend of Podesta

Mike Morrison (not his real name) grew up in surfing crowd at Bondi Beach with Podesta

Graeme Rooney (not his real name) MacKenzie's flatmate and drug user

Lisa Troost Lambert's girlfriend

Others

Joachim Blieszis supplies Levi with counterfeit goods for sale

Dr Allan Cala forensic pathologist who conducts post-mortem on Levi

John Carty father of murdered policeman; photographed with shooters at time of inquest

Magistrate Hugh Dillon hears cocaine charges laid against Podesta

David Mutton police psychologist who counsels Podesta, Dilorenzo and the police officers on the beach after the shooting

Magistrate Gillian Orchiston hears dangerous driving charge laid against Dilorenzo

INTRODUCTION

On 15 May 1997, a royal commissioner, Justice James Wood, QC, made public his six-volume report on a three-year investigation into the NSW Police Service. In conclusive terms, and with chilling insight, he declared Australia's oldest and most controversial constabulary to be rotten to the core, riddled with corruption and in need of complete overhaul.

Almost lost in the thousands of paragraphs and footnotes, Justice Wood proposed that police shootings be independently investigated; and he also gave three pages over to deplore the emerging trend of young policemen partying at nightclubs, and using and selling drugs. Six officers from the police station at Bondi, in Sydney's eastern suburbs, were adversely mentioned. On 26 May, the beachside station's commander reported secretly to his superiors that another of his constables, Rodney Podesta, was probably also into drugs. Investigators at Internal Affairs were told that Podesta should be put under surveillance because he was spending too much time at a Bondi Beach restaurant, the Liberty Lunch, a place linked to the cocaine trade. The Podesta investigation, code-named Borden, was immediately ranked alongside another Internal Affairs drugs inquiry, Operation Addlestone. The latter dealt with a senior constable from the same station – Anthony Dilorenzo.

On Saturday, 28 June 1997, at 7.31 a.m., Podesta and Dilorenzo gunned down a bedraggled Frenchman, Roni Levi, in the most dramatic of circumstances – in front of scores of horrified onlookers on Bondi Beach. Levi had been brandishing a kitchen knife when three shots barrelled into his ribs and chest, sending him down onto the cold morning sand. One last bullet, curiously, went into his back, tearing into his perineum, between his scrotum and anus. The shooting stopped the city. Because the killing had been captured by a freelance photographer and witnessed at arguably Australia's most famous location, it caused instant alarm from a distrustful community still reeling from the shock of the royal commission's findings. The shooting, frame by frame, was front-page news, broadcasted throughout the world. There was a yearning for answers: why hadn't Levi been shot in the leg? or had sand thrown in his face? or simply been covered by a net? The seriousness of the public spectacle, and its unfortunate timing so soon after Justice Wood's warnings, demanded the most searing, objective and well-resourced police inquiry.

This book seeks not so much to question whether Podesta and Dilorenzo were right to have killed Levi – the coroner stopped the inquest after finding there was a prima facie case against the shooters, and the director of public prosecutions (DPP), after studying the police force's case, said that a jury, properly instructed, would not be able to reach a conclusion beyond reasonable doubt. Rather, I have concentrated on the police reaction to the killing, and the botched response to allegations that the Bondi shooters were involved in drugs. The book adheres to the argument that a more thorough and impartial investigation of the shooting, and the shooters, could and should have been undertaken – and that a more detailed and accurate brief of evidence could have been assembled. This story allows a diverse cast of larger-than-life Bondi characters – policemen, prostitutes, drug dealers, security guards and surfers – to describe in their own words the heady months leading up to the shooting, and the panic-filled aftermath when rumours swept the promenade at Bondi. It is a world of drugs and alcohol and notorious nightclubs, in which Podesta and Dilorenzo freely mixed. Before and after the killing.

This task was made easier by the fact that so much about the Levi saga has been placed on the public record. More than 60 witnesses were either interviewed by or gave statements to the police at the time of the death. Scores of people also gave testimony under oath. The shooting was the subject of a four-week coronial inquest. The Police Integrity Commission held three separate hearings over eighteen months into various aspects of the Levi case, producing witnesses and evidence to explore whether the shooters were under the influence of drugs at the time they discharged their revolvers. All of this material has been used in this manuscript. I have also drawn on personal interviews as well as a wealth of other previously unreleased material from classified Internal Affairs files – including secret telephone conversations and exchanges recorded on bugs hidden in the homes of drug suppliers.

Of course, Dilorenzo and Podesta have denied being high at the time of the shooting. Dilorenzo was sacked from the NSW Police Service in June 1999 for failing to properly explain why he spent so much time with known drug dealers; however, despite the disgrace over his dismissal, he has steadfastly denied using prohibited drugs. Podesta resigned from the force in March 1998, days after the coronial inquest, when the Levi case was sent to the DPP for consideration on murder charges. He later pleaded guilty to attempting to supply cocaine, and was sentenced to four months of periodic detention in December 1999. Podesta insisted, however, that he snorted cocaine and took ecstasy only *after* the Levi shooting. Both men, through their legal counsel, declined to be interviewed or to assist in the preparation of the manuscript for this book. The narrative therefore seeks to record fairly their versions, given repeatedly under oath. Yet against this backdrop there is evidence from friends and relatives of Podesta and Dilorenzo that paints a completely different story.

Even after so many official inquiries and such apparently detailed examination, many questions have not been sufficiently answered, and some may never be addressed. Vital opportunities have thus been lost. One thing is abundantly clear though: the Levi case was mishandled from the start. What should have been an example of investigative excellence – coming so soon after the tabling of the royal commission report, and with public expectations so high – turned out to be a debacle.

The catalogue of calamities started on the beach, where an incomplete forensic examination was conducted. The crime-scene examiner determined that the shooters had been 5.2 metres away from Levi when the firing started – outside the three-metre zone of danger referred to by police instructors. But this crucial information was relegated to the officer's notebook, and not included in his statement to the coroner. Workmates of the Bondi shooters, contrary to specific orders, were brought in to work on the police inquiry, taking statements in the moments after the killing. Back at the station, the two traumatised officers were not segregated, as required to ensure their versions would not be tainted. Moreover, Podesta and Dilorenzo were allowed to telephone friends and family, Podesta using his mobile phone to call several of his drug-using friends and nightclub associates. (A convicted heroin dealer even walked in to talk to him before Podesta had been formally interviewed.)

And there were other travesties. The Bondi commander, despite only a month earlier having nominated Podesta as a suspected drug user and seller, somehow neglected to inform detectives of his concerns; as a result neither officer was obliged to give a urine sample. Worse still, the same commander gave a crafted and incredibly detailed account of the shooting at a media conference – thus giving credence and life to an officially sanctioned version of the tragedy – hours before the shooters had even been interviewed.

The drugs inquiries were also wrecked affairs, almost lampoonable. So serious were the claims that Podesta and Dilorenzo were partying at the Liberty Lunch on the dawn of the shooting that Internal Affairs, with the blessing of the Police Integrity Commission, organised a secret meeting with the coroner to work out how the inquiry should be conducted. Somehow, despite two police teams being formed to investigate the matter, each squad left the meeting thinking *the other* was chasing the suspects and witnesses. The inquiry therefore stalled for five long months, with next to nothing being done. During this time Podesta was out snorting and supplying cocaine and popping pills, and Dilorenzo, with the aid of a publicist brother, was working the media. Both officers were on stress leave.

Throughout the investigation, lawyers acting for Melinda Dundas, the estranged wife of Roni Levi, were fastidiously filing away evidence and documents on the growing debacle. In a unique learning experiment, lecturers at the University of Newcastle Legal Centre worked with their students to help Dundas prepare for the coronial inquest. The students were learning the law by doing the law, not just by reading about it. After raking through statements and interviews, the self-styled crusaders had chronicled what they believed to be massive faults in the police case (in fact, their exposé would eventually lead to major changes in the law). Although the law students sensed that the police investigation was a flawed affair, they could scarcely have imagined the true extent of the cock-ups. Police intelligence about the Bondi shooters disappeared, often without a trace. During the coronial inquest, a man left his name and number with a police customer assistance operator, saying a friend of his had seen the shooters taking drugs just before the killing – but this information, despite being logged and recorded, was misplaced. By the time it was discovered, some fifteen months later, the witness had died.

There are countless more examples of chronic mishandling, so many that conspiracy theorists could be excused for concluding that there was an orchestrated operation to bury the truth. Personally, I do not take such a disturbing view, however tempting – because the evidence has never been that conclusive. The continual bungling in the Levi affair was inexcusable, however. The investigation into the shooting on Bondi Beach and the claims surrounding illicit drug use should have been cutting-edge investigative operations. Instead, the police effort was a disgrace, a further blemish on the already deeply stained pages in the history of New South Wales policing.

Sydney, April 2001

ONE
THE LIBERTY LUNCH

'It was a general thing that
people went there regardless. You
knew that if you went there,
someone would be there.'
Robert Gould (not his real name),
referring to the Liberty Lunch cafe and restaurant,
Police Integrity Commission, Operation Saigon,
3 November 1999

Bondi Beach is an exhilarating spot, a place of soaring con-
trasts, of history and celebrity, excitement and aspiration. It is
an Australian institution and, due in no small part to the
2000 Sydney Olympics and the beach volleyball, it now
assumes something close to international icon status. It is a
must-see for tourists and, for the city's trend-conscious glit-
terati, it is a must to be seen at. It is an almighty location,
where so many elements of Australia are bundled up
together, where so much about the national identity and
psyche can immediately be appreciated.

Easily Bondi's most famous landmark, among many
natural and man-made wonders, is the brilliant stretch of
sand. It is laid out like a pure blond carpet between two
turret-like headlands, presenting a spectacle of waves and
wind and golden crystals. The rocky outcrop, Ben Buckler,
juts out at one end of the beach; the concrete sea pool and

clubhouse for the Bondi Icebergs (a cult-like club of swimmers, young and old, who confront the ocean daily no matter what the conditions) is the noticeable feature at the southern end. The beachfront spans almost two kilometres, all glorious, glittering sand. Even by Sydney's high standards – Whale, Narrabeen, Bronte and Cronulla – Bondi is a great beach.

Added to this, it is backed by a stellar pedestrian promenade, Campbell Parade. Here, restaurants, bars, juice stalls, ice-creameries, delicatessens and every shop imaginable provide sustenance and succour to the thousands of visitors who religiously pound its pavement. Everyone is eager for experience, a passing sensation.

And it is here along Campbell Parade that the locals, a rich assortment of characters and rogues, rub shoulders. Almost all slices of life are represented – all preened, styled and on display. Indeed, it would be difficult to find a more eclectic scramble of society than that at Bondi Beach. There are the yuppies, bronzed surfers, film and music stars, millionaires, well-heeled professionals, backpackers and blue-collar workers. And there are the gossipers. And the top-shelf celebrities, the 'A list', who guarantee valuable social-page column inches: Russell Crowe cruising in his latest car; Jason Donovan swimming with his baby; Claire Danes riding a scooter. Even James Packer, the son of Australia's wealthiest man, and his glamorous wife, Jodie – a former swimsuit model – call the beach their home.

Unsurprisingly, paparazzi photographers snap their best candid shots here, for the beach and its lively surrounds throw up a veritable visual feast. Bondi Beach enlivens the senses and there is no better place in Sydney to dine, to gaze out at the surf and pry on the habits of the rich and famous . . . and infamous.

Although spoiled for choice, the Liberty Lunch cafe

and restaurant was a coveted favourite. It was *the* place. If it was cool to be seen at Bondi Beach, it was cooler to be seen at the Liberty. Constantly countering the fickle fads of Sydney diners, by the start of 1997, after a mere three years on the block, the Liberty Lunch had acquired the sort of reputation that advertising cannot buy. There were, of course, other 'name' eating sites on the sunrise strip, and some more further down at Bronte. Among these establishments were the Beachwood, just next door to the Liberty Lunch; the Lamrock Cafe, at 76 Campbell Parade; and the hip juice bar, Sejuiced, at 487 Bronte Road. But the Liberty was spoken of in more excited tones. This was a place to be noticed, a place with the right people, the right atmosphere.

The Liberty occupied the ground-floor section of a larger complex at 102 Campbell Parade. There was a handy office upstairs, and beyond it, a clutch of modern home units, some with breathtaking views. Inside the club, a trendily decorated and dimly lit hang-out, were about 30 tables and, at the time, due to New South Wales's restrictive liquor laws, customers were obliged to order something to eat before being able to buy a drink. Refreshments were served from the bar closer to the rear, near the toilets. There was good food, outdoor dining, great cocktails and loud, groovy dance music. It was a place that 'attracted energetic people, people who had a lust for life'.[1] It became accepted that if you went to the Liberty Lunch, 'someone would be there. No-one really ever had any arrangements for that . . . people just went there regardless.'[2]

The Liberty was owned by a highly successful Sydney property developer named Kieran Brian O'Connor. It was managed by Easton Barrington James, a big, tall black man and an imposing and beguiling presence who oozed a cocky charisma. James kept the peace and he always had the right line, skills he had learned from years of front-door security at Jacksons on George, a 24-hour liquor barn near The Rocks, a place used to scuffles. Known to his effusive friends as TC, the rorting but lovable cartoon street cat, James ruled the Liberty Lunch with O'Connor's absolute trust and carried out the master's instructions to the letter. The two men were close.

At first, the operators of the Beachwood also ran the Liberty Lunch, as a next-door affiliate. O'Connor eventually took over the business – but not without heartache.

Things got messy early on between O'Connor and the Beachwood operators. 'We had to get administrators in. We were the major creditor. We were owed about half a million dollars; and had not received one bit of rent.'³ The situation was dire. TC became very familiar with O'Connor's tensions, especially when the indebted parties sent in a couple of burly blokes to 'encourage' O'Connor to back off. TC was one of the few who supported him. 'From that day onwards,' O'Connor would later say, 'he became a loyal friend . . . as close as a brother could be.'⁴ They ate out and drank together, went to the football and fished.

Three others helped TC to build the Liberty's reputation as the place to go. Stephen Langton (not his real name) worked as another of the managers, and Allan Graney and Peter Richardson (not their real names) poured drinks and took orders at a normally crowded and gregarious bar. This quartet – TC, Langton, Graney and Richardson – cultivated much of the place's infectious mood.

Graney was popular with the happy crowd because, like many of the Liberty's customers at the time, he enjoyed using cocaine. Even while mixing drinks and trying to work, Graney could see no problem with 'doing a line' or two.⁵

When the urge came and the opportunity arose, he would race from the bar to the toilet – where he'd busily crush up the white powder before sniffing it through a rolled-up paper note or straw. The drugs usually came from customers who apparently thought he was a friendly barman in need of a lift.[6] And he wasn't alone: at any time, day or night, Graney could have glanced over the partition of the toilet cubicle he so often occupied, and sighted a familiar face . . . doing a line.

Cocaine was everywhere at the Liberty Lunch, and for some of the masses, this was the 'something else' that was driving them in. It could be found in women's purses and men's wallets. It was behind and in front of the bar, and in pockets or tucked into underwear. There was no hiding from it. A lot of customers presumed that, because 'everyone' used cocaine at the Liberty, it was fine to join in.[7] One of the waitresses reported hearing snorting in the cubicles when she had gone to the toilet,[8] and some people felt so blasé, they were even snorting it off the tables. Cocaine made its users feel incredibly emboldened. Ecstasy, the so-called 'hug drug', was also popular in the back rows. It was a more discreet drug to consume – you didn't have to pull out a straw.

By January 1997, O'Connor and TC, fuelled by the street talk that cocaine was on offer at their place, were the talk of the town. The Liberty's reputation had swelled right under their noses – literally. O'Connor knew about the drugs,[9] as did TC and the rest of his managers.[10] But it was basically considered too hard a problem to solve, so overwhelming was its popularity. Besides, O'Connor didn't want his staff searching customers or barging into toilet cubicles – 'I don't believe it's . . . legal . . . to do that'.[11]

So the crowds kept coming. TC and O'Connor had one of the best cafe/restaurants in the eastern suburbs. It had become an up-market, trendy site for young money and beautiful people. It had also been transformed by fate into a drug haven, right in the middle of the strip.

Rewarded for its service and popularity, the Liberty Lunch boasted many regulars. In addition, the staff had some very special guests, top-rate customers who had access to a secret bar tab and free or discounted drinks. These customers received preferential treatment at the bar when it was particularly busy, and had access to a key to the office upstairs for 'more VIP-style treatment'.[12] The VIPs at O'Connor's restaurant could stay back after closing time with staff and their families, joining in in hip unofficial parties where they could 'stay in the back bar and drink until morning'.[13] These parties often brought complaints, and the Liberty's workers soon became accustomed to visits from Bondi police officers. One of them, Senior Constable Anthony Stephen Dilorenzo, fielded frequent noise complaints from the residents in the units above the club – 'We were there probably every Thursday, Friday, Saturday night trying to get the music turned down.'[14] Rather than fend off the invidious police attention, O'Connor actively encouraged it – he *loved* having them in his place. It gave the establishment a nice feel, a legitimacy. In view of the club's reputation for cocaine use, O'Connor thought that the presence of local police officers was good for business.[15]

The police station at Bondi was a nondescript, haphazardly extended bungalow, in Wairoa Avenue, about a thousand metres from the surf, in the relative backblocks. It was close enough to the action on the main drag but as far away as to be anonymously suburban. The location meant few off-the-street enquiries. Still, the place was always busy – sun, surfing and alcohol always seem to attract conflict and colour.

Like most cop shops, the station had long outgrown

its usefulness, with far too many officers crammed into its poky offices and corridors. In 1997, a big year of corporate rebuilding for the NSW Police Service, the rank and file officers at Bondi were feeling about as drab as their accommodation. Almost overnight, Justice Wood's searing royal commission had turned a previously trusting community attitude into widespread suspicion. The Bondi officers shared the depression of their 13 000 colleagues throughout the state, and the heat they were copping on the streets.

The guys and girls in blue at Bondi felt a special kind of taint, however: they were part of a *druggies'* station, a place that had been singled out and exposed by the royal commission. In the past year the Bondi cops had watched as six of their workmates confessed to using and dealing in a cocktail of prohibited substances: marijuana, cocaine, ecstasy, amphetamines and steroids. Some of the testimonies (given by codenamed police witnesses from the eastern suburbs) described off-duty coppers, in outrageous party-mode, congregating at fancy nightclubs and gyrating to techno-beats under the influence of synthetic drugs and too much alcohol. This was a new police culture, far removed from the after-five beer swilling at hotels that had been favoured by their older colleagues. Law enforcers were now wantonly breaking the law.

The Bondi commander, Chief Inspector Richard (Dick) Raymond Baker, had to deal with the royal commission revelations, and the suspicion and wild rumours that flooded his ranks. He was a firm enough, affable leader, doing his best to mend a fraught and fractured gang. He knew all too well that 'morale was very low' at the station, and that 'the staff were divided and generally it was in disarray to a high level.'[16] His superiors, including the new British police commissioner, Peter James Ryan, required of him absolute vigilance, however.

Baker's first test came with the Liberty Lunch.

According to the education officer at Bondi, Senior Constable Michael Cooper, it gradually became 'common knowledge' that some officers went to the Liberty after knocking off for the day.[17] Such frequent socialising presented obvious and awkward problems for Baker: as well as the issue of noise complaints from angry tenants there were 'innuendoes in relation to . . . illegal trading hours [and] drug activity'.[18] It was apparent to Baker and others in the force that by attending a venue that breached its licensing laws, Bondi police officers were giving the place 'tacit approval'.[19] The close contact gave a perception that the local coppers were in the Liberty's back pocket and on the take. And that couldn't last.

Constable Rodney Joseph Walter Podesta was in the position of being the most easily tempted by this potential for corruption, and was probably the restaurant's most prominent police guest.[20] In fact, he was so well regarded by O'Connor and his managers that he was on the restaurant's VIP list, one of only half-a-dozen privileged clients. Podesta had met TC while studying to be a policeman;[21] while O'Connor first met the rookie cop sometime in January 1997, when the Liquor Licensing Tribunal became involved over noise complaints from a tenant above the club at 102 Campbell Parade.[22] Stephen Langton bumped into him in late 1996. For a policeman, he seemed to mix rather easily with the yuppy coke-snorting set.

Podesta grew up in Bondi Beach, surfing and adventuring. As a teenager, he helped his father at the Piccolo Bar in Kings Cross, the city's red-light district. The Piccolo was a drug-dealing den, the place where you could score virtually anything, anytime. Podesta and his father had tried everything to prevent the dealing and had had plenty of contact with the police as a result: 'If anything was obvious, then the police were called, but I didn't see anything like that myself.'[23]

While still at school, Podesta mixed with the boisterous beach and board-short crowd on the promenade at Bondi. One of his better mates was one Mike Morrison (not his real name), and it is known that the pair liked to smoke marijuana.[24] Podesta's other major twenty-something acquaintance was Madison Mander (not her real name). They were soul mates. She first noticed Podesta – handsome, aged 23 and carefree – when she worked at the Cauldron nightclub in Darlinghurst. They would party together and, she claims, consume ecstasy and cocaine.

When Podesta decided in 1995 that he wanted to join the police – motivated by the experiences of his uncle, Inspector Harley Donahue, who had served the force for nearly 30 years – his friends were aghast, perplexed by this apparently out-of-character decision. Morrison counselled him on his loose attitudes and lifestyle, and told him he would need to completely turn himself around.[25] Mander also gave Podesta a lecture on his responsibilities, surprised by his choice of vocation – although Podesta himself also initially questioned the wisdom of his decision. Mander remembered him saying that he didn't want to take drugs anymore and that by joining the police force, he'd be able to do good and help people instead: 'I sort of hoped it would straighten him out a little bit, I think, more than anything. He needed a kick up the arse and I thought that might be it for him . . . I thought it might mellow him out a bit.'[26]

In May 1995 Podesta entered the Police Academy, the breeding ground for Australia's oldest and most notorious police organisation, at its sprawling campus at Goulburn, 200 kilometres south-west of Sydney. One year later, he was one of them, with all the accoutrements: the uniform, the gun, the

powers of stop, search and arrest, the discretion not to arrest
and the huge responsibilities that follow the taking of the oath
of office.

At first he was posted to Rose Bay, the extraordinarily wealthy harbourside enclave in Sydney's east but six
months later, still raw and inexperienced, Podesta was back at
the beach on a secondment. Back at Bondi, where he believed
he belonged. It gave him the chance to police the same
people he had grown up with, with whom he had surfed and
laughed and played. And it gave him the chance to get in
even closer with the Liberty Lunch crowd, two of whom, TC
and Stephen Langton, he had met recently.

Two of Podesta's closer chums, part of the after-dark
drinking set, were Ronald James Quin and his girlfriend,
Renee Rose Robertshaw. They both liked coke and ecstasy, as
well as other drugs. Robertshaw was a waitress at the Liberty,
and consequently the group would see one another all the
time.

Podesta and Quin were regularly hitting the Oxford
Street and Kings Cross nightclubs, where drug abuse was rife.
Quin would pick up his cocaine from any number of dealers
in the clubs but was careful to conceal his drug-taking behaviour.[27] In the pubs and clubs, Podesta came across as 'the type
of guy that likes to big note himself' like he was 'on some sort
of power trip'.[28] He was into spontaneous excitement – and
he liked the heat of the moment, the surge that came in those
steamy nightclubs.

One of the pair's mutual friends was Zac MacKenzie
(not his real name), a medium-level drug supplier, dealing in
ecstasy, cocaine and amphetamines. MacKenzie's flatmate,
Graeme Rooney (not his real name), who also had a decent
appetite for drugs, often saw Quin and Podesta at MacKenzie
and Rooney's place in Marrickville, an ethnically rich and

vibrant suburb in Sydney's inner west, but a bit of a hike from the convenient coast. Because the four lads met up so often, MacKenzie and Rooney drifted into the Liberty Lunch crowd and sometimes joined Podesta and Quin on their nocturnal excursions.

They'd hit Byblos, the Q Bar, Dancers (a nude lap-dancing club in Kings Cross) and the Black Market. The last of these was a day club up near the railway lines in Regent Street, Chippendale, just over the road from the historic Mortuary Station. The Black Market was infamous in the clubbing scene, both for having one night a week set aside for devotees of sadomasochism and for its illicit drug use.

Early one morning, Rooney went to the Black Market with Zac MacKenzie's girlfriend to try to catch up with MacKenzie. It was always a good place to start looking for the drug man. But instead of catching MacKenzie, Rooney collided with Podesta, already in the middle of a big night and apparently looking for more action. At some stage, Rooney would later say, he took up Podesta's invitation to go to a flat at Darling Point with a posse of guys and girls. There was great anticipation, lots of chatter.

On arrival at the flat, it became clear what all the fuss was about: 'some guy turned up and pulled out a bag of cocaine and . . . offered the girls lines of cocaine'.[29] Rooney immediately took a place in the queue as cocaine was poured out for sampling on a coffee table in the lounge room. For Rooney, it was an incredible experience, not least because there was an off-duty copper in the midst of it all. At a real-life drug party. And Podesta 'wasn't in police mode; he was definitely in human mode'.[30] Rooney considered it a case of 'first in, best dressed . . . and if you were quick to get to the front of the line, I suppose you got one. I don't know where Rod [Podesta] . . . was in the line, whether he missed out or he had one. There was a group sitting down in the lounge room. There was people out on the balcony and there was people in the kitchen'.[31]

The Darling Point party became part of the rich and growing Liberty Lunch folklore. Podesta was by far the most popular policeman in the Liberty set, but by no means the only officer welcomed with open arms.

Anthony Dilorenzo, an officer with nine years' experience and commendations for bravery and outstanding performance, was regarded as the de-facto chairman of an unofficial police club – the Living Dangerously Club. Its members sometimes dressed up in military fatigues and played paintball skirmish with toy guns on weekends; at night they'd drink at nightclubs until the sun came up and were regular gawkers at the lap-dancing salons. Indeed, their partying got to such an organised state that flyers appeared on noticeboards to highlight upcoming events.

Membership of this elite subculture was more secretive than the publicity suggested, however, and was never advertised. One of its flock remembered that the distinctive name started up the road at Waverley police station.[32] The regaled personalities in the LDC were Constable Patrick Eduardo Brown and two other young constables, Ted Shea and Paul Begbie. But Podesta and Dilorenzo, referred to in some parts as 'the Awesome Twosome',[33] were the LDC's heart and soul, its nucleus.

Dilorenzo, married with a child, and with another baby on the way, was streetwise and calculating – but his standards were slipping. Baker, the station commander, had recently disciplined Dilorenzo on his increasingly poor disciplinary record, despite considering him overall to be 'an excellent officer'.[34] It was noted that he often arrived late, with a dishevelled appearance, and frequently reported in sick.[35] But lateness and absenteeism were the least of Dilorenzo's concerns. For close to a year, Dilorenzo had been the subject of a special investigation at Internal Affairs because he was felt to be hanging out with the wrong people – those linked to the drug trade. The inquiry, Operation Addlestone, had pieced together an unorthodox jigsaw of family, friends and peculiar contacts.

Internal Affairs could not help but notice Dilorenzo's engaging brother, John, who preferred using the surname of Lorenzo. Perhaps it better suited his work in the media, where he had obtained in-depth knowledge about how television bulletins and newspaper stories and headlines are assembled. He had learned plenty about public relations also. He was a smooth operator, knowing how to manoeuvre the media to get his best results. Another Dilorenzo brother, Mark, had also adopted the Lorenzo surname – but because of his notoriety rather than for media purposes.

Mark Lorenzo had seen a different side of life from his brothers, spending more than two years in jail for the most serious of crimes: supplying heroin. Indeed, he had only just been released from custody – taking refuge with his family in this difficult time of adapting to a life on the outside. With his past history, Mark encountered great trouble finding a stable job, but had $45 000 in the bank, welfare benefits and a caring mother, with whom he lived, to soften his aches.

Naturally, Mark loathed police officers, as he would confirm later at the Police Integrity Commission: 'I want to make that clear straightaway . . . they're not friends of mine.'[36] The exception to the rule was Anthony's mate, Podesta. Anthony immediately accepted that the pair were friends and reported that 'they used to go bowling, to movies . . . [and] they liked to get out and chase the girls'.[37] Mark and Podesta were always on the phone, chinwagging over all sorts of things. Podesta called his pal fifteen times in January, thirteen times in February, 24 times in March and 43 times in April. And he'd ring at all hours: at 3.43 a.m. on 23 March and at 4.33 a.m. on 12 April; and then at 12.06, 12.19, 1.24, 1.29 and 4.31 a.m. on Anzac Day alone. It was very regular contact, at odd hours. Podesta and Mark Lorenzo were familiar faces at Sydney nightclubs such as the Cauldron, Rogues, Sugar Reef, Byblos and Dancers. Mark would go 'wherever the young girls were, where there was a nice bar and the people were decent'.[38] He also favoured places where he could get free drinks;[39] and certainly, he admitted, if cocaine was offered, he'd have a line.[40] But Mark Lorenzo wasn't into the tradition of barricading a toilet cubicle with a friend and going for broke. He was 'not that low', instead he'd go 'outside, or to my car'.[41]

In April 1997, Chief Inspector Baker called together the troops to give 'a clear direction that no staff should attend the Liberty Lunch or the neighbouring area, [the] Beachwood'.[42] Officers quickly got the impression that the place was under surveillance 'for the licensing problems it had or the noise complaint problems, or anything else that was going on in there'.[43] There was no 'grey area' about the commander's order, no ambiguity or leeway – the place was *off limits*. This caused mock alarm. Incredibly, many of the younger cops didn't get the logic behind the Baker ban – that Bondi police couldn't be seen to be properly responding to noise complaints (and 'anything else' illegal that was happening) if so many of them were inside boozing.

Constable Brown was particularly incensed since his fiancée had just booked the Liberty Lunch for his birthday.[44]

It was happening in four days' time and friends had been invited. At the suggestion of Senior Constable Cooper, the station's education officer, Brown took the matter up with Baker, who backed down once assured that no other police officers would be attending the party. Brown was given permission to blow out the candles, so to speak, at the Liberty Lunch. But only once.

While Brown was let off lightly, Baker took Dilorenzo and Podesta aside for separate warnings, not least because his beat officers had expressed particular concern about the pair hanging around the Liberty Lunch.[45] The edict put pressure on Podesta and was always going to be a hard promise for him to keep: not only was Podesta a special VIP guest but he was now also TC's landlord, the Liberty's likable manager having recently moved into a premises owned by the cop. It was not long therefore before Podesta started returning to the restaurant and the people he adored, carousing again at the bar with his friends – people like Robert Gould.

Gould, a former security guard turned local real estate executive, quickly became good friends with Podesta in the autumn of 1997. Gould was also friendly with Kieran O'Connor, the Liberty's proprietor. His other constant companions were alcohol, cocaine and ecstasy. With a $130 000 salary, plus commission from projects and property sales, Gould threw loads of cash after the white stuff.[46] He would snort it in the toilets of the Liberty Lunch, in the upstairs office, and in the bathroom at O'Connor's penthouse. He later agreed to the suggestion that he went to parties at O'Connor's place 'where people would quite openly use cocaine'[47] – a charge O'Connor denies. Gould sometimes supplied the coke, he said, but on other occasions, 'plates would just show up on tables with lines already cut up on them'.[48] On Saturday nights, after golfing together, Gould would invariably accompany O'Connor on what became the regular weekly visit for dinner and drinks at the Liberty Lunch. While the proprietor normally kept his wits, Gould would get smashed. Gould had heard all the rumours 'on the Bondi grapevine' that Podesta liked coke, and remembered one night in the Liberty's upstairs office when he joined TC and Podesta in a session of snorting.[49] The off-duty copper, the manager of the nightclub and the real estate exec all getting high on cocaine.

Podesta had a string of female companions. He was a true ladies' man.[50] For a while Podesta was engaged to Kylie Kummings (not her real name), a local girl, but he was 'very seldom on his own' and 'always had different girl-friends'.[51] According to TC, he liked 'to go out and pick up girls . . . He always bragged about that. He was one of those people that rated himself as a macho man.'[52] Podesta made many of his female conquests at the Liberty Lunch and sometimes went out with the waitresses and regulars.[53] One of the girls he met there literally did 'work' at the place – she was a high-class prostitute, a callgirl known as Samantha (not her real name).[54] They met in February 1997, when she lived in one of the home units above the Liberty. TC was immediately taken by her charming ways and gave her shiatsu massages, until he found out what she did for work. And others soon found out, it seems: 'She was with different people all the time . . . People complained that she was soliciting.'[55]

O'Connor was astonished that his place was being used by a prostitute and 'instructed the managers not to allow her in'.[56] A hooker was bad for business. But TC didn't pay any attention to his master's command,[57] and so Samantha started coming back with the management's consent. TC told his cop buddy to stay away from Samantha but the advice turned out to be worthless.[58] Samantha said she met Podesta one night at the Liberty Lunch. Later, they returned there to have an intimate dinner, at the policeman's suggestion, and he offered her cocaine, which they shared in the toilets. But it was not an altogether pleasant night. O'Connor spotted Samantha and Podesta, and he took them aside. The proprietor informed the constable that his female dining companion 'wasn't allowed in the premises and the reason she wasn't allowed in the premises was that she was barred.'[59] Moments later, now out in front of the restaurant, an argument started. O'Connor described the scuffle that followed: 'Another gentlemen stepped in. The beat police came in. There was a fight that ensued. One of the police officers lost his actual police hat.'[60] Podesta and Samantha later retired to her home and had sex. They kept in touch for the next month, she claimed (often at the same peculiar hours that he called Mark Lorenzo), and regularly got together to snort cocaine and take ecstasy. She said she once saw him with a 'sandwich bag [of cocaine] . . . about an inch thick', and that 'on average' Podesta would have 'about five grams' of the drug with him.[61] It was a short, action-packed fling and there was no animosity at the end. The pair 'just went our separate ways'[62] seeing each other occasionally.

It was around this time that Podesta moved back in with his parents at Matraville, further away from the beach. The reason for the change was, sadly, quite simple. He was needed on the home front – his father was dying of cancer.[63] Podesta did what he could to help, in the bathing, cleaning and feeding, and would sometimes rush home from work midway through the day. He was a treasure to his mother, Charmaine. Podesta had a flat below the house, with his own separate entrance – but he 'usually came through the front door anyway,[64] to see his parents. Neither his family obligations nor the anguish over his father's decline overly curbed his social strengths, however. Here he stood, precariously, almost at the end of his short-lived police career – at the start of his journey to ruin.

TWO
LIVING DANGEROUSLY

'It isn't a club; it's just a
fallacy, really. I suppose it was
just a name for all people in
that command . . . Being a
policeman is living dangerously.'

Rodney Podesta, Police Integrity Commission, Operation Saigon,
2 November 1999

Like the Liberty Lunch, the Soho Bar nightclub in Kings Cross had a cocaine problem; but, in vigorous contrast to the Bondi Beach restaurant, the Soho was trying to do something to control it. One of its security officers, Simon Duncan (not his real name), a former policeman, had been specifically instructed by the owners to regularly inspect the washrooms and forcibly open cubicle doors, if necessary, and to crack down on the scourge.[1] Despite the security patrols, coke connoisseurs couldn't resist the temptation to trundle off to the toilets.

It was at 1.30 a.m. on 10 May 1997, when Duncan spied three new sets of feet under the doors on one of his tours. As was his standard, he banged hard on the door and barked at those inside to open up. The door was not locked, but Duncan couldn't budge it, as someone was leaning hard against it. He then yelled again at the occupants and even

19

'mentioned the fact that there were police outside'.[2] All of a sudden, three lads 'came out and mentioned that they were the police, and there was a police badge shown'.[3] It almost got stuck in Duncan's eyes and he took great 'offence at the police badge being shown, being an ex-police officer'.[4] Duncan told the three toilet users they would have to leave, and he started to escort them out of the building, beyond the bar.

Looking more carefully now, he actually recognised the dimwits – or two of them anyway. One looked liked Rodney Podesta, and another bloke bore an uncanny resemblance to Mark Lorenzo. Duncan had never actually met Podesta in person, but understood his increasingly significant reputation – that 'quite a few people that worked at Bondi police station . . . didn't like him very much . . . that he was a bit of a rogue'.[5]

On the way to the Soho's exit door, Duncan stopped suddenly when he spied another Bondi policeman, Anthony Dilorenzo. Duncan never realised they were all part of the same crew until they all became huddled together. The ex-policeman had stumbled on a night out with some members of the Living Dangerously Club. Duncan had had an unhappy experience with Dilorenzo and Internal Affairs, although he believed that was water under the bridge, 'But I still didn't expect him to be as happy and jovial as he was. He put his arm on my shoulder, we shook hands. He generally appeared to be intoxicated.'[6] He talked for a while with Dilorenzo and almost certainly mentioned the unedifying spectacle in the toilets, and why he was showing his friends the door.[7]

Dilorenzo remembered the night differently – not even recalling the chat with Duncan, nor any of the subsequent kerfuffle. Dilorenzo claimed to have seen somebody snatching a woman's bag: 'I grabbed him and the doorman came in and we took him outside and a couple of other police arrived and I explained to them what had happened and they took him away.'[8]

Regardless of what really occurred, the affair was serious enough to spark an entry in the police force's computerised incident report system. At 1.45 a.m., Constable Spencer from the Kings Cross station jotted up the fracas in his notebook: 'Police spoke to male . . . police . . . S/C Dilorenzo . . . Constable Hughes . . . Constable Podesta . . . Bondi police.'[9] At 2.19 a.m., moments after being kicked out of the Soho, Podesta found cause to have another chat on the mobile with Mark Lorenzo.

A few days later, Duncan thought he should report the incident to his bosses, and the Internal Affairs branch also learned of it. Things were getting hot.

On 15 May, Justice Wood presented his royal commission report to the premier, Bob Carr, a six-volume critique on the ill-health of policing. The royal commissioner said a permanent watchdog, the Police Integrity Commission, should be created to keep corruption and crime in check, so endemic had the problem become. Justice Wood also paid special attention to Bondi police station, as stated previously; and to the problem of drugs and alcohol, noting that 'insufficient training had been given [to officers] . . . as to what was expected in relation to their association with recreational drugs . . . [and] that police were attending, on a social basis, various inner city nightclubs and dance parties where drugs were known to be openly and readily available.'[10] There were only three pages devoted to the growing trend, but it was prophetic stuff; and it put all serving officers on notice.

Wood's findings were right on the money. There were plenty of clubs where drugs were readily available. One was the Soho. Another of them happened to be the Liberty Lunch. In this post–royal commission context, with the police supposedly on high alert, Chief Inspector Dick Baker learned that one of his flock, Podesta, was disobeying his orders. The beat cops had told Baker that Podesta was spending too much time with drug dealers.[11] Baker called the rogue officer back into his office. But Podesta, confident as ever, gave him 'a plausible reason why he went there. He also told me he had booked the Liberty Lunch for a birthday party, and I informed him that I didn't think it was wise for him to continue with that'.[12]

In the weeks spanning the police ban, the Liberty Lunch had changed ownership, with Kieran O'Connor selling to a couple from Gladesville, Stanley and Susan Dowse. The Dowses previous business venture had come in the form of packaging alfalfa for supermarkets, so jumping in with the groovy set was a big change. Dowse was considered a bit old-fashioned. He was different from O'Connor, who was 'a lot more of a people person. Stan and Sue, I believe, hadn't run a business like that . . . and were unaware of the PR side of running a bar and treating the staff in an appropriate manner'.[13]

While O'Connor pulled up stumps in a business sense, he still kept visiting the place. The same staff, and many of his friends, were always there – and so was the cocaine and ecstasy. Podesta was foolishly still drinking and eating there and there were 'quite a few occasions early in the piece . . . where Kieran [O'Connor] . . . would come in . . . [on] Saturday nights, usually, and nine times out of ten Robert Gould was with him. They'd been out prior'.[14] There may have been new owners, and new attitudes, but on the cocaine front, everything was still the same.

On 26 May, Baker called Internal Affairs to report Podesta's insubordination. Assistant Commissioner Malcolm

(Mal) Brammer, the new boss of the corruption busters, was trying his best to refocus the squad, the butt of incredible ridicule at the royal commission. Brammer accepted it was 'a rather difficult command . . . and certainly there were a lot of deficiencies.'[15] Like all commanders in the harried post–royal commission environment, Brammer was often tied up with the frenzy of implementing reform. He was trying to shift the command from, in his words, 'the old approach of dealing with complaints in a sort of draconian reactive style . . . into a more proactive role' but conceded that this was quite a challenge 'given the resources . . . the exposures and the limited opportunities the investigators had been given at the time'.[16]

He'd encouraged patrol commanders to get active in the crusade against bent cops – and, by reporting Podesta, that was exactly what Baker was doing. He spoke to Brammer's personal legal assistant, Inspector Robert Ian Martin, about the concerns he had 'in relation to Constable Podesta's activities with some people that are known to be involved with drug activity within Bondi'.[17] Martin arranged for a private appointment with Brammer's top offsider, a civilian head-kicker named Gary Richmond, who was the new bloke in charge of running covert raids and investigations. Baker went to the meeting with Senior Constable Cooper, the education officer, and a bloke [I could] 'trust with my life'.[18] Baker wanted Cooper 'fully aware of what strategies . . . would take place . . . [and he] was basically a good medium to inform the constables that they should not talk about issues if they do know it, but come directly to me'.[19] In the interests of Constable Podesta, Baker said, 'it would be wise to have him targeted under surveillance, or whatever measures they thought fit . . . to eradicate the innuendos'.[20] Richmond agreed, and went directly to his computer, authoring a memo to approve an official Internal Affairs investigation.

On 30 May, Richmond gave the reference to one his team leaders, Detective Inspector Paul Douglas Jones, the coordinator of a small unit of officers. The note was headed: 'Allegations the police officer is using and dealing in drugs.'[21] Richmond informed Jones that Podesta was believed to be dealing in drugs and that he frequented the Liberty Lunch, on Bondi's Campbell Parade.[22] Jones now briefed his investigators and Operation Borden, a full-blown inquiry into Podesta and his drug-using cohorts, was started. The Borden team consisted of Detective Sergeant Christopher Keen, Detective Sergeant Wayne Thorn and Detective Senior Constable Duncan Tchakalian, each assigned various duties.

Keen did most of the legwork. He spoke to Detective Senior Constable David Minarik about the other Bondi drugs inquiry, Operation Addlestone, 'and just to assist us with a bit of background with the inquiry, he told me certain things about his investigation' into Dilorenzo.[23] Like many of his overworked colleagues, Keen had other inquiries to juggle. At first, with his time so limited, all the detective sergeant could do on Operation Borden were background checks – until 'there was an informant that came to my knowledge' and the investigation picked up momentum.[24] On 5 June, Baker rang Richmond to get an update on the Borden file. There was 'positive information' cropping up, Baker was told. Richmond thanked the Bondi chief because his 'information was useful and . . . it linked to some of their inquiries', and, most importantly, 'that they were continuing with that inquiry'.[25]

On 17 June, Tchakalian was given the task of trying to find the Soho nightclub security guard, Simon Duncan, the guy who had allegedly witnessed the badge-pulling episode in the toilets. Although Duncan had reported the matter to the Soho's owners, '[I] didn't believe they would report it because I couldn't understand why an owner of a hotel would let the police know there was possible incidents happening on the premises.'[26] He thought it more likely that Internal Affairs officers themselves had seen Podesta and Dilorenzo kicked out of the Soho, that the two cops had been under surveillance all along.[27] Having an interview with Internal Affairs was not what Duncan had intended but he told Tchakalian, albeit reluctantly, that he would cooperate and tell the investigator what he knew. However, he failed to keep his appointment on 19 June, 'for business reasons'.[28]

Two days later, having postponed the interview with Internal Affairs, Duncan thought it would be a good idea to talk to Dilorenzo. Duncan left a message for him at the Bondi police station and, at 4.44 p.m., Dilorenzo, from his home, rang Duncan on his mobile phone. Their conversation lasted for five minutes and 23 seconds. Duncan later admitted he 'could have' revealed to Dilorenzo the presence of Internal Affairs and the interview that was to have occurred but insisted that the nature of the call was far more innocent than that: 'Tony was the only person I sort of knew to say: "Look, as an ex-police officer saying to a current police officer, that was a stupid thing to do." And I just basically told him that . . . I took offence to it.'[29] Duncan claimed that Dilorenzo said he understood but that 'He was just there having a drink . . . and . . . he had nothing to worry about.'[30] And that was the end of the matter, although later Dilorenzo could not recall such a chat. Regardless, the presence of Internal Affairs meant the Living Dangerously Club was in dangerous waters.

At the precise time Internal Affairs was after Dilorenzo and Podesta, Commissioner Peter Ryan was unfurling massive plans to improve police performance, with the overly bureaucratic organisation being restructured, downsized and ripped apart. The strategy was fewer middle layers and more officers on the beat. It was touted as the means to guarantee greater supervision and more autonomy. Every station was affected.

From 1 July, new commanders had been assigned to take over, to rejuvenate the deflated and pilloried ranks. Bondi 'was being absorbed into the Waverley patrol'.[31] The restructure was specifically designed to make Waverley 'the mother station' so that 'everybody else on general duties went to Waverley as the main station and people that were doing beat duties remained at Bondi'.[32] Under the changes, Baker was heading off to Mount Druitt, in Sydney's far-flung western suburbs, and Superintendent Robert May had been picked to take charge of the restructured eastern districts, including Bondi. In the time prior to the handover, Baker and May had several discussions to assist with the baton change. Baker spoke about what he had done 'in relation to Internal Affairs' and how he had 'some concerns in relation to those activities'.[33] He put May on notice: a major Internal Affairs investigation was under way.

On Thursday, 26 June, it was decided to commemorate the Bondi–Waverley amalgamation with a booze-up. Everyone from the two stations was invited to the Coogee Legion Club for a night of revelry. It had been decided that 'as Bondi was not an autonomous police station in its own right any more . . . the social club would be stopped and the . . . [rest of the] money spent . . . at an associate function'.[34] Michael Cooper, who coincidentally had put in his retirement papers and was two days away from leaving the job, had $1140 of the kitty which, he arranged with the club management, would go towards financing an open bar.

It was a wake of sorts for Bondi, the end of an era –

and the emotions were running high. There were even a few fights at the bar, but 'almost everyone was in a happy mood', with jokes, awards and speeches further lightening up the proceedings.[35] Cooper, who had the social club cheque in his pocket – and responsibility for keeping a lid on the excitement – was pacing himself on light-alcohol beer but observed that his restraint was not being universally embraced. Like any open bar, there were 'some other fellows who were buying triples – and, of top shelf, which didn't make me very happy'.[36] It also meant tongues were being loosened.

Cooper distinctly recalls one conversation that night: a chat involving himself, Patrick Brown, Podesta and Dilorenzo. Cooper noticed that Podesta appeared to be upset: 'He was quite incensed that he'd just learned Internal Security had been down to the Liberty Lunch restaurant making inquiries as to whether he was involved in the sale and supply of drugs from the restaurant.'[37] According to Cooper, the chat was an intense exchange:

Brown: Yes, why, what's happened here? . . . Why are they doing it? Rod's not doing this type of thing, so whey are they doing it?
Dilorenzo: Shut up. Rod, I told you, we're not going to talk about this.
Podesta: Why are they doing it? What information have they got?
Cooper: I don't know, I don't know.
Dilorenzo: Fuck 'em, let 'em prove it.[38]

When the Legion Club closed, many of the officers went over the road to the Coogee Bay Hotel. Brown went to Dancers with some other Bondi officers while Dilorenzo walked off into the night. Podesta reached for his mobile. At 11.45 p.m., he made a quick call; at 1.20 a.m. on Friday, 27 June, he called the number again. The number belonged to his new best friend, his partner's brother and a former heroin supplier – Mark Lorenzo.

THREE
THE NIGHT BEFORE

'He was high on cocaine. He looked
very agitated. He couldn't sit
still.'

Witness SA2 (Samantha), on her purported meeting with
Constable Rodney Podesta late on the night before the shooting,
Police Integrity Commission, Operation Saigon, 10 November 1999

Just after 7 a.m. on the last full day of his life, Friday, 27 June
1997 (barely hours after the diehards from the Bondi police
station wake had partied themselves into bed) Roni Levi woke
from his slumber at 59 Brighton Boulevard in Bondi, to begin
his final, fateful mental descent, his spiral into oblivion.

Levi's world was falling apart. His thoughts were
muddled, his speech patterns contorted and incoherent and,
for a normally passive, friendly conversationalist, the Frenchman was suddenly becoming incredibly introspective. He was
withdrawn, constantly worried and emotional, and often
could not perform the most rudimentary of tasks. Unknown
and misunderstood, Levi was in the grips of a terrifying
mental breakdown – a collapse in his powers of reasoning. He
was on the verge of a psychotic episode. He knew neither
where he was nor where he was going. Nothing made sense.
Nothing seemingly could be done.

Levi's flatmate, Warren Brunner, was well aware of the problems. Perhaps more than most he understood his friend's quickening mental disintegration, this journey to the edge of rationality. Brunner had watched Levi turn from a gregarious, caring man into an unconfident embarrassment in need of help. And, although the flatmates had only been together for a few months, sharing a modest two-bedroom dwelling near the beach – a short stroll from the North Bondi Surf Life Saving Club and the police station in Wairoa Avenue – Brunner knew Levi well enough to appreciate that, on this day, there was something seriously amiss. Levi was close to falling apart.

Brunner's worries for Levi started intensifying on the evening of Thursday, 26 June, when he passed on a message. Brunner relayed a call from a man called Joe, who had phoned to express his irritation about Levi's failure to show up at a prearranged meeting. Levi virtually erupted with anger, saying that he felt he was in trouble. While accustomed to the tantrums, Brunner had never before witnessed such a depressed, wild episode. He knew vaguely of this Joe, and that Joe had been pestering Levi. Other friends had heard of this colourful character; one spoke of Levi being 'under enormous strain . . . in huge fear . . . because he was being stood over by a Sydney man'.[1]

Joe, the standover man, had helped Levi, an otherwise upright citizen, to get a criminal record. Ten days earlier, at the Melbourne Magistrate's Court, Levi had been fined $100 and given a six-month good-behaviour bond after being found guilty of selling two caps, pirated against copyright rules, at the Formula One grand prix. Levi had been 'among a dozen people arrested for selling the merchandise without consent'.[2] Joe had given the contraband to Levi, promising him a $2 commission for each item he sold. It was not a heinous crime, it had nothing to do with drugs, drink driving or sex and violence. Nonetheless, the arrest was something that Levi – a spiritual, if not religious man, a Jew, someone respectful of the law – would not have enjoyed.

Perhaps because of his upset and shame, Levi concealed the arrest from his wife, Melinda Dundas, from whom he'd long been estranged but continued to speak to, as an intimate friend and someone who would listen. Dundas learned of her husband's brush with the law only when police visited her Melbourne home to serve a summons. Joe was always niggling Levi 'for money he owed him after supplying him with counterfeit T-shirts and caps'.[3]

Roni Levi, 33, was born in Ashkelon in Israel, 50-odd kilometres south of Tel Aviv. His parents, Richard and Rebecca, hailing from Egypt, had been 'proud Alexandrians until they joined, under the presidency of Arab nationalist Gamal Nasser, a Jewish exodus'.[4] Like many of their countrymen, they fled to Israel. When Roni was two, the family moved on to Paris.

There were four children: Roni, the eldest, and brothers Ilan, Remy and Laurent. They lived in a prestigious suburb, part of the upper middle class, with the parents managing a successful fur and leather shop. Roni 'celebrated the Jewish holidays and until 13 attended a private Jewish college for instruction twice a week'.[5] He was closest to Ilan, the pair separated by only eighteen months. Both were excellent swimmers and, in family photographs, 'the two are forever locked in an easy embrace'.[6] Levi developed into a gentle, artistic person, a health-conscious vegetarian who never smoked and rarely drank alcohol, except for big celebrations. He was not involved in illicit drugs.

In 1988, after an unspectacular school life, Levi went

to college to follow his love of photography. The following year he journeyed to London in pursuit of his dream, finding a job in the photographic profession, and met the woman who would become his wife.

In Europe on a working holiday, Melinda Dundas was working with Associated Press in its London office when the serious dating started. The couple 'fell in love and returned to Paris, where Mr Levi picked up photographic assignments. His work appeared in glossy magazines and fashion catalogues and in house material for France's largest retailer, Galarie la Fayette'.[7] But good jobs were hard to find so, in reality, he found it extraordinarily difficult to find steady work. In a pattern that would invariably repeat itself, Levi was forced to find casual work and odd chores to boost his wages. All sorts of things kept Levi busy and beyond the brink of destitution: he worked as a pharmacy assistant, a brochure and community newspaper photographer, in clerical duties and part-time waiting. To most, he impressed with his commitment and friendly nature – a rare commodity in the casual labour market.

In 1991, Levi and Dundas were married in a civil ceremony but the relationship was dogged by difficulties and tension. Religion was a powerful obstacle and the relationship with Levi's parents was strained: Levi's father had not attended the wedding, and the pressure of marrying outside the Jewish faith was considerable.

The relationship also suffered from other misgivings. Once, Levi attended a self-awareness course in a bid to find direction in his life and more confidence. When he returned from the weekend workshops, Dundas had found him, literally starving, raving about his prolific insights – and claiming he could actually read the mind of a waiter at the cafe where they sat. Dundas, although concerned, had thought little of the episode at the time and considered 'it was a delirium brought on by hunger'.[8]

In late 1992, the couple's relationship foundered and Dundas returned to Melbourne, homesick and hoping. It was an amicable parting; the pair remained close friends. Indeed, when Levi migrated to Australia in 1993, the couple tried to make a go of it again, but the attempted reconciliation eventually dissolved. They were friends, not lovers.

Always restless and never settling down, Levi wandered the land: Sydney, Adelaide and Melbourne would all play host to the affable Frenchman over the next three years. He ventured home to France, attending two weddings and giving no hint of the trouble that had started to fester inside his mind.

On his return to Sydney from Adelaide in late 1996, still desperately seeking direction, Levi initially stayed at city short-term hostels before moving into a share-accommodation house at Annandale, in Sydney's inner west. But 'it wasn't long before arguments broke out over what his flatmates saw as a failure to pay his way'.[9]

In February 1997, Levi made his way to Brunner's place at 59 Brighton Boulevard. But the move to Bondi coincided with the most pronounced deterioration in Levi's mental condition – with his depression and anguish starting to foment. He'd seen a career counsellor, had enrolled at the East Sydney campus of TAFE to study English and office administration, was still actively engaged in all manner of part-time jobs, had undertaken work experience with a film documentary house, and was doing still pictures on the side for the *Australian Jewish News*. He was trying everything. However, he had also seen a psychiatrist in an obvious quest for answers to his mental confusion. Levi could feel himself slipping away: 'He . . . told the psychiatrist that "people don't understand me' and confessed to feelings of low self-confidence.'[10] In the last frustrating month of his life, Levi was out of luck, working in patchy and unfulfilling jobs, and looking in all sorts of places for clues.

In his last week, Levi's crumbling innermost world took on physical manifestations. There were many prolonged silences, even under intense questioning from close friends, and an inability to communicate, keep his mind focused and finish sentences. He also seemed very self-conscious. On Tuesday, 24 June, Levi went to work at five o'clock in the afternoon at a document-copying business. But, after making a string of straightforward errors, and not heeding his supervisor's warnings, he was sent home. His mind was patchy, drifting, somewhere else. Later that night, Levi's family called the Bondi flat from Paris. His parents were due to arrive in Sydney in a week's time, for a holiday and a reunion. They too noticed dysfunctional behaviour. Levi's 'responses were slow and wandering; his mother later described a strangeness that she felt about the whole conversation'.[11] Ilan felt that his brother 'sounded distant, as though something was wrong, but I doubt he was mentally ill'.[12]

On Thursday, 26 June, Levi started reaching out, crying for help. In the afternoon, Levi spoke to a friend, claiming – in a muddled-up babble that was impossible to decipher – that he had been hypnotised over the phone and that someone else was controlling his thoughts and actions. He also tried to reach his wife, leaving a message on her answering machine in Melbourne: 'I need to talk to you.' The collapse of all balance was upon him.

On Friday, 27 June, at 10.30 a.m., Levi bumped into some friends as he walked along Campbell Parade. His mate Daniel Hagege spied Levi and invited him to coffee with his partner, Tina Dalton. Levi said he had a 11.30 medical appointment he had to keep, and mentioned it repeatedly. They sat down at the Gelato Bar at South Bondi, a stone's throw from the Liberty Lunch, where the trendy waiters were just getting ready for the regular lunchtime crowd. Hagege could detect nothing wrong with Levi but, involved in a deeper conversation, Dalton became concerned: Levi could not speak properly. His expression was awkward, and there were pregnant pauses and a lot of mumbled words.

She urged Levi to come to dinner, concerned by his demeanour and isolation. Two visiting French doctors, Freddy and Caroline Atlani, were coming over for the evening. It was to mark the start of a week of specialist medical conferences in Sydney, followed by some sightseeing. Levi was told he was most welcome to come along. But he declined the offer and rushed off mysteriously for the pressing engagement.

Levi missed his 11.30 appointment at the Double Bay Medical Centre, an encounter that would have informed him that his HIV test results – an annual occurrence – had proved negative. At 3.30 p.m., four hours after leaving the Gelato Bar, Levi rang up the casual job agency seeking a shift. They suggested he take a spot at the horse trotting, at Harold Park Raceway in Glebe. Moments later, despite having only just committed himself to working the evening in Glebe, Levi rang up Daniel Hagege to take up the dinner offer. He told Hagege that he was losing his mind, and wanted some help. Hagege, who lived only streets away, insisted that he would come over to pick him up, becoming concerned at the shrill and awkward tone in Levi's voice.

Minutes after the phone call ended, at about 4.30 p.m. – just fifteen hours before his death – Levi banged on Hagege's door. His problems were now impossible to disguise. Thankfully though, given his state, Levi could not have been in better hands. The Atlanis, trained doctors, and his two close friends –

all of whom found Levi incoherent and rambling, even when the dialogue switched to French – were studying his every movement. Levi's health was the main topic of conversation and they prevailed on him repeatedly to get professional medical assistance. Levi agreed it was time he sought help but insisted that it could wait until after prayers. Freddy Atlani, Hagege and Levi set off for the synagogue to think things over.

After worship, Levi's mood worsened. Despite gentle prodding from his companions over dinner, which he ate heartily, Levi would not (or could not) reveal his troubles, instead gibbering away in semi-sentences and words and half-words. At about 9 p.m., Freddy Atlani asked Levi if he would like to go to the hospital, saying it would be best if someone had a look at him immediately. Levi nodded meekly. They arrived at St Vincent's Hospital Emergency Department in Darlinghurst just before 9.30 p.m.

Back at Bondi Beach, Dilorenzo and Podesta – the two officers who would shortly discharge their firearms, fatally wounding Levi – were finishing their dinners. They were each scheduled to be back on duty the next morning at seven o'clock.

Dilorenzo observed a family tradition on Friday nights, almost without fail. It was a takeaway fish dinner with his wife Annabelle's aunt and uncle, Nola and John Preston. Since his daughter Claudia had been born three years earlier, the Prestons would come over to the Dilorenzos' house on Fridays to mind Claudia, staying into the evening for a family meal. It was a casual, albeit organised affair, with other family members and friends sometimes joining in.[13] On Friday, 27 June, the Dilorenzos and the Prestons were joined by only Barry Rutter and possibly Angelo Astudillo (known as Chill).

Dilorenzo arrived home from work about 4.30 p.m. and then sat down to watch a video replay of a rugby league show. Just before 8 p.m., Dilorenzo and John Preston drove up the road to Ocean Foods in Vaucluse where they were on first-name terms with the proprietor and collected the take-away order. Dilorenzo ordered his regular dish: tuna marinated with sweet chilli. After the meal, Dilorenzo was safely in bed by 9.30 p.m., ready for the early shift. But his mate Podesta was still out on the town. It was soon to be Dilorenzo's partner's twenty-eighth birthday – and he was celebrating.

Podesta was with his friends, Ron Quin and Renee Robertshaw, having a small pre-birthday dinner at a Thai restaurant in Campbell Parade, just the three of them. The get-together was planned because Robertshaw could not attend the next night's planned mega-festivities. Podesta, having just completed a twelve-hour shift, met Quin and Robertshaw at Terrific Thai at around eight o'clock. It was a busy haunt where no reservations could be made, so Quin and Robertshaw had arrived about half an hour earlier to get one of the celebrated outside tables. Podesta, like many officers who have just completed their duties and do not wish to be conspicuous, was most likely in 'partial police trousers with a T-shirt on, because I went straight from work'[14] and he probably also was wearing his police-issue 'Baxter boots . . . and a blue and white sort of windcheater jacket.'[15]

Robertshaw bought a chocolate cake, with 'Happy Birthday Rodney' scrawled on top in icing. Quin might have taken along a six-pack of beer as well but it was a subdued affair as 'Rodney wanted to have a quiet evening. He was going out with all of his police friends for his birthday the following evening.'[16] When they finished, near nine o'clock, the three continued on to the Beach Road Hotel, to the upstairs section for a 'game of pool and a beer'[17] but they 'didn't even finish their drinks,'[18] and Podesta left, telling them he wanted to see his father.

At about 10 p.m., Podesta later claimed, he arrived home to see his parents. Podesta's father made a special effort to sit up at the table, where they shared some slices from the chocolate cake. After a while, Podesta helped his father back to his sick bed, and then told his parents that he was going to lie down.

Samantha, the prostitute girlfriend, claimed Podesta did not go to bed that early, however; and that he was actually seeing her that night. Although the Police Integrity Commission later suggested Samantha might have got her dates confused, she remembers seeing Podesta at her flat above the Liberty Lunch at around 10 p.m. Podesta was dressed in his police uniform and was 'high on cocaine . . . very agitated', and told her he had just ingested some coke.[19] Podesta now only had eight hours until he was due to report for duty. He'd been up until all hours in the previous few nights. But there was one big shift to come.

At St Vincent's Hospital, the situation was much more sombre. Levi's fate was hanging in the balance. After being examined by a nurse and a doctor, he was considered clearly unwell. Hagege and Atlani had helped convince Levi that it would be best to take up the suggestion to stay in hospital for some tests. Dr Elizabeth Meagher noted that Levi was cooperative, but confused. Levi asked her early on: 'Do you think thoughts can come down the telephone line from one person to another?' The doctor replied that she did not but asked him what he thought. 'Oh no,' Levi insisted. 'No, no. Of course not.'[20]

Hagege and Atlani farewelled Levi with a reassuring hug, promising to visit him later. It was now about midnight. By the time he was seen by Nurse Purnell, who had been assigned to do a fuller medical examination, he was becoming agitated and starting to speak about voices. He told the nursing staff that he wanted to leave, but at 1.30 a.m., Levi's plan to depart was stalled with the sudden arrival of the Emergency Department's registrar, Dr Brennan. The exchange went as follows:

Brennan: Are the voices telling you to do anything?
Levi: No.
*Brennan: Do you feel you might do harm to yourself or to
    another person?*
Levi: No. You enjoyed asking that question, didn't you![21]

Levi again motioned to leave. But Dr Brennan pleaded with him to wait until he got further advice. Brennan quickly spoke to the resident medical officer at Caritas, the hospital's psychiatric wing, recalling the features of Levi's demeanour. Although Levi accepted Brennan's direction, Levi walked for the next few hours, seemingly without purpose, in and out of the hospital.

He was seen by a security guard at 2.30 a.m. on Burton Street. And then just before four o'clock, he approached Nurse Purnell, asking if he could make a reverse-charge call to his family in France. As soon as Purnell connected with the operator, however, Levi declined to proceed, walking off to see someone else.

Later he spoke to the night nurse, John Palmer, about his problems. He 'was still very restless and agitated . . . [and] was not completing his sentences . . . He asked me if I could hear the voices talking to him.'[22] Then, Levi suddenly asked for a pen and paper and retired to his room. At about 4 a.m., Nurse Palmer saw him sitting on the bed, writing contentedly. But by 4.30 a.m., Levi was gone, nowhere to be seen. He was officially missing from the hospital.

At 5.30 a.m., a call was apparently made from the hospital to Brunner at the Bondi flat, to let someone know that Levi was on the run. It was a pity no-one answered the call, for Levi was heading in Brunner's direction.

The Frenchman was racing speedily towards Bondi Beach on foot, a lengthy seven-kilometre hike from St Vincent's Hospital – and a difficult and challenging exercise in the early-morning winter air. Levi would have been freezing, and uncomfortable. He was also almost blind, his vision impaired at the best of times, despite the fact that he wore glasses. Now Levi was on the street – semi-blind, sweating, disoriented, almost certainly scared, and in the throes of his worst mental episode. Levi's time had arrived.

FOUR
A BEAUTIFUL DAY

'It was a beautiful day . . . and
I clearly remember paddling over a
wave . . . I heard what I believe
to be three or four shots in
succession . . . '

Mike Morrison, Police Integrity Commission,
Operation Saigon, 3 November 1999

At 6 a.m. on Saturday, 28 June, with the sun faintly smearing the Bondi Beach horizon with a golden yellow, Roni Levi emerged from the eerie morning darkness. Right next to his apartment, at 59 Brighton Boulevard – without his keys and without a clue. Just before dawn is always the coldest part of the day, as well as the quietest. It was just 8 degrees.

Levi's flatmate, Warren Brunner, was sleeping soundly but an enormous thundering on the bedroom window quickly roused him sufficiently to get him to the door. When the door opened, Levi strode straight ahead and into his bedroom – and then went straight back out of the flat. Brunner had watched the behaviour grow weirder by the day, but this was as bad as it had ever been. It was manic.

Bleeding, sweating and panting, Levi roamed the streets of Bondi at dawn. Dishevelled and unkempt, dressed in dark pants with a brown jacket and a long overcoat, he remained largely out of sight for the next 30 minutes – except for a chance spotting of him in Wairoa Avenue by Pascal Czerwenka, a university student making deliveries for the Ben Buckler Newsagency. At 6.30 a.m., almost exactly to the half-hour, Czerwenka spied Levi for the second time, just about to bang again on the door of his flat.

When Brunner again opened the door, Levi ignored his bedroom and this time went to the kitchen. Brunner, still at the front door in nothing but his boxer shorts, started hearing the shaking of cutlery as Levi rustled around in one of the drawers – perhaps he was looking for a knife. Brunner's first reaction was to head down to the street, for his own safety.

Levi reappeared clutching the commonest of kitchen utensils: a black-handle Wiltshire Staysharp with a 21-centimetre blade. He couldn't avoid seeing Brunner, shivering and shaking. 'It's not for you,' Levi told his flatmate. Czerwenka witnessed the streetside chat, returning to his red Ford Laser. He noticed Brunner was trying to reason with his friend, trying to pacify Levi and deal with the knife. Levi refused to listen and instead sped off towards Wairoa Avenue, with Brunner now in pursuit, yelling repeatedly: 'Roni, I want to help you.'[1]

It was 6.40 a.m. when Levi hit the end of Brighton Boulevard and turned into Ramsgate Avenue, as if he was heading back in the direction of the beach. Levi passed a morning walker, Arnold Payment, and, a short time later, Brunner hurtled past Payment in hot pursuit. Brunner started pointing at Levi. 'That guy over there,' Brunner gesticulated, 'is going to do something and he's got a knife.'[2] Payment could see nothing alarming about Levi's appearance at first, and suggested that Brunner 'call the police and then stay a safe distance away from him'.[3]

It was at about 6.50 a.m., at the bottom of Ramsgate

Avenue, at the corner of Military Road, when Levi crashed into Lani Jensen, walking south on his way to work at the Bondi Hotel. Jensen noticed Levi was sweating and spitting, and blood was over his face and nose. Seconds later, Brunner surged past Jensen, yelling out to Levi. The pair caught up with each other, walking in staccato style – stopping and starting – further up the road.

They were heading north up the Military Road incline, a steep walkway on the way to North Head, witnessed by staff at Sean's Panorama cafe. Levi and Brunner walked up and down the length of the road twice, at one point catching the attention of Lieutenant Commander Noel Pont, an officer in the Royal Australian Navy.

By this time, Levi's overcoat was falling limply over his shoulders and he was still sweating and panting. Pont recognised that Brunner was seeking to get his friend to put the knife away. The mood was tense, but Brunner seemed at times to be prevailing, gently getting his point across. But then, when Brunner got close, Levi raised his arm and started moving the knife around.

It was 6.54 a.m. when Brunner, having done all that he thought he could, eventually turned his back on Levi and sprinted off down Military Road, on the way to the police station. Levi started to run along the beachside promenade, pondering the pounding surf.

At 6.56 a.m., Brunner reached the station at Wairoa Avenue. Outside on the verandah, enjoying a cigarette, was Senior Constable John Lewis Jones, just about to finish the twelve-hour overnight shift. He was the first to see Brunner sprinting in to make a report. Sergeant Graham Taylor was also outside. Anthony Dilorenzo had just arrived for duty on the changeover, and was inside, sorting out his belongings. Brunner told Taylor and Jones how his flatmate had just threatened him with a knife and might be trying to kill himself, adding that Levi had 'just snapped' and was 'running around the streets near Brighton Boulevard with a large knife'.⁴ Jones, realising his shift had not ended, rostered himself back on for duty. There was one more job to go. He barked out for Dilorenzo.

At 6.57 a.m., Dilorenzo grabbed the keys to the paddy wagon and motored out the door – leaving behind his hat and jacket in the rush to action. Brunner, still freezing in his boxer shorts and 'a bit hysterical . . . very frightened . . . [and] yelling and screaming',⁵ was ushered into the rear passenger-side seat to act as lookout. He directed the search, briefly retracing their earlier walk down Ramsgate Avenue and into Military Road. But there was no sign of Levi.

They then decided to have a search of the flat in case he was hiding there. At 6.58 a.m., Jones got on the police radio. 'Bondi One to VKG,' he began, and then launched into a description of the situation:

> *Radio, we've got a job from the station. A male gone berserk with a knife. We have the informant with us. At the moment, we're in Brighton Boulevard . . . over here at Bondi. The male is described as wearing a black raincoat and carrying a large kitchen knife at this stage. We're just looking around for him, if there might be another vehicle in the vicinity.*⁶

At exactly the same time Czerwenka – having forgotten an important newspaper delivery – was returning to an apartment near 59 Brighton Boulevard. On his way back to his car, Czerwenka noticed Bondi One's lights flashing on and off at him, signalling him to move his vehicle quickly. As soon as he had sat down in the driver's seat, however, Dilorenzo was pounding on the windows. Nervous, Czerwenka piped up: 'I just wanted to tell you that I saw the guy.' 'Where?' Dilorenzo demanded, asking for identification while Brunner shook his head in denial. 'I haven't seen him here,' was all Czerwenka could muster.[7] At 7 a.m., Brunner, Jones and Dilorenzo raced into the flat, hoping to find Levi – the police officers with their revolvers drawn and at their sides.

Constables Christopher Goodman and Geoffrey Smith took to the air in Paddington One, saying they were on their way to Bondi to help in the hunt, having heard the earlier radio message. The target, Roni Levi, bloodied and messy, was not in the flat but down on the beach, being watched by joggers and early-morning walkers on his stagger down to the sand from the promenade. Running north on his fourth lap of the beach, Danny Weidler, a newspaper journalist, noticed Levi literally charging into the water. Levi began to splash around and walk aimlessly, fully clothed, in the frosty surf.

At 7.01 a.m., Dilorenzo and Jones, started searching each of the rooms in the flat. Back at the station, Rodney Podesta had just arrived at work for what would be the biggest day of his life. After a quick briefing on the situation, Podesta jumped into a paddy wagon, Bondi Two, and followed Sergeant Taylor – heading towards Ben Buckler, the big headland where Levi had been earlier sighted. At 7.02 a.m., Dilorenzo found a photograph of Levi in the apartment and then a motor vehicle licence – useful identification to give to VKG, which he did.

Meanwhile, Podesta swung Bondi Two into Brighton Boulevard and in the direction of the beach. Levi was still on the beach, bouncing about in the freezing waves, when Podesta turned the corner. At 7.02.58 a.m. (logged precisely to the second by the VKG police radio), Jones depressed the button on his portable:

– Bondi One to VKG.

– Bondi One.

*– Surname spelt Lima-Echo-Victor-India. Christian name
    Roni. Romeo-Oscar-November-India. Date of birth:
    six, one, 64.*

– Six, one, 64. And do you have that person with you yet?

*– No, negative, radio. If you do a check, you might do it on .
    . . he's got a Victorian driver's licence.*

– Copy that. We'll put it through National names.

The transmission ended at 7.03.49 a.m. Podesta may have
missed the exchange – he was out talking to some joggers,
getting an eyewitness account of Levi's latest encounter. It
was either in Brighton Boulevard or near Military Road when
Podesta says he was approached and told that there was 'a
crazy man with a black jacket on . . . [who] was threatening
them [the witnesses] with a big knife' and who had then run
off and gone into the water'.[8] Leo Hamlin, a council cleaner,
noticed the exchange as Podesta talked to, in Hamlin's
words, the 'two local swimmers who I often see at the beach
. . . [They came] out of the surf and hurried over to a police
car which had just arrived in Ramsgate Avenue right in front
of the North Bondi RSL.'[9]

Podesta was trying to take everything in, but really
'didn't know what was going on'.[10] He would later recall that
one of the swimmers noticed the suspect in the water with his
clothes on, and pointed him out to the policeman – 'and I
saw the gentleman come, walking up the beach'.[11] Things
began moving very quickly now. Podesta went back to his
vehicle to make the broadcast, catching sight of Levi walking
towards him. But in the excitement and confusion, Podesta
mistook his car sign as Bondi One – not Bondi Two. Static
soon filled the airwaves as Podesta's transmission interfered

with the real Bondi One. At 7.04.48 a.m., VKG told (the real) Bondi One that the criminal database search on Levi had yielded nothing. Here is how the dispatches were recorded, starting with Jones's reply to that message from VKG:

7.05 a.m.: Yeah, copy that, radio. He was last seen in the vicinity of Campbell Parade. We're just going to have a patrol around the beach and Ben Buckler.
7.05.10: (Static. Simultaneous talk.)
7.05.12: Yeah, to the car calling.
7.05.14: (Static. Simultaneous talk.)
7.05.16: That car calling?
7.05.28: I've got that person up here on Bondi Beach on the corner in front of the surf club. I'm just going over there to approach him now.
7.05.28: That car that's in at Bondi Beach in front of the surf club, your call sign?
7.05.33: The other Bondi car. I presume I'd be Bondi Two then, if the other car's calling as Bondi One.

As Podesta, Bondi Two, drove over for a closer look, Dilorenzo and Jones, Bondi One – hearing Podesta's dispatch – hurtled down to the beach. Podesta kept his focus on Levi, who 'was actually running up the beach . . . the gentleman must've seen my vehicle'.[12] Podesta described his first brush with Levi in an interview later that day: 'He ran across the Campbell Parade. I drove the vehicle up to him, about 10 metres away, when he stopped . . . I saw he had a big knife in his hand. I . . . opened the door of the car . . . asked him to stop and then he ran back across the road towards the beach.'[13] The search now became a chase, and the cops moved in for closure.

Behind the wheel of Bondi One, Dilorenzo acceler-ated the car so it mounted the kerb, clearing away a growing crowd of spectators. The doors were hurled open, and Dilorenzo and Jones jumped out in pursuit of their suspect. 'Stop. Police!' they both yelled as Levi descended from the promenade to hit the sand, dashing back for the water.

Podesta, still tetchy with the adrenalin racing, abandoned his police vehicle on the wrong side of the road – with the door left wide open – and sprinted off to catch up to the action. Dilorenzo, clearly the quickest runner, was gaining on Levi with each pace, hoping to tackle him before the water. But about a metre or so from the surf, Levi suddenly turned around – brandishing the knife at the policemen for the first time. He then headed into the water, striding out until he was half submerged, the chilly waves tossing him in all directions. It was now nearly 7.07 a.m. and the beach, almost like an amphitheatre, started to stage a macabre real-life scene for the growing throng of onlookers.

Levi, having lost his essential spectacles in the rush to avoid the police, had a penetrating, menacing look in his eyes. Lost, unable to focus properly, he desperately tried to find his bearings as he stood out in the water. He started waving the knife around in figure-of-eights and making strange noises. And then, turning the knife towards himself, Levi 'pretended . . . like he was gonna push it straight through his stomach region'.[14] By now, having left their valuable batons either in the cars or at the station, Dilorenzo, Jones and Podesta had their revolvers out, trained on Levi's stomach. The guns were all they had to defend themselves, should they need to. Podesta's weapon was particularly impressive – soon after leaving the academy, he had taken the gun to a shop in the city to have a rubber grip attached to the handle. It made the revolver fit more tightly into the heel of his hand.[15]

By this stage, Sergeant Taylor had arrived at the beach and was watching the disturbing events unfold with

Brunner on the promenade. He was the most senior officer in sight, 'the commander there to oversee the situation and to report to the radio the resources we may need'.[16]

At 7.07.18 a.m., Taylor hit the radio button to speak to VKG to make his one and only call for back-up: 'It might be an idea if we get an ambulance down here for when he comes out of the water,' he suggested. No reinforcements, no dogs . . . no negotiators. Taylor considered there was little chance of things getting out of hand. Indeed, so calm did the situation appear that Taylor declined to even quarantine the crowd – both to guarantee their safety and deny them the view.

By 7.08 a.m. the Paddington officers, Goodman and Smith, had joined in, but were covering Levi at a distance. It was five against one.

At 7.09 a.m., Dilorenzo, on the portable, contacted VKG, keeping an eye trained on Levi all the while. 'Yeah, radio,' Dilorenzo shouted. 'I was wondering if there was any boat, Water Police or someone that could come out . . . he keeps going out. Don't know when he's going to come back in, this bloke.' Eight minutes later, the police launch *Intrepid*, based in Sydney Harbour, commenced the journey to the Heads, and round to Bondi Beach.

At 7.18 a.m., the VKG operator called Dilorenzo with a helpful, albeit belated, suggestion: 'Bondi One, do you require the negotiators there now?' the operator asked. 'Yeah, I think it might be a good idea,' Dilorenzo replied. 'He doesn't seem to want to listen to anyone else.' Two minutes later, the first of five pager messages were sent. Two minutes after that, a police negotiator and counsellor, Sergeant Terry Dalton, trained in defusing hostile situations, responded to the plea for help – and headed down to his car. Dilorenzo was told negotiators were on the way. But by the time Dalton reached his garage, Levi would be dead.

Meanwhile the cops on the beach employed their own tactics and did their best to calm Levi and encourage his surrender. Soothing phrases were made in dulcet, conciliatory tones. Each of the key participants – Jones, Dilorenzo and Podesta – tried to coax Levi to come out of the cold wash, where he was being dumped and rocked. However, it was only when they retreated a distance from the shoreline, creating a largish free patch of sand, that he obeyed. Dilorenzo told his colleagues they had 'plenty of room', that they should 'just break off, let him do what he wants to do'.[17]

It was 7.21 a.m. when Levi moved in from the water, his clothes drenched and heavy and freezing, his head spinning from side to side. He had been in the cold surf for 14 minutes. The knifeman suddenly became conscious of the five officers that surrounded him and started heading north, up to the surf club where he'd first been spotted. Dilorenzo stayed on the inside, the nearest to the beach wall, about five metres away to Levi's left; Podesta skimmed the water's edge with his boots, staying on the right also about five metres away. Jones kept ahead of Levi, more than ten metres in front, with the walk dragging naturally towards him. Goodman and Smith were further away still, at Levi's rear. It was formed as a triangle of safety, with support. The revolvers were not pointed at Levi so much as they were drooped, somewhat casually, down by the sides, ready for immediate use.

The cajoling continued: 'C'mon Roni,' 'drop the knife', 'It's the police here, we're here to help you' – literally every conceivable line was used. Jones, Podesta and Dilorenzo were the chatterers, but mainly Dilorenzo, who 'screamed a hundred times, "Please, please drop it." "Roni, please drop the weapon." . . . Everyone would've heard me. I was screaming it out.'[18] At times, Levi was menacing, contorting his face meanly, aggressively; at other moments he turned his back defiantly on his pursuers, and stared serenely and passively out at the waves.

Levi never responded to his pursuers remaining silent throughout the perplexing ordeal – apart from all manner of garbled noises. He wore a 'stuck-in-a-runaway-train expression . . . [that] registered not only psychic, but raw physical pain'.[19] Dilorenzo described him as being 'like a lizard flicking his tongue in and out in a real fast motion and his eyes looked like . . . devil eyes'.[20]

Constable Grant Seddon, a welcome reinforcement, had also been busy at work. Arriving soon after the two Paddington officers, Seddon had been sifting through sand close to the promenade, looking for something Levi was thought to have dropped on his initial scurry. (His glasses? Pills perhaps?) When the search proved fruitless, Seddon acted as go-between, ferrying items to and from the officers on the beach. At one stage, he fetched Podesta's keys so that the truck Podesta had discarded could be moved onto the correct side of the road, parked and locked up – away from the punters listening to the police radio. He came back with two long metal batons. The ultimate confrontation was looming, all of it within the gaze of a swelling congregation.

Joggers had given up watching the drama from the sidelines and had returned to their laps on the sand, skirting precariously close to the police pod directly in the line of fire. As Dilorenzo recalled: 'There was a lady jogging who was no more than 50, 60 foot [about 15–18 metres] away from the incident.'[21] It had become a chaotic scene: guns, uniforms, a washed-out and drawn lone figure, and people all around.

There was also a photographer on the sand who'd originally gone down to film the famous Bondi walls. Subdued and studious, and a Frenchman (ironically enough) Jean Pierre Bratanoff-Firgoff was now capturing the dramatic images, flicking off frame after frame. At 7.26 a.m. Dilorenzo got onto his radio. 'Yeah, radio,' he said. 'If we can just get further cars down here. This bloke's walking up and down the beach following joggers and persons on the beach. We just want to secure them away from him.'

Levi's trek up and down the beach now headed south again, back to where he had first left the water. His demeanour was becoming more active, volatile; his noises sounding more anguished. The mood on the foreshore had become more strained than before as the rising sun from the north-east corner started to cast lengthy shadows. Levi was now bordered on his left by the water, with Jones, Dilorenzo and Podesta encircling him on his right, in a triangle. Goodman and Smith were well behind this human spear, still acting as the outer cordon.

At that point Levi pushed the knife back towards himself again, into his stomach, as if he wanted to kill himself. He paused only to flick the weapon from hand to hand, juggling it almost. Jones, dropping his gun in a gesture of backing down, walked forward and pleaded with Levi to return to the promenade for a chat. 'Everyone get back. Get back!' Dilorenzo yelled out as Levi marched dramatically at Jones, taking two or three quick steps in the policeman's direction and jabbing with the knife. Suddenly he stopped on the spot, staring. Jones started to squeeze gently with his fingers on the trigger as Levi turned again – back to the north.

And then, about this time, 'according to a key witness, as the minutes ticked away and the sun crept over the northern head to light up the white cubicle of Australia's most famous beach, their demands turned scabrous: "Listen you fucking deadshit. Drop the knife." '[22] This was no longer a nonchalant waiting game. Levi, now sparked, was clearly 'becoming more agitated, just the stare in his eyes,' Constable

Goodman later reported. 'You could sort of, like, feel the frustration with him.'[23]

At 7.29 a.m., Levi headed west, towards the promenade . . . and, in so doing, he moved directly towards Podesta and Dilorenzo. Jones and Seddon – who had rejoined the group after an absence – now split themselves apart as flanks on Levi's right – behind and in front of his shoulder axis. Goodman and Smith watched from the left, at a much longer distance. Everything was moving more quickly now; Levi was certainly surging faster than before.

And then he stopped, throwing his arms dramatically apart like clock handles at 2.45, on the three and the nine. Crucifix-like. Dilorenzo and Podesta positioned themselves about five metres away from Levi, fifteen feet, two body-lengths from the knife. An uneasy silence followed with Levi remaining in this paralysed pose for five to ten seconds. A long pause when so much had already occurred so quickly. Seddon moved in from behind Levi for another baton hurl, smashing the calm. Incredibly, Levi caught the advance in time, spinning around to confront his attacker. The opportunity gone, Seddon backed off, and Levi went on the march again.

He turned and strode, almost galloping, towards Dilorenzo. The cop – with his gun drawn and targeted, his portable radio hitched to his equipment belt, and a mouthpiece clipped to his shirt – found himself walking backwards, quicker and quicker. Up the beach. Towards the wall, the barrier, and the crowd. With nowhere left to turn. Dilorenzo felt Levi 'coming faster and faster', the constable even having to 'jog backwards to get away from him'.[24] Podesta also felt him 'picking up the pace . . . [because] he had the knife. He was wielding it. We were backing up'.[25]

As they hit looser sand, away from the high-tide line, marked by a string of seaweed, Dilorenzo actually slipped over, but then quickly regained himself. Not before Levi had made his boldest challenge, however, with a couple of quick leaps forward with the knife. Seddon moved in, attacking with the baton. But Levi moved away before he could strike. Seddon reeled back defensively while Levi 'turned and moved forward much quicker than before with the police continually moving backwards'.[26] Now it was Podesta's turn: 'I saw Levi lunge forward and push the knife further out, directly at Constable Podesta.'[27] At this point Bratanoff-Firgoff clicked off a few more precious frames, transfixed by the tension and the expectation.

All of a sudden the knifeman's attention returned to the hapless Dilorenzo. As the policeman would recount later that day: Levi marched 'that fast at me, I couldn't run any further back and I had this wall behind me and . . . next thing I know . . . the blade was coming at me and I thought: Fuck, what do I do?'[28] Levi advanced again and, Dilorenzo recalled: 'I saw my wife and my kid flash through my eyes'.[29]

It was 7.30 a.m. The sun now completely coated the sand in a bright pale shade. The waves pounded in, roaring in in smallish-size sets. An ever-congested beachfront of spectators gazed out in awkward wonder, and then in horror. Even at this sickening moment, Bondi Beach was magnificent and inspiring.

Podesta's drug-taking teenage mate, Mike Morrison, was similarly awestruck as he woke up to the morning on the waves, blissfully ignorant of the drama on the shore. He thought it was a 'beautiful day – I'll never forget it. I was in the southern corner of the beach. There were about three or four other surfers in the water at the time and I clearly remember paddling over a wave and I heard what I believe to be three or four shots in succession.'[30] There were four shots in all, Podesta and Dilorenzo doing the firing. Levi collapsed onto the sand. Paramedics sprinted to the scene. And then Morrison caught the next wave in . . . to a bloodied beach.

FIVE

AFTER THE SHOTS

'He lunged at them and they both
fired their weapons . . . I
believe it was the only action
they could take at that particular
time . . . It was a most
appropriate action.'

Chief Inspector Richard Baker,
12.18 p.m., 28 June 1997

Podesta's first shot hurtled through the cool beach air with frightening force, smashing the knuckle on one of the fingers of Levi's left hand before colliding with the thumb. *Bang!* Spearing in on a slight angle from the left, the bullet kept powering away into the exposed right side, puncturing the chest just below the right nipple and into the heart, spraying blood. The metal jacket tore a 2.5 centimetre hole in Levi's aorta, the size of a 20-cent piece, and just kept on going; gnashing through his body and splitting a rib before resting in muscle.

In that split second of pain, power and brutality, Levi was propelled back and off balance, spun slightly towards north. Then *pow-pow!* – two more shots were fired. Two taps in succession, this time from Anthony Dilorenzo. These shots hit in roughly the same spot – in the ribcage on Levi's left side – spinning him back and around, this time to the south, straight back towards the officers and dropping him down towards the sand. One of the bullets whirled through the lungs and destroyed several ribs, ripping them apart. The bullet spiralled further still, eventually smashing out through Levi's back and into the corner of a damp black jacket, filling with blood. The other bullet also created maximum devastation: the chest, more ribs, the oesophagus, liver and spine, all were mangled and attacked by its withering speed.

A fourth shot ended the salvo, Podesta's second shot, perhaps only a second after his first, interrupted by Dilorenzo's quicker trigger finger. This final round connected with Levi as he was crashing to the sand, at first only to his knees. The thunderclap of bullets sent a roaring echo across the sand – *bang-pow-pow-bang*! – that bounced back loudly to the promenade. Podesta's second shot caught Levi in the bottom – or, to be medically precise, it punched into the knifeman's perineum, the tender gap between the anus and the scrotum. The bullet heaved up through the rectum, coming to rest in softer buttock tissue.

In the second or so of gunfire, Senior Constable Jones didn't 'recognise them as gun shots at first . . . Out there they were very quiet at first. I didn't realise – I thought it was, but . . . [then] I thought "No" because he was still standing . . . still holding the knife'.[1] Even in his thud to the ground, on his knees, Levi's knife would not budge. To Sergeant Taylor, the senior officer at the scene, who was standing some 250 metres away from the action, the shooting took place so quickly that he reported seeing only 'the male waving the knife around' and then hearing 'what appeared to be two shots'.[2]

After the noise had died down, Goodman and Smith rushed to their colleagues. Seddon had got to the bleeding Levi first, however, immediately swinging his baton at the shot man's right hand – going for the knife. He pressed his baton on Levi's wrist. With crucial seconds ticking by, Jones hurried in, stamping one of his heavy boots on the knife hand, and using his other foot to kick the weapon away. Dilorenzo also charged in quickly, and instinctively stood on top of his victim – pressing Levi's bulk into the beach – suddenly shocked into thinking 'he was going to jump up with the knife when he was on the ground and go at us again'.[3]

But Levi committed no such miracle. He lay there motionless and face down, his head cushioned roughly but peacefully into the cold, loose sand, breathing faintly. Blood spewed out. The pulse slowed.

Podesta was dumbfounded, shocked to the spot. At 7.31.15 a.m., Dilorenzo spoke into his portable radio: 'Radio, this male's charged us with a knife. We've had to discharge our firearms. He's on the ground near. The ambo's down here now.'[4]

The VKG message started a chain reaction. Copy staff at Sydney newsrooms, listening in to police exchanges on radio transmitters, yelled out the action to reporters and photographers. All the buttons were pushed, with investigators, crime-scene analysts, coronial staff, government contractors and police media representatives all being called. So too were senior officers – patrol commanders, district commanders, region commanders, assistant commissioners – and the offices of the commissioner, Peter Ryan, and the NSW police minister, lawyer and Labor stalwart Paul Whelan. The news flashed across the country. The first reports were light on detail, but clear enough: police had just popped a guy waving a knife in front of people on Bondi Beach.

Two paramedics, Craig Payne and Gregory Sikkens – who had watched the drama for sixteen minutes – raced down to the beach, kneeling alongside Levi. Immediately, they spotted three gaping wounds to the chest but the pulse, once reported as weak, had gone altogether. He was unconscious, on his way out. With all this going on, Taylor arrived on the beach, as did a third paramedic. Various resuscitation techniques were attempted – nothing.

This was no longer a semi-comical dance up and down the beach. The adrenalin of the moment subsided, and what seemed like a deafening silence took over. The ambulancemen were looking worried and worked away feverishly – 'putting tubes in him and hooking him up, pumping into him'.[5] It was all too much for Podesta: 'Rod burst out crying . . . He was starting to crack up a bit.'[6]

The young officer bawled uncontrollably for minutes that seemed much longer – too distressed and overwhelmed with the enormity of what had happened. And what was about to happen. Dilorenzo grabbed his partner by the hand and took him to Taylor for consoling, and to get him out of the way.

With the revival attempts still going on, and the minutes preciously ticking over, Jones grabbed a notebook and started rounding up the witnesses. Names and numbers were jotted down and statements taken from the scores of people who could possibly give evidence on this very public killing. Five people volunteered their names to Dilorenzo; others wandered off to speak to other officers. Busy chattering and gesticulations filled the promenade; people exchanged viewpoints and observations on the surreal sights and sounds of that winter morning at Bondi Beach.

Some people walked away. Some stood in silent contemplation. Others remained with eyes glued to the waves and the beach, not knowing what else to do. But the ultimate voyeur, the person with the most critical observations and information, Jean Pierre Bratanoff-Firgoff, knew exactly what to do. Having just recorded on film the most dramatic of moments, a death, all in sequence, his thoughts were racing. He coolly took out the film and tucked it down near the bottom of one of his socks. Hiding it from view; sensing its immediate value. He then walked up to Jones, and left his contact details before racing home. To his darkroom.

The paramedics gently lifted Levi from the sand, clipped him onto a spinal board and wriggled his frame into a pressurised medical suit, to at least try to keep the blood with his vital organs. At 7.40 a.m., the body was carried from the sand to the shore. Police officers lent a hand, with Dilorenzo carrying an oxygen apparatus. Up they lifted the body, and into the back of the van. At 7.43 a.m., the ambulance vehicle exploded in a shimmer of lights and horns before dashing off to St Vincent's Hospital in Darlinghurst where the victim's terrifying morning had begun.

It was 7.45 a.m. Dilorenzo walked back to the beach to caucus with the other cops and see what needed to be arranged. And then he saw 'a couple of media cars show . . . just vultures . . . [coming] in straightaway'.[7] This acted as the cue to exit the scene. Seddon grabbed Podesta and Levi's equally shaken flatmate, Brunner – the man who had lived a lifetime in the past 105 minutes – and drove back to Bondi station. Seddon also grabbed the guns for forensic examination. Jones went to the station in a car with Dilorenzo, but they 'didn't really feel like talking about it [and we] didn't really say much on the way back. We were, how can I describe it . . . remorseful.'[8]

Podesta was placed in the sergeants room and Dilorenzo went to an office in the detectives area. This was an attempt to ensure the officers were separated and that their testimonies would be free of any collaboration between the two.

Two officers from Bondi, Detective Sergeant Adam

Michael Purcell and Detective Senior Constable Murray James Wilson, took control of the initial, and crucial, part of the investigation. They were the first senior officers on the scene. But they were not *in charge* – or at least they were not supposed to be. In accordance with strict police guidelines, the duty operations inspector (DOI) – the overall commander of operations as-they-happen, the officer who lives in a central communications bunker, coordinating resources as transmissions are received – makes that call. After the shots were fired, the DOI, Inspector John Warren Kent, got on the phone and paged the on-call homicide investigator for the designated area, Region South.

The message served as a wake-up call that morning for Detective Senior Sergeant Robert Norman McDougall. A seasoned investigator with 32 years' policing experience, McDougall started the ring-around. Local officers could not be used. That would give some people the wrong idea. Indeed, the Commissioner's Instructions specified that only investigators from outside the area could be approached to work on killings by police officers. There was no ambiguity in the directive. The outsiders rule was an important corruption-prevention strategy, especially at this time, in the immediate aftermath of the Wood Royal Commission. It was essential, McDougall knew, to use cops who had no connection to those who were involved.

McDougall called his understudy, Detective Senior Constable Michael Fitzgerald, who lived in Coogee. Fitzgerald was asked to go straight to the station, to hold the fort until his superior officer had got his lot together. While McDougall got changed, he made other calls but could only manage to raise Detective Constables Comans and Allison. The Bondi commander, Richard Baker, also took a call. It should have acted as a jolt – two officers he suspected of being drug users and suppliers had just popped a guy on the beach. Internal Affairs also got buzzed to intervene. Detective Inspector Peter Thomas Fitzpatrick picked up the call in his car in Elizabeth Street in the city and headed down to the sand as the Internal Affairs review officer. He had the most important job of all: to be the impartial observer, to guarantee compliance with the rules. Fitzpatrick's duty was to make sure that McDougall and Fitzgerald got it right, that they did everything the right way.

And so it was that by 7.50 a.m., barely seven minutes after Levi's body had been dragged from the sand, all of the ingredients were down at Bondi or on their way. This was to be the first big test of accountability, just weeks after the humiliation of the royal commission. It was explained to reporters that the police would look diligently, and impartially, at what had happened and how it could have been handled differently.

It was 7.55 a.m. when Levi was wheeled inside the hospital doors, 24 minutes after hitting the sand. Dr Reginald Lord, the general surgery registrar in Emergency, had just finished scrubbing and was ready to insert a chest tube and perform an emergency thoracotomy. It was their only chance. On arrival, 'the patient had no blood pressure, no heart rate, no respirations and no sign of neurological function'.[9] But despite his pathetic condition, the fight to recover his life continued for another twenty minutes. One of the nursing staff, still on duty from the overnight shift, recognised Levi as the patient who had absconded just three hours earlier.

Nurses Rachael Meek and Sharon Renshaw helped with the resuscitation efforts and took notes to chronicle the ordeal for the record. Dr Lord later recalled that 'four teams worked simultaneously. The first team managed the endotracheal tube and ventilation, another doctor inserted a chest tube into the right chest, relieving a right non-tension pneumothorax. The third team attempted to insert intravenous cannulae'.[10]

While the doctors and nurses pushed on, glancing at their monitors for a sign of hope, Detective Wilson, a close workmate of the shooters, was taking control of the initial police response at the beach. He relayed a message on his radio to VKG at 8.09 a.m., fourteen minutes into the Levi operation. He explained that, from initial conversations, it appeared that one of the officers had fired twice and another officer just once – with one of the shots hitting the chest.

At 8.19 a.m., Roni Levi was recorded as dead. Nurse Meek collected the puncture swabs and took a blood sample, as per procedure. When Levi was rolled over to remove his clothes, 'a small metal object was found between the shirt and the patient's back'.[11] It was Dilorenzo's bullet.

Word of the shooting spread quickly. All along the promenade and in the cafes and breakfast houses on Campbell Parade, talk centred only on one thing.

Senior Constable Dave Rose from the Police Media Unit, the dreaded information controllers, found himself in the invidious position of trying to please both his police peers and the journalists he was paid to accurately inform. Rose arrived at the height of the drama and joined a growing ensemble of officers near the sand. Some were guarding the crime scene, keeping the stickybeaks at bay, or acting as sentries. Other officers were continuing to take statements from witnesses, as the impatient journalists had also started to do.

The Channel 9 camera team found Leo Hamlin, the council cleaner who had witnessed the race to the beach, the walk and even the shooting. The reporter asked him simply if he'd seen Levi 'lunge at all at the police at that stage . . . just before he was shot'.[12] Hamlin had a quick think and then said, 'Well . . . I'm not too sure.'[13] It would turn out to be a crucial conversation.

With journalists racing around for quotes, Rose appreciated that the police side of things needed to be quickly explained. Rose wanted a talking head, someone in a uniform that he could put in front of the cameras, for the nightly news bulletins. He thought he would try his luck with Baker. After all, he was the boss of Bondi, and a guy who knew all about the shooters.

Rose first spotted Fitzpatrick, the Internal Affairs reviewing officer with whom he thought it proper to clear things. Interviews were extremely sensitive topics and needed high approval. They could prejudice investigations or be criticised later in court. 'Peter, I'm gathering the information at the moment,' Rose informed Fitzpatrick, '[and] things are pretty hectic. As you can see, there is a large crowd here. What I intend to do is see Dickie Baker later in the day and we will do a stand-up in front of the media later in the afternoon.'[14] Fitzpatrick, who was there to enforce compliance with the rules, did not stand in the way of this potentially prejudicial moment. Instead, he turned on his heels and returned to the station, where the major players were assembled.

All six officers in the shooting party – Podesta, Dilorenzo, Seddon, Jones, Goodman and Smith – had already been ordered to keep apart and not speak to one another about what had occurred. But that was hard in the poky Bondi station, with no room to move. Podesta was in the sergeants room; Dilorenzo occupied the detectives room close by; and the four other officers filled up other hastily created compartments. On occasions, some of them sat at opposite ends of the *same* room in a feeble attempt to observe the non-communication edict. Of course, the intended separation became a charade.[15] Incredibly, when Fitzpatrick arrived to supervise the investigation, shortly after Levi was pronounced dead, Podesta and Dilorenzo were sitting down together – in direct contravention of police orders. The Internal Affairs man noticed that Podesta 'was upset . . . [and] looked as if he'd been tearful' and so, instead of taking them to task, Fitzpatrick politely 'asked questions of how their welfare was . . . I just asked some general questions because I didn't want to jeopardise any form of the investigation at that point in time, so early in the day.'[16]

By 8.13 a.m., Rodney Podesta had recovered sufficiently to start hitting his mobile phone. Friends and family needed to be informed of his predicament. Dilorenzo was also on the blower, devastated and concerned for his pregnant wife, Annabelle. He told his wife that Levi was in a pretty bad way in hospital and she later told a journalist, 'I was in shock . . . putting on video tapes for our three year old daughter, and I just said: "Do you want me to come down?" He later called me . . . to say the man had passed away.'[17]

Podesta's first thought was to ring Ron Quin, the cocaine-using friend he had been with the night before. Podesta placed the call to Terry Voto's mobile, which was a regular way of contacting Quin due to the lack of a telephone in the flat shared by him and Voto. The call lasted ten seconds. Quin's girlfriend, Renee Robertshaw, was about to leave for work when the call came through. The short stroll down Campbell Parade, dropping in quickly at the Liberty for a coffee, and off to her other job at a local real estate agency, was a ritual. It was Saturday, the busiest day in the property week, and she had to be in early.

It was now about 8.30 a.m. Inside the Liberty Lunch, waiting for her coffee, Robertshaw picked up the vibe on her previous night's dinner partner, Podesta. And it wasn't pleasant. The shocking news came from either 'Victor . . . [or] Robert Gould. It could have been Jason, it could have been anyone who goes in there and has a cup of coffee'.[18] The conversation was singling out Podesta for his behaviour, and Robertshaw, incensed by the ill-informed criticism, briefly had 'an argument with some people about the shooting. I didn't think it was fair that Rodney was getting the blame'.[19]

The Liberty Lunch now became a hive of activity and rumour-mongering. It was gossip central. At 10.07 a.m., a person using a mobile phone belonging to Stephen Langton, the Liberty's effervescent floor manager, called Podesta's mobile. After this call, all sorts of phone calls were made to a small gang of Liberty regulars. At 10.20 a.m., Langton's mobile was recorded ringing Langton's home, where his girl-friend, Joanne Diamond (not her real name), was staying.

Three minutes later, the Langton mobile called Robert Gould, who, as usual, had been out late at the Liberty Lunch the night before. After all, it had been a Friday. Indeed, Gould had used his mobile only hours earlier, check-ing his voicemail for messages three times from 1.48 to 2.35 a.m. on 28 June, presumably to see if a lady friend had called. Gould had, as was his usual practice, experienced 'excess drinking and indulgence in drugs'[20] and was obviously feeling it. When he found out, in his morning-after haze, that Podesta and Dilorenzo had just killed a guy on Bondi Beach, his jaw nearly hit the floor. Gould, the cocktail prince of the eastern suburbs and savvy real estate executive suddenly had disastrous thoughts. Thoughts of what might have gone on with Podesta in the twilight of the night before.

'Oh shit, that's not good!'[21] he said to himself. Gould thought that it was entirely possible he and Podesta might have been drinking and doing coke together the night before the shooting. But he couldn't be sure it happened. Now Gould began to panic. He tried to call Victor Mainwaring (not his real name), a Bondi identity and Liberty regular. But the line was engaged. Mainwaring was already catching up on the latest gossip, from the person using Langton's mobile.

At 10.32 a.m., Mark Lorenzo, the former heroin dealer, rang Podesta on the mobile. He too wanted to find out what was going on, and how his mate was feeling. The Bondi shooter, supposedly under investigation and apparently segregated from other officers (but not from the rest of the world), was taking and making all sorts of calls.

At 10.33 a.m., seconds after hanging up on Lorenzo, Podesta took a call from Gould. Three minutes later, after speaking briefly to the shooter, Gould started alerting other people about the tragedy. His golf and dining partner, Kieran O'Connor, the Liberty's former owner, had just 'got back from elephant trekking in Burma' when 'the drama queen of Bondi, Robert Gould' rang him up with the news.[22] It only momentarily broke his concentration. O'Connor's trusty partner, TC, also got the word when he got to work at the Liberty. 'This is the last thing they need,'[23] he exclaimed.

McDougall, the detective in charge, got to the scene relatively late and so met the coronial representatives down at the beach, going 'into the actual scene beyond the tapes.'[24] The coroner, Derrick Hand, and the deputy coroner, John Abernethy, gave an impromptu briefing, declaring that independent legal counsel would be appointed to supervise the case.

Hand and Abernethy also attended Baker's office at the police station, receiving a crisp briefing on what was known about the tragedy, and what was being done. The coroner was now technically in charge, with the police under his command. However, despite appreciating the significance of the coroner's responsibilities, Baker remained silent on his suspicions about the shooters. He never uttered a word to the coroner or his own police superiors; neither did he contact Internal Affairs for guidance. Baker left the running to the Homicide Squad. And he left them alone – without details of all that he knew.

By 11 a.m., with the formalities with the coroner completed, McDougall got down to business. The district commander, Chief Superintendent Bob Waites, 'said he was willing to supply investigators from other patrols to assist' so as to keep the investigation independent and at arm's-length and above board.[25] McDougall told Waites that this wouldn't be required, however. He had a team of four that could handle the load.

McDougall explained that he and Allison would interview Dilorenzo, and Fitzgerald and Comans would interview Podesta. Completing such formalities with the shooters was rightly deemed the major priority. The remaining four officers, Seddon, Jones, Goodman and Smith, were told they could make statements. It was desirable, but not essential, that they be separately interviewed, but there were not enough officers on hand for that.

McDougall considered the next day, Sunday, would provide time for focus,[26] but things moved faster than McDougall could contain. Calls were coming in from everywhere and 'because of the large number of witnesses . . . presenting themselves there and then for the purpose of making a statement . . . I involved the other . . . [Bondi] police.'[27] The Commissioner's Instructions on independent inquiries, explicitly written up and underscored in bold black letters, were now being breached.

At 12.15 p.m., Baker took up the offer to say something important about them to the media, to give an explanation of the actions of the Bondi shooters. Baker could have said several things, cautious and respectful of the fact that the coroner was officially in charge of the investigation. The script had been used successfully, and without discourse, countless times before: 'It was a terrible tragedy, a regrettable incident . . . We extend our condolences and sincere regret to the families involved . . . The officers involved will receive full welfare assistance . . . An independent shooting team has been established to investigate the matter . . . And, because the inquiry is now in the hands of the coroner, that is all that can be said.' Dave Rose, the media advisor, almost certainly reminded him of the script.

Baker was feeling more adventurous than that, however. He gave Podesta and Dilorenzo – even though they had not been interviewed and given an official version of their actions – the full backing of the force. Prejudging the coroner in his inquiry, Baker said the police action could be completely justified and was appropriate in the circumstances. He said it was something that had to be done. And, contrary to police instructions, Baker described in great detail the morning's events. He talked about the fear of hostages being taken, the pursuit up and down the beach and in the surf and negotiation attempts and a baton strike.

The Bondi chief put an official version on the table, before any of the facts had been established, one that was hard to counter. He said the police certainly didn't want to shoot people unnecessarily: 'The two officers took this action because they feared for their lives. That's the bottom line. It was the only action that was available to them to repel the very fact that their lives were in danger.'[28] Baker put the blame squarely on Levi's shoulders, saying his officers had taken 'all the necessary precautions to prevent the incident until the person lunged at them with the knife'.[29] Before the shooters had even been questioned, it came across that the

puzzle of Levi's death had already been answered – at a kerbside press conference, before a pack of cameras. It was the
knifeman's behaviour, Levi's lunge, that had encouraged the
gunfire that ripped through the cold morning air.

THE REMAINS OF THE DAY SIX

'Well, as I was told, the night
of the shooting, I did excessively
drink . . . I was that drunk . . .
I drank excessively . . . to
forget about what had happened
that day.'

Anthony Dilorenzo, Police Integrity Commission,
Operation Saigon, 2 November 1999

One of the more eager members of the Living Dangerously Club, Constable Patrick Brown, who had partied with Podesta and Dilorenzo at the police 'wake' just two nights earlier, was woken by his fiancée to be told about the shooting. She hadn't mentioned which of the officers had been involved and so Brown was drawn down to the station, overtaken by curiosity. It wasn't long after parking his motorbike that he learned their identities.

Although Detectives McDougall and Fitzgerald had stressed to the officers that they remain isolated, the smallness of the station at Bondi rendered that a virtual impossibility. And if any of the detained officers had bothered to switch on a radio, they could have heard their commander, Richard Baker, providing a script of what had occurred.

There were many visitors to the station. Dilorenzo's wife, Annabelle, came to offer her support. Brown talked to 'numerous people' and to 'Tony Dilorenzo and Rod Podesta as well'.[1] Podesta and Dilorenzo were outside 'having a break . . . a smoko break, or something'[2] and, probably not thinking of its relative triviality, Brown asked whether Podesta's birthday booze-up was still on the cards. 'Obviously I could see he was upset,' Brown would tell the Police Integrity Commission. 'He said: "This is going to take ages. I won't be turning up." I said: "I don't think so. It is still going to be alright. It is still going to go ahead."'[3]

At 12.22 p.m., the person operating Stephen Langton's mobile phone called Podesta for another chat, their second conversation of the day. At some stage, Podesta even called one of his drug-taking mates, Graeme Rooney – Zac MacKenzie's flatmate from Marrickville – to say he had killed someone.[4] At 12.33 p.m. and again, twelve minutes later, Mark Lorenzo called Podesta. They apparently had much of common interest to talk about. Lorenzo even went to the station, one of the sea of visitors who were allowed to dart in and out; seemingly at will.

McDougall, trying his best to keep things tidy and uncontroversial, was appalled to learn that a woman from police welfare 'had come in and they'd had a group meeting during that morning or that afternoon prior to the interview . . . I think it was the six police on the beach'.[5] He became concerned at the detail with which the group might have discussed the events of that morning, and how this would obviously lead to each officer's version of the shooting being tainted. So, despite McDougall's gag order and a directive that all officers be separated, the effort to prevent contamination had become a fiasco. Baker had already given a detailed public critique of the shooting at the press conference and now the six officers had swapped versions about the shooting under the apparent guise of a counselling session.

By lunchtime, everyone in Bondi knew, or could have known, what had happened on the beach – and, all of a sudden, rumours of boozing and drug-taking were snow-balling. The same thoughts Robert Gould had contemplated in his mid-morning blur were now being spoken about, openly but with feigned secrecy, in the coffee shops and bars along the promenade. It was particularly feverish at the Liberty Lunch. The new owner, Stanley Dowse, started hearing 'from staff or customers' rumours that Podesta and Dilorenzo 'were under the influence of either drugs or alcohol and that they'd been to our premises on the night before.'[6] While the shooters waited for their questions, the word was on the street.

At 2.30 p.m., Wilson and Purcell, the two Bondi detectives, went to St Vincent's Hospital, where they had inspected Levi's body earlier in the day. Their attendance was required a second time to complete the important reporting formalities. Wilson assumed the status of 'the officer discovering death', a formal legal title giving him responsibility to report the death and its circumstances to the coroner. It was a serious obligation.

Nurse Rachael Meek handed over three bloodied 'puncture wound swabs' and '1 × purple top of blood and small metal object',[7] together with other items that had been recovered from the operation. The policemen then escorted the body on the trip to the morgue. At 3.04 p.m., Levi was placed in the custody of the coroner and an autopsy was scheduled. Wilson completed the p79A form, which constituted official advice to the coroner. He echoed Baker's remarks about the efficacy of the police conduct – and again the word 'lunged' was adopted. Wilson told the coroner,

Derrick Hand, that Levi had 'walked from the water and lunged at one of the officers with a knife. Two police officers then fired a number of shots from their service revolvers. The deceased sustained three wounds in the chest region and one in his left hand'.[8]

It was just after 3 p.m., while Wilson was typing up his form, that McDougall accompanied Dilorenzo to Waverley police station to ask him some questions. At 3.47 p.m., the electronic interview machine was activated and McDougall and Robert Allison, one of his hand-picked detective constables, began the crucial interrogation of the senior shooter. One minute later, down the road at the Bondi station, Fitzgerald invited Podesta in from the verandah for a similar ordeal.

Both teams used the ERISP machine ('electronic recording of interviews with suspected people'), which had only been introduced a few years earlier. The improved technology of such machines provided investigators with a valuable record of a subject's demeanour, whether interrogators were being oppressive or degrading, and if the expressions and movements of a witness, suspect or victim were indicative of something else. But all was not well with the ERISPs today. The machine in Dilorenzo's interview had no sound and picked up none of the voices in the room. At Bondi, with Podesta, the audio was fine but the vision was fuzzy and unrecognisable. For these most critical of interviews, the recorders were malfunctioning.

Podesta's interview with Fitzgerald and Comans was surprisingly short. It took only 36 minutes. By contrast, Dilorenzo's interview went for more than an hour and stretched to 186 questions. He was even invited by McDougall to draw a diagram of the beach, highlighting the officers' positions, to give the team a better understanding of what had taken place. Dilorenzo was quizzed on whether he had been drinking or was on 'prescription drugs'; Fitzgerald, however, declined to ask Podesta this simple question.

Although McDougall could have forced the shooters to provide a urine sample – as new laws introduced just four weeks earlier empowered him to do – Podesta and Dilorenzo were given no such instructions. Instead, they were both asked about police rules and regulations, their firearms training and the gravity of their powers. McDougall put the situation starkly to Dilorenzo: 'Are you aware of the conditions that a police officer is allowed to use his firearm?' Dilorenzo's reply:

Yes, I am. I know the powers come from common law and also if . . . I have a fear that . . . they or myself are going to receive grievous bodily harm or death, then in order to stop that I can discharge my firearm . . . if I didn't shoot him, I was the one that was going to get the knife through my guts. He was that close. I mean, if I . . . had a video on him, you wouldn't believe it. I mean, I can't believe I let him get that close to me.[9]

Despite the differences in the questioning, a strong common theme emerged, the same opinion that some of the officers had already shared with each other in their chats on the verandah: *Levi had been asking for it.* The shooting, they deduced, was a police-sponsored suicide, or 'suicide by cop' as the apparent phenomenon is known. Podesta remarked that Levi 'knew what was going to happen . . . this gentleman wanted to commit suicide and we were his best option to do it. We believe he used us to do his dirty work'.[10] Dilorenzo was similarly eloquent in assessing Levi's rationale: the knife-man had acted like 'he wanted to die . . . he kept turning the knife around on him and attempting to stick it into him and then . . . maybe he said: "I'll try to stab one of them and they'll finish it for me." And that's all I can think. I mean, I pleaded with the guy for 30 minutes.'[11]

With the interviews over, after eight hours of supposed isolation, Podesta and Dilorenzo were excused from further duties – but not before being reminded that they were not to discuss the incident with anybody. Dilorenzo went straight home. Podesta, still distressed, followed his partner, so they could talk in private. According to Annabelle Dilorenzo, the younger officer was 'basically a mess. They talked about [the shooting] over and over again. They had the tapes from when they were interviewed and they played them and spoke about them.'[12] This was, of course, quite an inappropriate thing to do, in direct contravention of his orders.

Podesta then returned home to his distraught mother and father, who had 'been waiting all day for him to come home' and were understandably very worried.[13] Charmaine Podesta's shooter son was upset and jittery when he arrived at Matraville, but nonetheless committed to keeping his engagements. He'd been persuaded to drown his sorrows with his mates and celebrate his twenty-eighth birthday in style.

At 4.44 p.m., twenty minutes after he'd finished his interview with Fitzgerald, Podesta got another call from Mark Lorenzo. At 5.40 p.m., Podesta rang TC at the Liberty Lunch, and also stopped by the restaurant later on for 'a little chat with . . . and expressed his disappointment in what happened. He said there was no way he could have avoided it'.[14] Podesta told TC to pop along to the birthday do if he finished work early. It was a group booking, for about fifteen people, at Tak's Thai restaurant on Oxford Street, Paddington, a place where the cops often got takeaway orders. At 5.50 p.m., Podesta got active again, phoning Mark Lorenzo.

Early in the evening, Podesta went to the Beach Road Hotel in Bondi to catch up with some people for a pre-dinner drink. Indeed, this was a night requiring a lot of drinking. Podesta was with 'five or six people'[15] when Terry Voto, Ron Quin's flatmate, spotted him up near the bar: 'he turned around and said hello to me . . . I asked him had he heard about the shooting on Bondi Beach and he replied something like, "Yes, I shot the person" or something like that.'[16] It was the start of a long night. The television news bulletins were chock-full of stories on the Levi drama. Cop controversies always rate highly, and this was compelling stuff.

Angelo 'Chill' Astudillo, who lived in Dilorenzo's apartment block and often shared the Friday-night fish dinners, was immediately affected by the television reports. He visited his friends that evening after he'd phoned Annabelle Dilorenzo and had been told that her husband was involved. Dilorenzo told Chill simply that a guy had pulled a knife, and had had to be shot.[17] And then he turned to face Astudillo and said: 'Look, do you want to come to a birthday party? I wouldn't mind if you came with me.'[18] At 7.27 p.m., Mark Lorenzo rang Podesta's mobile again. Another night of intoxication and exuberance was about to begin.

Much earlier on that Saturday, Melinda Dundas had tried to contact Levi after hearing her husband's message from the night before. So when the telephone rang in her Melbourne home and her sister, Fiona Christopher, answered it, 'Melinda, hovering in the background, thought it was Roni on the phone returning her call, until she noticed her sister shudder and take a deep breath. Melinda still couldn't believe it. "What they mean is that Roni's been shot and he's in hospital," she insisted.'[19]

Late that afternoon, Senior Constable Wilson, the Bondi detective who had done so much of the legwork, collected

Dundas and her sister from the airport at Mascot, and took them and a family friend, Jane Cole, to the morgue at Glebe. To view the body. Wilson's partner, Purcell, informed reporters waiting outside the morgue that the family was 'very distressed at the moment'.[20]

Wilson stayed with them for most of the evening too and together with McDougall, advised them on how the investigation was proceeding. Dundas then 'made tentative arrangements to attend the police station for the purpose of supplying a statement to assist the coroner'.[21] At 8.40 p.m., Wilson dropped Dundas and her supporters at Thellen Lodge, where they would stay for the night, to try to sleep with so many thoughts rushing through their shocked minds. He then clocked off duty, finishing a long day.

At 9.25 p.m., Wilson got on the blower to Podesta, to find out where the birthday celebrations were taking place. When he arrived at Tak's Thai – 'as a last minute thing, owing to the day's events, to show a bit of support'[22] – the party was in full swing. Everyone was buying drinks for the Bondi shooters, as an act of solidarity. There were loud across-the-table discussions, whispers in ears, and all sorts of mobile phone calls, coming and going.

At about 8 p.m., when the first orders for curry, noodles and stir-fry were being taken, Podesta picked up a call from Senior Constable Jones, his colleague from the beach that morning. Jones had just finished a stressful 22-hour shift, but more than that, he was worried. He wanted to make sure that Podesta was feeling in control of his faculties, 'because he seemed to be the most upset immediately after and throughout the other occasions I'd seen him on the day. Tony appeared to be handling it all right, but I was concerned about Rod's welfare'.[23] At 9.02 p.m., Podesta got another call full of comforting words. It was Mark Lorenzo . . . again.

The party became an event with two purposes: blowing out the candles for Podesta's birthday and trying to forget about what had happened. Podesta, the party boy, was joined in celebrity, in notoriety, by Dilorenzo, his fellow shooter. One of the other officers on the beach, Christopher Goodman, was also in attendance, as were Patrick Brown, Senior Constable Bobby Reed and Constable Bal Dadley from the eastern suburbs. Astudillo, Dilorenzo's mate, and Mark Lorenzo were also at the table.

The night soon turned into an inebriated affair. Dilorenzo drank heavily and Podesta had copious amounts of Jack Daniels and ended up 'very heavily intoxicated'.[24] Just after 9.25 p.m., Podesta called Graeme Rooney, his effervescent drug-using mate from Marrickville. Later still, at 11.53 p.m., Podesta called another Bondi drug dealer. Within seconds of that, he got straight back on the phone yet again, to Mark Lorenzo, from whom he'd become separated since leaving the restaurant.

The night was full of dishevelled drinking episodes, and nightclubbing: Byblos, Dancers and a place called the Temple, in the Exchange Hotel on Oxford Street, were visited by the Bondi shooters. They hovered near Taylor Square in Darlinghurst, where the first editions of the Sunday newspapers were just being hurled.

SEVEN
WASTED TIME

'Our systems have had a failure.
We have to learn . . . so that we
lessen the chances in the future
of this situation recurring . . .
I guess it is possible that
mistakes will occur.'

Acting Police Commissioner Jeff Jarratt,
1 July 1997, ABC Radio

The shooting received saturation coverage. And so there was instantaneous saturation community debate. Both of Sydney's Sunday newspapers gave it top billing, with considerable spreads on inside pages, although at this stage, the names of all those involved were withheld.

French photographer Jean Pierre Bratanoff-Firgoff, who sold his pictures to the *Sunday Telegraph*, had his most powerful image 'severely cropped and enlarged' all over the front page.[1] It was a harrowingly real illustration that captured the frenzy of the moment – the panic, the danger, the loneliness of the beach. Deep shadows, projected by the early morning sun, spilled across the sand. The shooters, slightly hunched and tight together, with their legs apart and guns raised, sat in foreground to the right. Their target, Roni Levi, his drenched jacket dangling from his elbows, loomed over Anthony Dilorenzo's left shoulder, staring straight ahead at the shooters, and leaning forward, like he was on the move. Jones and Seddon, one racing off with a baton and the other aiming his revolver at Levi's head, were racing forwards on the left of the frame. Goodman and Smith could not be seen, their presence on the left cropped by the back-bench newspaper editors.

It was a photograph that required more than one viewing, not just a passing glance. And it appeared to tell a different story from the one provided by Chief Inspector Baker's media conference. Levi didn't look in the pictures as if he was surging quickly up the beach; he appeared as a less mobile figure, restricted in his movements.

The opposition publication, the *Sun-Herald*, offered a special insight, using Danny Weidler, a senior reporter and eyewitness to the events the previous morning, to talk in his own words about the slaying. Using the banner headline: 'Shot dead as I watch . . . Our reporter sees police kill man on Bondi Beach', the newspaper recited, in great detail, Weidler's impression of the bizarre 35-minute showdown on the sand:

> *I was jogging along Bondi Beach at 7 a.m. when I saw a man run into the surf fully clothed. Moments later, six police arrived and stood at the water's edge. An ambulance pulled up soon after. I kept on jogging. Then on my way back from my lap, I stopped to watch. I turned to another jogger and said: 'Surely, they aren't going to shoot him?' Then the man fell to the sand, blood oozing from his clothing.*[2]

Both newspapers recorded a raft of responses from police officers, politicians, civil libertarians, eyewitnesses. Everyone was approached to have a say and express a view on the tragedy. Indeed, a lot of people volunteered an opinion, such was the force of the moment.

Undoubtedly due to the killing's very public nature, there was an explosive community reaction. It was the gossip in coffee shops, bars, workplaces, dinner parties and sporting fixtures. Contrasting views, expressed in equally vociferous language, filled letters pages, and the switchboards of radio talkback stations lit up with agitated listeners. On one hand, there was a spirited defence of the officers' actions: they'd been courageous, they had no alternative, it was argued. On the other, there was incredible fury. Between these two viewpoints, an overwhelming sense of community disquiet over the policemen's conduct would quickly leap to the fore and grab the ascendancy. The Levi shooting was seen as a brutal and excessive act, and it was incredibly 'hard to believe . . . considering he was surrounded by half a dozen policemen with guns drawn against a man armed with a knife'.[3]

The disbelief produced predictable criticism. Why didn't they just shoot him in the leg or the arm? Why didn't the police simply throw sand in his eyes? How come they didn't all use their batons? Why didn't they use a net, or bring in a four-wheel-drive vehicle to run him down? Couldn't they have charged him en masse? Anything but their revolvers . . . So soon after the Wood Royal Commission, with public suspicion so acute, the failure by the police to settle the dispute triggered great emotion. Irate citizens phoned Bondi police station to vent their anger, leaving officers 'disgusted by hundreds of . . . threatening phone calls'.[4] There was no middle ground here: the unnamed cops were either murderers or heroes.

Conscious of the potential for adverse political fallout, the Police Minister Paul Whelan pledged that there would be a thorough and exacting inquiry and emphasised its independence. He put a comfortable spin on things, however – mindful perhaps of pricking a negative reaction from the 13 000 officers he administered, many of whom saw themselves on that beach. Whelan seemingly justified the police action, saying the death was 'very regrettable but, faced with a threat, officers have to react . . . Police put their lives at risk to protect others. We can ask nothing more of them than that'.[5] The acting police commissioner, Jeff Jarratt – overseeing, in the absence of Peter Ryan, the entire geographic and political restructure of the organisation – commented that new training procedures for high-risk situations were about to be made compulsory for all officers and that better batons would soon be introduced. There was mention of capsicum spray and Jarratt even made a visit to the police station at Bondi.

These gestures and assurances rang hollow somehow – not least because 'most members of the public have taken it for granted, for many decades, that police were being given special training to deal with such situations.'[6] The Council for Civil Liberties condemned the shooting, as did health authorities, fighting to develop a better community understanding of people suffering from mental illness. The Liberal Party's Opposition police spokesman, Andrew Tink, said that given the public's concern, it was probably appropriate for the Police Integrity Commission (the new independent watchdog recommended by Justice Wood) to investigate the matter.

An official police media spokesman, Senior Constable Mark Hargraves, 'disputed reports suggesting the man did not understand police warnings to drop the knife . . . "There was no problem with his English," he said'.[7] But running commentary like this only served to deepen the community's concern – for Levi, as had been made clear, had not spoken a word on the beach. It suggested that police media statements were being slanted against a dead man who could not speak for himself.

Detective Senior Sergeant McDougall appreciated the weight of public expectation, that his investigation would need to be meticulous, nothing could be missed or left to chance. Only the most scrupulous inquiry would be sufficient to douse the suspicion that the police could not be trusted to investigate their own.

There was apprehension, built on the police force's historical inability to keep its focus in such matters, that the investigators would support their blue brothers by producing a voluminous and impressive-looking report, but one that lacked content or credibility: it would satisfy all of the coronial requirements perhaps, but none of the community's demands. Now Levi's widow, Melinda Dundas, joined the chorus of disenchantment, desperate for answers. She rang the police to tell them she would not be available for an interview. Not just yet.

On Monday, 30 June, Coroner Derrick Hand appointed a barrister, David Cowan, to effectively take charge of the investigation, to direct police enquiries and coordinate the brief of evidence for a coronial hearing. The gesture underscored the (apparent) independence of the case, sending the clear message that the police would not be able to collude or cover up with such a prominent member of the Bar in play. Cowan's inclusion guaranteed that this would be no normal investigation. He had experience in police shootings, having played a role in the inquiries into the shootings of David Gundy and Darren Brennan.

The coroner's jurisdiction is peculiar. Unlike the

criminal or civil courts, it is not bound by the strict rules of evidence. Witnesses can refuse to answer questions on the grounds that they might incriminate themselves. Greater flexibility generally prevails, and investigators are encouraged to think outside the square. Even hearsay evidence, rarely allowed in the criminal sphere, is tolerated – anything that gets to the heart of the matter, that allows the cause of death to be established. Technically then, the coroner, through Cowan, his advocate, was at the helm of the quest to unearth the full circumstances behind the shooting. The primary collector of evidence, McDougall, was their foot soldier. He was in charge of the inquiry, but subject to Cowan's direction. This was the firm understanding from the start.

As was to be expected, on the same day that Cowan wriggled into the saddle, there was a flurry of activity: the newspapers' 'front page photos [caused] every Tom, Dick and Harry . . . [to keep] ringing the police station with information or supposed sightings, or whatever. It was just a matter of all hands . . . on deck because it was a madhouse because of all the press it had received.'[8] A special media hotline was established to unclog the station's other lines.

Amid the mayhem, the chief police psychologist, David Mutton, was lucky enough to commandeer a spare room to hold a meeting, a counselling session, with the officers and the ambulancemen involved in the shooting. Mutton urged them to relive the incident if they could, blow by blow, in a cathartic attempt to assist in their ultimate rehabilitation. It soon became clear to Mutton that Podesta and Dilorenzo were despairing and feeling 'dreadful' about taking a human life: 'They have families themselves, so they are acutely aware of distressed relatives. But their greatest fear is of being judged, by the public, by their own police force, by the courts.'[9] Such judgments were being made, mainly in the media.

Although it was the police force's highest-priority case, requiring briefings for the minister, McDougall was paddling pretty much alone. There was his team of three from the South Region – Detectives Fitzgerald, Allison and Comans – and the officers he had borrowed, in contravention of police guidelines, from the home-town station of the shooters – Purcell and Wilson and Constable Morris. But that was it. This represented the entirety of the police response. And, as the hours turned to days, they found themselves dealing with the most burdensome of loads: the processing and evaluation of statements, the location of relatives and friends, the assessment of forensic data and the correlation of leads, and investigating discrepancies. And taking calls – *hundreds* of calls.

No request was made for extra officers, but there was also no offer of a taskforce, no suggestion from senior commanders that extra bodies might be needed to deal with the extraordinary tide of enquiries and information. After all, there were scores of witnesses and infuriated citizens wanting to be interviewed, pleading to have their say.

McDougall realised the Levi shooting 'was a very unusual incident' and felt that 'the number of statements from completely independent witnesses . . . would highlight any indiscrepancies [sic] . . . that might appear in the police statements.'[10] It was therefore obviously crucial, he insisted, with the matters still vivid in the mind, that these witnesses be interviewed as soon as possible. Yet on the day after the killing, only two people from the veritable throng of possibles managed to secure an officer and make statements. The inquiry croaked, rather than roared, into action.

In these early days, McDougall was distracted, sometimes out of touch with what his colleagues were discovering. He chose to remain with Melinda Dundas and the distressed parents, Richard and Rebecca Levi, who had recently arrived in Sydney from France. He had helped them avoid the media at the airport. McDougall also won approval from coronial authorities, after being contacted by Levi's uncle, Emanuel Meschers, to delay the post-mortem 'due to requirements of the Jewish religion'.[11] He even arranged a meeting for the Levi family, their rabbi and Dundas with the coroner and key forensic staff.

He also made it clear he had a serious job to complete, however, obtaining an order from Coroner Hand to give him the right to search 59 Brighton Boulevard and seize items of interest. Dundas insisted that she be present during the visit and a time was arranged for that afternoon.

When McDougall arrived to execute the coroner's direction, Dundas was already inside, along with the Levis, Warren Brunner and Brunner's mother and family friends. There was a confrontation, Dundas refusing McDougall permission to enter her husband's room. The policeman returned with Cowan, another lawyer and Chief Superintendent Bob Waites, McDougall's boss. And then, in the presence of a solicitor representing the Levi family and Dundas, Michael Marx, the search was conducted.

They took notebooks, computer disks, old infringement notices and his bail undertaking from the Melbourne courts. All this was bundled up and taken to the station for formal tendering. At 7.45 p.m., Dundas witnessed the exchange of Levi's personal belongings. It was countersigned by the police's receiving officer, Patrick Brown – the closest of mates with the shooters and a loyal member of the Living Dangerously Club.

McDougall's initial business left his understudy, Michael Fitzgerald, effectively alone, in charge of taking statements, contacting friends and associates of the dead man, and building up a picture of why Levi had threatened the officers. Between Saturday and Tuesday, in the absence of other helpers, Fitzgerald did his level best to cope on his own, but he was obliged to again use the Bondi officers, Podesta and Dilorenzo's workmates, to type up important initial statements. Fitzgerald's helpers, Wilson, Purcell and Morris soon grew accustomed to a constant procession of people, shuffling in and out of the station's abandoned intelligence office.

The search for any, and all, witnesses was detailed and efficient: advertisements were placed in local newspapers; a blue and white police bus was installed on Bondi Beach; charter bus companies were contacted; and a guest list from a four-star hotel that overlooked the beach, with 157 names, was obtained and checked. Many of Levi's associates were approached. Even the man known as Joe, who had preyed on Levi in the days prior to the shooting, was located. He was interviewed, identifying himself as Joachim Blieszis, 'a middle man buyer and seller of tickets for scalping . . . and associate of a group of English males who are believed to be a major group involved in the production, distribution and sale of the goods'.[12]

While Levi's private affairs were heavily scrutinised – with investigators seeking a motive for, or insight into, his erratic behaviour in the moments before his death – the colourful life and times of the shooters were never even considered. It was the dead man they wanted to learn about, not his police assailants. The Awesome Twosome, the targets of secret investigations into claims of drug use and dealing, were not deemed worthy of background checks or deeper analysis. It was felt that they should be left alone in their grief, that they had already been interviewed. Neither McDougall nor Fitzgerald were encouraged to dig deeper.

The Bondi commander, Richard Baker, who had taken the brash lead in the media, praising the pair for their killing of Levi, remained astonishingly silent in his new command at Mount Druitt, in Sydney's far western suburbs. So did some of his superiors. He'd neglected to mention both the existence of the Internal Affairs investigations and the fact that Podesta had disobeyed his order to stay away from the local drug haunt, the Liberty Lunch. The Internal Affairs commander, Assistant Commissioner Mal Brammer, logically 'assumed that Chief Inspector Baker, who'd come to us with the information about Podesta, would raise that . . . [drug] information with the relevant shooting [investigation] team, him being present on the weekend shortly after the shooting'.[13] But, for whatever reason, Baker was mute – and Brammer didn't bother to check if these vital details on the shooters had been passed on to his representative, Peter Fitzpatrick. The latter's task of course, was to ensure that McDougall's investigation was done by the book. But Fitzpatrick was effectively working with his eyes wide shut. Because he was not working at head office, Fitzpatrick was not privy to the vital information that his department was hunting Podesta and Dilorenzo.

Brammer's more junior officers, the heads of Operations Borden and Addlestone, worried about the silence – and wondered if they should start talking to McDougall's people, 'to let them know we were looking at them [the shooters]'.[14] But there was an overriding 'concern that releasing any information to the investigations team would compromise any proactive inquiry [against Podesta and Dilorenzo] . . . that we were attempting to commence'.[15] So nothing was done.

McDougall was therefore not only understaffed, but also under-informed. Although he was particularly mindful of the notoriety of Bondi cops in general (courtesy of the recent royal commission), he later admitted he would have adopted 'a completely different approach' if he'd been given a scintilla of information, a confidential briefing, on Internal Affairs' investigations into Dilorenzo and Podesta.[16] So while customers at the Liberty Lunch continued to spread the rumours about the night before the shooting, the scenes still fresh in their minds – the perfect time for interviews to have taken place – the police investigation shuffled on ignorantly. During these first days, the identities of both the shooters and their victim remained confidential. This inhibited unwanted publicity, of course, but it certainly didn't stifle the public clamour for answers.

When Roni Levi's name was released to the press, the pace of the case and the pressure for answers intensified markedly. Journalists started to piece together the knifeman's contorted final 36 hours: the dinner, the trip to the hospital and the scramble to the beach. The dead man's identity meant there was now so much to record. Levi's parents were seen visiting 59 Brighton Boulevard, and the morgue. A photograph of the dead man, looking carefree and beaming, was also printed in newspapers, sourced through the startled Jewish community.

In an email message to the ABC, Levi's three brothers, Ilan, Remy and Laurent, seemed to sum up the community's shock, deploring the fact that 'there were no other alternatives than killing him . . . [such as] catching him or hurting him in a leg or in an arm'. And there was no mistaking the brothers' feelings towards the shooters: 'Because you are in a uniform with a gun, you cannot play cowboy . . . You cannot as a police officer judge someone only on 20 minutes of his life.'[17] With the weight of emotion increasing, public opinion moved against the policemen. But still no-one knew their names, except for those in the know.

On Tuesday, 1 July, McDougall attended the post-mortem at the Glebe morgue. He took along Wilson, the officer discovering death and signatory on the p79A form, for the sake of formalities. The procedure was conducted by Dr Allan Cala, a respected forensic pathologist, and witnessed by a police forensic officer, two ballistic experts, an autopsy assistant and a religious observer. Three bullets were extracted from the body, two 'in the left back region and one in the left upper sacral region at the top of the left buttock near the natal cleft'.[18] The doctor concluded that the shots had neither come from close range nor an intermediate distance but had been 'fired from a distant range (greater than 1 metre), as there was no gun powder stippling, muzzle abrasions or soot in the wounds or on the clothing to suggest contact.'[19] He observed that 'chest and finger wounds were inflicted first' and, significantly, that Levi may then 'have lost balance, crouched over or fell to the ground and, in the process of this, received a gunshot wound to the perineum.'[20] That was the final shot, Podesta's second.

That same day, McDougall finally got reinforcements. But three days had been lost and many opportunities wasted. McDougall lost Detectives Allison and Comans, who'd helped interview the shooters on the first day, and was able to relinquish the three Bondi officers – but he gained nine equally experienced investigators. And so now there were eleven, rather than seven officers, examining the Levi case. And, at last, none of them were from the home station.

This was a clear benefit, as well as a belated recognition of the rules but the Bondi gang – Wilson, Purcell and Morris – had already conducted a mountain of work, contrary to the Commissioner's Instructions. They were aware 'that there were guidelines that local police were not to direct the investigation – and conduct the investigation . . . [but we were] of the opinion that we could be . . . gophers . . . utilised, in the event of lack of resources, as assistants'.[21] In reality though, they were intimately involved and did more than just fossick – they took crucial statements.

Wilson interviewed the council cleaner, Leo Hamlin, an important witness. Moments after the shooting, Hamlin had told television news reporters that he wasn't sure if Levi had lunged at the police, yet, after seeing and reading Baker's descriptive comments, Hamlin had somehow grown more precise about the officers' conduct. He even adopted Baker's language, suggesting in his chat with Wilson that Levi had 'lunged at [Dilorenzo and Podesta] . . . with the knife in an outstretched hand'.[22] Other witnesses gave statements to the home-town boys, with the police claiming they had instituted a priority system for interviewing those who had seen the shooting.

So many days after giving his details, Bratanoff-Firgoff had lost all patience with the police. He believed he was a high priority: he had the revealing images, concrete evidence, and yet he had not even been contacted. Suffering nightmares and hearing gunshots in his sleep, the Frenchman questioned the apparent laxity in the investigation. Why his photos had not been requested, and in sequence. Bratanoff-Firgoff said he had 'nothing against the police and I don't think it is fair to accuse them of anything. But this shooting was obviously a mistake. It's something that happened that shouldn't have'.[23]

With the acting police commissioner, Jeff Jarratt, the pressure was telling. Although the killing should not have been discussed, especially with the media, Jarratt held a number of press conferences and a radio interview – as if to emulate

Baker's prejudicial and premature strike. Despite initially tacitly supporting the officers, Jarratt's tone by the Tuesday had become different. In a live interview, he conceded that the Levi incident, from all the briefings he had received, had been a mistake. In a lengthy and freewheeling discussion on the ABC, Jarratt said the police had 'to learn from this experience. Our systems have had a failure – we have to learn . . . to correct those so that we lessen the chances in the future of this situation recurring . . . Obviously young people are involved in making critical decisions in the short time and I guess it is possible that mistakes will occur'.[24]

The interview sparked shock waves; and there was instant reaction. The police union kicked Jarratt hard and pleaded, legitimately, for such detailed analysis to be delayed until after the inquest, 'where we believe the actions of our members will be vindicated'.[25]

In response the coroner issued a press release, urging calm and silence, and demanding respect of his authority. Hand said the rash of public statements was likely to colour the recollections of 'witnesses, some of whom may not as yet have come forward . . . [and] may have a tendency to interfere with the proper administration of justice in connection with the inquest'.[26] This was legal code for contempt or subverting the law.

Although the shooters remained unnamed and beyond the public's reach, they were getting belted all the same. They had their supporters and sympathisers but the media's portrayal of their actions – and the angry talkback tattle – was predominantly slanted against them and showed no signs of slowing.

Levi's family had been joined by Dundas in publicly condemning the police actions. Unmoved by a meeting with the acting commissioner, she called for the shooters to be suspended and described the shooting as 'excessive . . . appalling . . . and unjustifiable'.[27] She was also keen to set the record straight on her husband's character: 'Roni was not mentally ill; he was not a drug addict and he was not ever violent. He was the most gentle person I know. It feels like Roni is on trial and not the police that shot him. The police are taking him apart, first his body and now his life.'[28] The widow's remarks reflected, in large part, the public mood being increasingly played out in the media. The police were in the spotlight, and not for the first time.

The newspaper letters pages were deluged. Just over a week after the shooting the letters editor of the *Sydney Morning Herald* succinctly set out the parameters of this most public debate:

> *At one extreme was the view that all the officers involved should be charged with murder. The opposing view held that anyone brandishing a knife or any potentially lethal weapon deserves to be gunned down. One bizarre letter suggested the police shot him because he was Jewish . . . there were letters which abhorred the waste of a young life and while in no way condoned the shooting, nevertheless acknowledged what incredibly difficult decisions and life-threatening situations the police face every day in their work.*[29]

Leo Schofield, the prominent social columnist, likened the killing to a 'form of elimination of non-conformists . . . [and it] could become a regular public event, another tourist attraction for Bondi. Just line up dimwits, feebs, the depressed and the demented and anyone else deemed to be out of line and gun them down publicly on a beach.'[30]

A former ombudsman, David Landa, wrote from the

other side of the ledger. He cited two powerful inquiries he'd been charged with reinvestigating. One involved a knife-wielding man who had murdered his wife and injured his children. Despite the experienced sergeant wounding the man with six shots, the man continued to move on the cop shooter . . . his life only saved by a fluke shot from his rookie partner. The other inquiry involved a policeman being admonished by his superiors for firing a warning shot, and not following his training of shooting to stop the offender. Landa's letter revealed a no-win world, with few answers on how 'to prepare police for such confronting and potentially dangerous situations'.[31]

Dilorenzo's brother, John Lorenzo, a man adept at media relations because of his television publicity work, now moved more closely into the scene. While Dilorenzo and Podesta would not be named in the media until day three of the coronial inquest, Lorenzo had been mortified as the hate mounted against his brother, who 'was recording the news and buying every newspaper'.[32] Free of charge to the family, and their shooter friend, Lorenzo seized control of the public relations campaign. His first task was to turn the game decisively back in his brother's favour. And he struck hard.

His first exercise, a masterful strategic ploy, was giving the largest circulation newspaper in Sydney, the *Daily Telegraph*, exclusive access to Dilorenzo's wife Annabelle, albeit anonymously. Lorenzo knew the emotional impact that would flow from getting her to talk. He knew his brother and Podesta were gagged, but there was nothing in the police rules to say that an officer's *wife* couldn't comment. Posing sideways on Bondi Beach, in a front-page photograph with her head tilted – her pregnant silhouette inviting sympathy – 'Jane' gave an emotional insight into her family's distress.

She spoke of having mild contractions after the

shooting – and went on at length about Levi's motives, police shooting training, her husband's psychiatric treatment and the horrific day itself. She said they were initially 'pretty numb' but 'it has been slowly getting worse as the days have gone on'.[33] As a result of the stress of the ordeal, her husband was now 'snapping and yelling . . . very agitated . . . He has no zest for life. He has got nothing to look forward to. He just sits and stares in front of him all the time'.[34]

Annabelle Dilorenzo also wrote an open letter to the same newspaper, printed in full with her name omitted, in which she repeatedly described Levi as 'the crazed man . . . about to stab my husband', and asked: 'Would the public rather have my photo on the front page as a widow who lost her gentle husband?'[35] The newspaper's celebrated columnist, Miranda Devine, even chipped in to add her considerable clout to the officers' cause: 'Grieving for Roni Levi doesn't have to mean blaming the police who killed him.'[36]

Annabelle's expansive interview wasn't all positive. In her naivety, she had revealed in the newspaper that her husband and the other shooter had returned home after the killing and played their taped interviews to each other. This was in clear defiance of police instructions and, accordingly, the sparks flew. Cowan phoned McDougall and demanded that the officers be severely reprimanded and a written order was served on them to disclose nothing further about the matter – repeating in sterner terms the direction they had been given on the day of the shooting. Sensing the seriousness of the breach, McDougall asked Cowan if he wanted the pair interviewed again, with a more forensic approach. Cowan declined. He saw no need to put them through the ordeal of another inquisition.

On Thursday, 3 July, at a memorial service at Woollahra in Sydney's eastern suburbs, just before Levi's body was returned to its ultimate resting place in France, about 200 mourners gathered to hear a tribute to the man, the artist, and to be together in their grieving and their shock. Rabbi Pinchos Woolstone, who'd been with the family throughout the ordeal, urged restraint from his sombre audience and spoke forcefully on the need, 'especially during this sacred moment, to avoid any feeling of vengeance and any desire for revenge . . . feelings . . . [that] are anathema to our Jewish value system'.[37]

It was lasting justice that they were seeking, he said, not retribution.

Despite being counselled on an almost daily basis, and reliving repeatedly the nightmare that must come from killing another person, Dilorenzo and Podesta were still partying hard. Just as they had been before the shooting. These days, however, the drinking and nightclubbing served to suppress their confused emotions. Podesta's close friend, Graeme Rooney, had caught up with them, in the immediate aftermath, along with Mark Lorenzo, Podesta, Dilorenzo 'and a couple of friends of Mark's and some other police officers, I presume'[38] to see lap-dancing performances at Dancers, in Kings Cross. The shooting was an obvious topic of conversation but, Rooney reckons, the talk also turned to drugs. And the question of taking pills. Podesta, he says, asked him for an ecstasy tablet, and he obliged – 'and then he came and asked me for another one. He said he wanted to give one to Tony because Tony never has any and he wanted to cheer him up'.[39]

This was not an isolated night of inebriation. Within a week of the shooting, Ronald Quin was calling Podesta at

2.09 a.m., and TC was also out with the shooters, on the prowl. In fact TC caught up with Podesta on *the day after* the killing.[40] That Sunday they'd partied with some people and ended up at Dancers.

Over at the Liberty, Stanley Dowse spotted Podesta and TC together in the days after the shooting as they wandered into the restaurant. Cognisant of the rumours that Podesta had taken drugs at his place before hitting the beach, Dowse watched the encounter keenly but noticed only that TC was drunk – 'he was supposed to be working that night. I shooed him off the premises'.[41]

On Friday, 4 July, in another part of town far removed from the beach and the shooting investigation, Simon Duncan, the Soho Bar nightclub security guard, finally found time to report to Internal Affairs about the cubicle incident. But, even after interviewing Duncan, incredibly, Internal Affairs stayed silent. McDougall therefore began a second week of trying to piece together the details of that horrific day on the beach without the most significant details.

EIGHT

THE SECRET MEETING

'The meeting was not actually to
provide documentation . . . it was
to go and discuss . . . what
Internal Affairs was doing . . .
and . . . the information that
we'd received in relation to the
intoxication of Podesta on the
night [before the shooting].'

Malcolm James Brammer (Internal Affairs commander),
Police Integrity Commission, Operation Saigon, 22 February 2000

By the middle of July 1997, just three weeks after the shooting, McDougall's team had ostensibly finished. The specially assigned investigators, their interviews and statement-taking completed, and even Fitzgerald, McDougall's sidekick, had returned to normal duties. McDougall himself was left again to his own devices; almost single-handedly compiling the brief of evidence for the coroner, a weighty dossier of documents, photographs and measurements. He kept in weekly contact with his notional boss, David Cowan, and was feeding briefings regularly to his police superiors. Everything appeared to be going according to plan. Despite its highly charged and controversial status, the Levi case still seemed to be an open-and-shut affair.

The investigation had been completed in lightning-quick time, with 39 eyewitness accounts and more than 30 of Roni Levi's friends, family members and former flatmates also being interviewed. The investigators had done an excellent job at researching Levi's profile and interpreting his idiosyncracies, in picking him to pieces. Their efforts produced an incredibly expansive picture of a man who was 'a sensitive human being; so full of charm, of joy and of so much life . . . a little unconventional, but very much an artist . . . so young, so full of joie de vivre'.[1] But while much information was elicited by the police on the dead man, barely an etching was devoted to the shooters. Without the crucial Internal Affairs files, Podesta and Dilorenzo, and their acquaintances and antecedents were never mentioned, let alone investigated. In that darkest of Sydney winters, with the community remaining fascinated and perplexed by the shooting, the Awesome Twosome – still anonymous and on stress leave – were all but off the hook. McDougall's role slowed to a stop. There was little more that could reasonably be done, he thought.

Melinda Dundas had not even thought about stopping. Struggling with understandable stress, and full of adrenalin and anger, Dundas, a journalist, questioned everything. Contorted inside by a potent mixture of emotions – her love for a dead man and the grief that came from reviving the reasons behind their drift apart – she hurled herself into a zealous quest for answers.

Michael Marx, a respected member of the Jewish community, a prestigious solicitor and a person not prone to stomaching matters without questioning them, had given Dundas instructive initial counsel. With little money, Dundas could only do so much. But then Marx took a chance call, from a lawyer representing a bunch of students: they felt they could help her research the case. 'Students?' Dundas had shouted out to Marx, outraged at his suggestion. 'We don't need fucking students – I want the best QC in the world!'[2] But urged on by Marx, she agreed to a meeting.

It was some 200 kilometres north of Sydney, at Newcastle, the coastal capital of the coal and wine-growing Hunter Valley, that Dundas found her refuge. The University of Newcastle Legal Centre, isolated from the swish city legal offices, had already studied the Levi case with a mixture of shock and distress. Dundas encountered lawyers who didn't work with a meter ticking away; here was a group of lawyers focused only on public-interest advocacy. They were about correcting matters of law, righting wrongs. At the end of their first meeting, full of emotion and heartache for Dundas, it was agreed that they should take over the case. On this first visit, the advocates were intrigued by the concerns raised by Dundas, a Melbourne woman a long way from home.

Bound by a nucleus of three men – a tireless and unflappable solicitor, John Boersig, an inquisitive lecturer and academic, Associate Professor Ray Watterson, and Robert Cavanagh, a rumbustious, unorthodox and fearless barrister – the Newcastle Legal Centre was seen as a pioneering, experimental institution. It had developed, within a teaching law school, as a hybrid community legal centre. It took on complaints and cases from clients like any other law firm or legal-aid body but it differed in that staff and students not only studied law, they worked in, and with, the law. They were students and practitioners at the same time, helping prepare submissions, conduct research and analyse witness statements. The centre's painstaking work and stubbornness – and its refusal to go away and give up or shut up – had prompted three separate inquiries into the police investigation of the rape and murder of Leigh Leigh, a teenage schoolgirl, at Stockton Beach. And they'd had other credible victories. This brought more kudos, and more work from the

marginalised. Now with Levi, they had their most con-
tentious case.

On 23 August, nearly eight weeks after the morning at Bondi
Beach was shattered, someone finally gave voice in an official
way to the drug and alcohol rumours about the shooters.
Despite the fact that word had been running rampant in Sydney's plush eastern suburbs since the very day Levi had
perished, they only got public ventilation after a chance
encounter across town. In Sydney's harsher and less appreciated inner west, and in the most clichéd location for
rumour-mongering: a hairdressing salon.

At 4 p.m., Robert Bromwich, a barrister employed by
the Commonwealth director of public prosecutions, sat down
to get his ears lowered, as it were, at Noddy's On King, at 88
King Street in Newtown. His regular clipper, Katrina Rafferty,
came to his assistance, and the conversation flowed liberally, as
usual, in unconscious rhythm with the scissor cuts. The Levi
shooting came up. Rafferty, Bromwich later relayed, told him
'something to the effect that one of her other customers had
told her that the police, or some of the police, involved in the
shooting had been drinking in Bondi until 3 a.m. on the day
of the shooting'.[3] The rumour could have been dismissed as
little more than idle gossip; however, the conversation would
cause a chain reaction, transforming the Levi case.

That night, Bromwich recalled the hairdressing discussion at a dinner party. Although incredulous, one of
Bromwich's friends said he would contact Stefan Bialoguski,
a friend of Levi's, to see whether the rumour was of any use.
Bialoguski, Bromwich's friend knew, would be eager to see if
the information fitted with any of the other tips that the
friends of Levi and the Jewish community were collecting.

Bialoguski, another journalist, worked for Australian Associated Press and happened to be a key figure behind the scenes in the bid to help Dundas get justice. Like Dundas, Bialoguski had been deeply affected by the tragedy. He was particularly close to Levi and was 'feeling cheated, not just because a friend has been stolen from me but because the closer friendship I felt growing between us can now never blossom. For a gentle man who walked so lightly on this Earth, his presence among us has left a deep imprint.'[4] He had been expecting Levi to come to his home for lunch on the day he died, and he and a group of friends had even talked about Levi's health at the synagogue, in ignorance of his fate, hours after he had been floored to the sand.

On 28 August, Bialoguski called Bromwich, asking for his hairdresser's name and anything else he knew. Bromwich obliged, but suggested he would call Rafferty first.[5] Rafferty now expanded on her original information, telling Bromwich 'that the customer who had told her the things she had told me . . . was someone who, at the time of the shooting, had owned a cafe in Bondi . . . but she may have said the customer [simply] knew the owner of the premises in which the police had been drinking'.[6] She added that the customer had since moved to Darwin, which, coincidentally, was where Bromwich was heading that very weekend. He asked Rafferty to get the customer's contact number so he could meet up with him in the Top End. Rafferty agreed to find the numbers, but unfortunately Bromwich's plane left Mascot before any details could be found, and so the meeting failed to materialise.

On 5 September, Bromwich got a call from Levi's widow. She asked about the Darwin trip (Bialoguski having passed this information on to her) but of course, there was nothing to report. Bromwich told Dundas that he felt the information about the officers' activities just before the shooting ought to be reported to 'whoever was going to be the counsel assisting the coroner'.[7] Dundas agreed and rang David Cowan herself to fill him in about these new allegations. At the suggestion of Cowan's instructing solicitor, Stuart Robinson from the Crown Solicitor's Office, Bromwich typed up a statement – and the Rafferty rumour now achieved the status of hearsay evidence, possibly admissible in the coronial inquest. The Coroner's Office now had knowledge that someone was claiming the shooters were partying on the morning of the killing.

Despite the seriousness of this new allegation, more than 30 days passed before Cowan's police troubleshooter, McDougall, was told about the rumour. For a man supposedly in the hot seat, McDougall was getting lukewarm intelligence and, as with the Borden and Addlestone files, he was being kept out of the loop.

Cowan not only had McDougall at his disposal. Deputy Commissioner Jarratt – his exciting time at the helm having finished with the return of the holidaying top cop, Peter Ryan – had given the counsel assisting extra resources to deal with the Levi matter. Jarratt had specifically assigned an Internal Affairs link man, Chief Inspector Bernard Roy McSorley, to act as 'a conduit for the supply of . . . information, a contact for Mr Cowan to speak to when he perhaps needed to know something or needed to be provided with guidelines'.[8] But while McSorley may have handed over photocopies of rules and regulations, 'an extendible baton, and other things, and reports on police shootings',[9] he was never asked to brief Cowan on what Internal Affairs was doing with the Bondi shooters, nor was he ever in a position to. And Internal

Affairs, conversely, never came to learn about the Bromwich statement. So, more than two months after the shooting, a breathtaking line of inquiry about the Bondi shooters – put down in writing by a barrister – was lying in a hole, seemingly going nowhere in a hurry. With every wasted day, the chance to strike grew dimmer.

It was not until 16 September that the Levi matter happened to come back into focus. Internal Affairs' Assistant Commissioner Brammer phoned his counterpart at the Police Integrity Commission, Assistant Commissioner Ernest (Tim) Sage, the leader effectively of the body tasked with rooting out serious corruption. Brammer gave Sage an update on the Borden and Addlestone inquiries but he also suggested, given that they had information about the Soho nightclub and the shooters' alleged bad conduct, that it would be a good idea to see the coroner. Brammer wanted to fill Derrick Hand in on the Internal Affairs inquiries and the information they had already accumulated. Brammer, of course, was aware of the coroner's incredible flexibility in admitting colourful testimony, but was not sure 'in what context they may use any sort of development of evidence, irrespective of whether it [was] . . . connected to that particular night or not'.[10] On 17 September, more intelligence about the Bondi shooters came to the attention of Detective Sergeant Christopher Keen, the main investigator in Operation Borden. At 7.30 a.m., Keen went to Bondi with Detective Wayne Thorn to meet an informant, Amanda,[11] who claimed she had some information about the shooters – allegations, 'albeit hearsay, that one of the officers involved in the shooting had been intoxicated the evening before the shooting'.[12] Amanda, Keen and Thorn had a two-and-a-half hour session at a coffee shop on Campbell Parade, where the whispers had long been doing the rounds. Amanda also gave the coppers the nickname of a man who could be helpful – Robert – someone who had been with the officers in the pre-dawn hours. Keen and Thorn then walked down the road, to the Liberty Lunch restaurant, to take a look at what all the fuss was about.

Things now became more urgent, and Keen – although not aware of the Bromwich statement, which mirrored this new information, of course – felt an immediate need to report Amanda's intelligence higher up the ladder. He spoke that afternoon with Gary Richmond, the chief of investigations in Internal Affairs, and to Inspector Robert Martin, the legal officer, about his quandary – whether McDougall should be cut in on the action or not. Keen's informant had made a serious allegation that directly affected the inquiry.

By the next morning, at 8.05 to be precise, Keen decided he could wait no longer. He believed certain people needed, and deserved, to know what he knew. He rang Inspector Peter Fitzpatrick, the Internal Affairs man on the Levi inquiry. Fitzpatrick later recounted the conversation for the Police Integrity Commission: ' "Peter, are you still the review officer for the Levi shooting?" And I said, "No." He said, "Well, can I just pass this on to you anyway?" '[13] Fitzpatrick had in fact already been removed from the case, less than a month after the shooting, and transferred to the Child Protection Enforcement Agency – a move that forced him to surrender to another officer the serious task of keeping an honest watch over the Levi case. Notwithstanding his lack of involvement with the case, Fitzpatrick told Keen he'd better get in touch with McDougall. It was one for him.

Keen rang the senior investigator minutes later and, rather coyly, 'told him I had information that was relevant to his inquiry, however, I didn't give him the full details of what information that I actually held'.[14] But at 8.25 a.m., before

Keen had a chance to give McDougall all the facts, Inspector Martin emerged from Brammer's office with a direction: only Brammer's staff officer, Chief Inspector McSorley – the link man with Cowan's chambers – and no-one else, was allowed to communicate with McDougall. The boss's word was final. Martin told Keen 'that a meeting was going to be arranged with the coroner and with the investigators from the shooting team and . . . a number of other interested parties and . . . [Amanda's] information would be exchanged then'.[15] Keen and the other investigators were told (contrary to what would actually occur) that McSorley would carry out regular information exchanges.

Brammer put absolute faith in McSorley, and encouraged the overly cautious security, because he was paranoid about leaks, and not just about the Podesta and Dilorenzo affair. Brammer and Police Commissioner Ryan, had agreed that 'whales in the bay [were] . . . a prevailing issue'[16] in his work – in reference to the code used by cops to alert colleagues that were under investigation. Brammer was forever ramping into his officers 'about the level of security and also the consequences of breaches of security in the eyes of the Commissioner . . . where investigations in relation to police corruption were compromised by the leaking of information or telling people who people trusted, and that was compromised by talk in the meal room, and so forth'.[17] Because of all of this, Brammer felt that he should deal with the Amanda allegations himself, or at least through his own delegate, McSorley, his trusted sidekick. This would help to formalise the matter, put it beyond reproach. Later in the day, McSorley called McDougall.

The two officers met at midday at Police Headquarters in College Street, Darlinghurst, named the Avery building after the commissioner who made the first substantive reform efforts. McSorley even took McDougall into Brammer's personal office, captured by the sensitivity of the moment.

Armed only with Keen's briefing notes, and no direct knowledge of the allegations, McSorley outlined the breadth of the Borden investigation, but only in the broadest terms. McDougall later remembered being told about 'the Liberty Lunch . . . as being the premises in question' and 'that a female had come to them with information and that there were other people involved as far as witnesses . . . and that they were under investigation for drugs' but, tellingly, 'I was never given any names'.[18]

Brammer's edict was badly misinterpreted – and he has accepted the blame for the bungle. Brammer thought Keen and Detective Inspector Paul Jones would provide progress reports to McSorley, who would pass them on to McDougall; and that McDougall would get in touch with Internal Affairs if he had further queries.[19] McSorley did no such thing; he'd been too secretive, too cautious.

While McSorley and McDougall chatted around the particulars of Amanda's information, Detective Thorn was out on the streets. He had already learned the identity of the person referred to by Amanda as 'Robert'. He didn't actually make contact with the man, but he was looking in all the right places. At 12.45 p.m., Thorn accompanied Keen to the same coffee shop at Bondi Beach as before to get more drum from Amanda. By the time they made it back to the office, Thorn had a message from their informant. Amanda had different news this time: she no longer wanted anything to do with the police. Something had changed her mind.

On 19 September, Brammer wrote to Tim Sage at the Police Integrity Commission, warning him of the past few days' developments. He attached the latest secret briefing notes and the Amanda allegations and now strongly urged for a meeting with the coroner. There were hot items to discuss, in private.

On 23 September, Cowan's instructing solicitor, Stuart Robinson, wrote to the Newcastle Legal Centre, about the upcoming coronial inquest. Robinson had already received a letter from Dundas's solicitor based at the centre, John Boersig, requesting any Internal Affairs papers on the Levi case. But the Crown Solicitor's Office simply replied that 'the police investigation has not yet been completed. However, it is anticipated that it will be completed soon. The brief of evidence will then be physically assembled, copied and made available for distribution'.[20] This suggested, as was the reality, that the Levi case was meandering along at a disturbingly unruffled pace. On 8 October, a month after receiving the Bromwich statement, Cowan finally passed it on to McDougall. Despite now having been given two flecks of information about his shooters within a three-week period, McDougall too seemed reluctant to leap into action and no spontaneous enquiries were made.

On 17 October, the secret meeting was held. The presentation was driven by Internal Affairs, with Brammer and Richmond doing most of the talking. The coroner, Cowan and Robinson listened on, as did Sage and another officer from the Police Integrity Commission. McDougall was the only other interested spectator. The meeting effectively turned into a demarcation exercise.

Brammer didn't want to interfere with the shooting investigation, nor compromise Operation Borden, and McDougall wanted to avoid 'a clash of information' and to make sure that 'we weren't crossing paths in our investigation[s]'.[21] Brammer wanted McDougall at the meeting 'so that he understood very clearly what we were doing without exposing him too much to . . . what Internal Affairs were doing . . . and also . . . the information that we'd received in relation to the intoxication of Podesta on the night and also the more holistic approach'[22] – whatever that meant.

The Bromwich statement was read at the meeting and McDougall picked up from Richmond's speech that Podesta and Dilorenzo 'may have been affected by drugs or involved in drugs'.[23] The coroner voiced the opinion 'that it would be helpful if we could conclude the investigation before the inquest occurred'.[24] Such a speedy conclusion depended on the meeting being a success, with the lines of demarcation being settled. But this had not been achieved; in fact, everyone was in more of a muddle than before they'd sat down to chat.

When Brammer left the meeting, he thought McDougall would liaise regularly with Keen.[25] This was news to McDougall, however. He believed he was 'investigating . . . [the Bromwich] allegations that one or other of the officers were under the influence of alcohol, but . . . allegations that either of the officers were under the influence of drugs . . . [were] something that Internal Affairs would investigate'.[26] If he found information they were drunk, he owned it; if they'd been high on drugs, then that was a matter for the corruption busters. McDougall considered there was an artificial divide over what was in reality the same issue: what Podesta and Dilorenzo had been up to in the pre-dawn hours before Levi was shot. Confusion abounded.

To make matters worse, Keen, the officer Brammer wanted McDougall to liaise with, also felt unclear about *his* responsibilities. He believed, after being instructed by Martin, that McSorley was the only one with the right to talk to McDougall. So he shut his mouth. Appallingly then, after what should have been a breakthrough meeting with Coroner

Hand, each of the parties that had attended, who had pushed their fingers into the pie, now pulled them out, confident that someone else was going after Podesta and Dilorenzo. Everyone thought they understood what was going on . . . with the result that no-one knew what was going on.

On 29 October, twelve days after the secret meeting and nearly seven weeks after Bromwich first gave voice to suggestions that the shooters might have been drinking, McDougall got himself in a position to investigate the allegation. He advised his new offsider, Detective Senior Constable Michael Sinadinovic – an officer with no previous exposure to the shooting inquiry – to look into the matter. Sinadinovic contacted Katrina Rafferty, the hairdresser who had sparked the kerfuffle, and learned that, although she couldn't remember the customer's name from whom she'd first received the gossip, she believed he was linked up with a trendy cafe in the Bondi area, Sejuiced. She also spoke about a place called the Liberty Lunch.

On 31 October, in a symptom of the chaos that had enveloped the investigation, more intelligence was mishandled. Keen had a discussion with a police administrative assistant, Susan,[27] who claimed 'Podesta was under the influence of drugs prior to the fatal shooting'[28] and 'that her son knew another person who knew another person who was friendly with Podesta'.[29] Susan even supplied the names, as if to link the dots in this puzzle. But nothing happened. Keen, nor anyone else at Internal Affairs looked into it, because 'the proactive stage of the . . . [Borden] investigation was continuing and we . . . didn't want to jeopardise anything that we were doing . . . by making any overt inquiries'.[30] Susan's information was put to one side and ignored. And it wasn't passed to McDougall, as Keen thought he was barred from communicating with him – but nor did Keen pass it on to McSorley to pass on to McDougall. There 'was obviously a communication problem, a misunderstanding'[31] – and another possible opportunity floated away.

New names and characters now came into the frame. On 3 November, on a visit to the Liberty Lunch, McDougall and Sinadinovic met one of the new managers, Damian Bell, who said he knew Podesta, but had no knowledge about the shooters being in the restaurant on the night before the Levi killing. No rosters could be provided as they were destroyed every couple of weeks but Bell suggested that the night manager, TC, might have a better idea. The cops told Bell they would return. McDougall and Sinadinovic moved on to Sejuiced, at Bronte, and more interesting information came to light. The owner, David Lucas, said he'd bought the cafe from a Bondi identity, Andrew John Ruwald, just three days after the shooting. Lucas denied knowing a hairdresser in Newtown called Katrina, venturing instead that Ruwald still owned a sister cafe, with the same name, near the Bondi Icebergs, but that he was staying overseas. Sinadinovic left a message for Ruwald with Craig Field, the manager of Sejuiced at Bondi.

On 12 November, McDougall and Sinadinovic went to the Liberty Lunch, and actually conducted a quick interview with TC, who said the officers were definitely not inside on the night in question. He knew for sure and was most vociferous, for he was working at the Liberty in the hours before the shooting.

The next day, TC was escorted to a police building in Strawberry Hills. He thought it was best to accept the offer from McDougall to undertake a formal interview and co-operate with the authorities, so as not to arouse undue suspicion. TC said he'd known Podesta and Dilorenzo for a

long time.[32] He said there was no way the officers were there
that night: around that time Podesta was 'not going out
because of his father's illness and he . . . [was going] to stay
off the booze for a couple of weeks until his birthday because
he wanted to have a big night that night'; as for Dilorenzo,
'his wife was pregnant at the time . . . [and] he wasn't going
out at all . . . he was under the thumb'.[33] TC was asked about
when he first found out about the shooting, his meeting with
Podesta on the fateful afternoon, and their rowdy drinking
session on the night after the killing when they'd all gone up
to Dancers. He was also asked about Andrew Ruwald and the
Sejuiced cafe. The Liberty manager answered all of the questions quite eloquently and repeatedly stood up for his copper
mates. At times, he was even protective, criticising anyone
who claimed the shooters had been partying at the Liberty
the night before the shooting – 'that person would be the
biggest liar I've ever seen and I would tell that person that in
front of their face. It's not true'.[34] It was a great performance;
and TC offered names to back up his story. For some reason,
McDougall didn't take up the offer to try to corroborate
TC's story. He must have felt that TC, the best friend of the
shooters, could be taken at his word.

On 18 November, Ruwald, having just returned from
overseas, rang Sinadinovic. He denied knowing the hairdresser
and was of no assistance – 'although he had heard a number
of different rumours about the police involved in the shooting
at Bondi Beach'.[35] And that was that. The following-up of
Bromwich's allegation was shelved. McDougall and Sinadinovic had spoken to a few people, taken one statement from
TC, an admitted friend of the shooters – and concluded that
there was nothing left to do.

On 24 November, the Crown Solicitor's Office wrote to the Newcastle Legal Centre and declared that the allegations 'have been investigated . . . [but] have not been borne out by the investigations. No lay statement concerning the allegations will be contained in the brief'.[36] No information about drugs would be presented at the coronial inquest. Three days later, the massive brief of evidence was given to the Newcastle lawyers. The cops had finished their work. A big blue line had been drawn under the matter; the hunt for the truth in the Levi affair had ended.

All of these developments sat uncomfortably with the legal centre, whose students started to pour over the witness statements and the various exhibits – quickly pinpointing what they believed were major deficiencies. Why had the Bondi officers been so intimately involved in the statements, contrary to the Commissioner's Instructions? Why didn't the police use photogrammatory techniques on the beach to produce more accurate measurements? Why had Baker made his media statement? And why had he gone into so much detail?

There was another incredible omission, although at first it was hidden from the legal centre. The crime-scene investigator, Senior Constable Clinton Nicol, had left out a key piece of information from his statement in the police brief: how far the Bondi shooters had been from Levi when they killed him. In his notebook, Nicol wrote that he believed Podesta and Dilorenzo had been about 5.2 metres away from Levi when they fired. This was more than two metres outside the 'ring of danger' referred to by police weapons trainers – the three-metre circle within which it was considered appropriate to shoot. Somehow, however, Nicol had failed to put this crucial fact in his official statement. Cavanagh picked it up when, during the inquest, Nicol's notebook was handed over at the last minute for inspection.

Together, the students and the lawyers, admittedly with the benefit of hindsight, engaged in a forensic sifting exercise. They documented every criticism and investigative failure, every breach of police rules and procedures they could find. Their gravest concerns centred on how the police had tackled the Bromwich hearsay allegation. On 12 January 1998, nearly six months after the shooting, the centre wrote to the Crown to say it wanted more information to help prepare for the inquest. The hearing was scheduled to start on 9 February, and time was ticking away.

The legal centre asked for the video interviews of Dilorenzo and Podesta, case running sheets, police policy documents, Internal Affairs paperwork and 'records of any criminal convictions, or disciplinary charges brought against any of the police officers in the incident'.[37] It also demanded all of the police material obtained as a result of the Bromwich lead. Three days later, the Crown sent back some documents, the entirety of McDougall's effort to get to the bottom of the rumours about the shooters. The parcel contained the Bromwich statement, a running sheet typed up by Detective Sinadinovic and the record of the interview with TC. The Newcastle lawyers – Boersig, Watterson and Cavanagh – nearly fell off their seats. They couldn't believe the police could content themselves with such a paltry offering of three brief documents. An extraordinarily serious allegation, admittedly hearsay, had only been given the most cursory of probes.

On 19 January, three weeks before the coroner was set to start taking evidence, the centre served its most vituperative salvo on those charged with investigating properly the Levi killing. It attacked McDougall and Sinadinovic for placing any faith at all in TC, 'an avowedly close friend of the subject of the investigation without obtaining appropriate corroboration',[38] and ridiculed the officers for not accepting TC's offer to produce names of people who could verify his story. The Newcastle lawyers stressed to the Crown that there had been 'significant difficulties with police officers stationed in the eastern suburbs in the past' and that, in this case, 'the close association by relevant police officers with licensed premises in this instance is a matter of grave concern'.[39]

NINE

PANIC

'He certainly wasn't happy . . . I'd
known him for many, many years and I
found it a little unusual. He
certainly expressed to me: "Well, why
haven't I been told this before?" and
McDougall may have even said . . . he
was going to complain about it.'

**Robert Martin, referring to the detective's reaction at learning that
Internal Affairs had withheld a vital lead on the shooters for five months,
Police Integrity Commission, Operation Saigon, 24 February 2000**

The days leading up to the coronial inquest were exciting, full
of tension and strain. There was a storm, more a cyclone,
before the relative calm of the court. Of course, there should
have been a much more assured preamble. But Cowan, the
counsel assisting the coroner, and his police investigators
were wading in murky waters. Despite its confident pro-
nouncements to the Newcastle Legal Centre, the Crown's
case was chillingly under-prepared.

One week before the inquest, despairing at the quality
of the police investigation, the Newcastle lawyers took the
unusual step of hiring a private eye. Not wanting to bumble in
where they were unwelcome, John Boersig alerted the Police
Integrity Commission of their proposal, just in case their
gumshoe might interfere with a sensitive inquiry. The PIC did
not deter their interest – and so the private investigator, Michael
Rumore, armed with cameras, video players, microphones,

binoculars, scanners and other electronic surveillance equipment, started his seven-day assignment at the Liberty Lunch restaurant. The Newcastle lawyers told Rumore that TC was the main target. He was the friend who had given the shooters their security blanket, their alibi. The swank eateries and bars of Bondi were a world away from Rumore's rank suburban office – a cramped, loosely organised room full of files, notes and papers – in Gladesville, in Sydney's north-west. Rumore, pronounced like the Italian word for love rather than the English word for gossip, had been briefed on what difficulties to expect as he delved into the shadowy strip of big money, beautiful young people and bags of cocaine.

Rumore arrived at the Liberty Lunch at 8.15 p.m. on Sunday, 1 February, and stayed for about two hours. He used a concealed video camera to film the interior, giving his employers in Newcastle a glimpse of the place about which they had heard so much. It was a revealing first sortie and Rumore noticed at least fifteen staff working a busy floor. He jotted down in a notebook that 'the patrons occupying the rear bar section, in the main, appeared to be regulars and the majority knew each other.'[1]

While things may have appeared vibrant, the Liberty's traditional character and allure had changed radically in the seven months since the shooting – or since Stanley Dowse, had taken the wheel. Things had gone downhill fast.[2] Dowse worked in the restaurant from morning to night. His presence and old-fashioned attitudes irritated a lot of the staff and the regular patrons. Kieran O'Connor was sorely missed.[3] Only months after starting, Dowse had lost one of his managers, Stephen Langton, after he 'was led to believe that . . . [Langton] supplied liquor to a person to take off the premises'.[4]

Dowse was taking on the frivolous behaviour that had for so long been accepted, and this brought about inevitable conflict.

Dowse was mortified that cocaine was being used in his restaurant, and was determined to see its apparently prolific consumption eradicated. Once, he found 'a small bag, a plastic bag, in the upstairs office, which I handed to the police to get analysed . . . so somebody that had a key to the office used the drugs'.[5] Dowse knew that only a few of his managers had access to the upstairs room. Increasingly disenchanted, staff and patrons felt that, in stark contrast to the good old days, when there had been 'nobody to give us a slap on the wrist', Stan and Sue Dowse's regular presence meant that 'it was very hard to do what you wanted to do'.[6] The barman, Allan Graney, resigned soon after the Dowses' arrival and so too did TC – and with their disappearance, so went the customers. The Campbell Parade cognoscenti felt 'the vibe of the whole place' was disappearing, that 'there was less of a social atmosphere there, so therefore there wouldn't be as high a use of drugs . . . When they . . . took over the place, that vibe and atmosphere slowly died'.[7]

By the time Rumore sat down to order a flat white in February 1998, although the place seemed to be bristling with the clang of plates and the tinkling of glasses, the Liberty Lunch was in reality well short of the peak of its trade – and nothing like it had been at the time of the shooting. He watched keenly as two women 'and two males, all aged in their late twenties to early thirties, departed the premises and were gone for approximately fifteen to twenty minutes. When they returned they proceeded directly to the bar at the rear'.[8] Intrigued, Rumore returned the following day, still hunting TC, but he was nowhere to be seen.

The Bondi shooters, destabilised and distraught, had been seeking professional help since the shooting, in line with contemporary welfare thinking. Both had been taking anti-depressants and other medication, to ease their strain.

Podesta was seeing a psychiatrist recommended and funded by police welfare experts, and was independently consulting a psychologist as well – such was the depth of his mental turmoil. The death in November 1997 of his father, succumbing after a long and nauseating fight with cancer, had only added to his heavy burden and his mother's distress also detrimentally affected him. They'd nursed him until the end. With all of these negative influences, Podesta was considered to be barely coping, even under the almost constant sedation of prescription drugs such as Aropax and Normison.

Podesta, a constable on stress leave, was seeking escape in other drugs as well: he was mixing large quantities of alcohol, cocaine and ecstasy – 'just cocktailing everything'.[9] He was still socialising, as was his habit, with a lot of people who were either taking or seeing lots of drugs. Podesta, at the height of his depression, was nightclubbing, gawking through inebriated eyes at glamorous dancing girls, and 'drinking excessive amounts of alcohol . . . [and] taking drugs to make myself feel better'.[10] He couldn't get by without his friends, and was keen to help them out whenever the opportunity arose.

In late January 1998, days before the inquest, Internal Affairs finally got NSW Supreme Court approval to place listening devices in Podesta's car. It had taken a long time to put a tail on the coke-head. This surveillance was, of course, unknown to McDougall, who was doing last-minute checking. Late in the evening on 31 January, Podesta jumped into his vehicle with Peter Richardson, the Liberty barman – with every bit of their conversation being monitored. (At this stage it might be useful to be reminded of some names: Kieran O'Connor (one-time owner of the Liberty Lunch), Allan Graney (another barman at the club) and Madison Mander (Podesta's Bondi soul mate). The Caves, also mentioned, is a nightclub at Star City casino.

At 10.46 p.m., in Podesta's first mobile call, he talked to a person about the O'Connors, to see if they wanted some tickets, some ecstasy:[11]

Podesta: Do you want me to . . . what do you want . . . like, for now? – Um, I can see what I can do for you – um, what . . . [O'Connor's wife] wanted . . . They want to go the party? – How many tickets do they want? – Yeah – Alright, well, listen, I'll go and do that now and then, um, I'll pick some up now and I'll just come around – But I'm with, I'm with Peter, OK . . . Cool? – Peter's cool with Kieran because Peter, we went, we all went to the Caves together last weekend – Oh, it's just that, that he's with me, that's all – OK. Well, yeah, we'll see you soon. Bye.

Podesta [to Peter Richardson]: [We can] . . . get together some pills and drop them up to Kieran and then we can get them to rack us up.

Richardson: Now?

Podesta: Why not?

Richardson: Shall I stay in the car?

Podesta: No, you fucking come up with me. Go up and get some pills and take 'em up to Kieran's . . . and get some . . .

Richardson: Kieran's place . . . mad?

The pair journeyed to Hall Street, and then there is silence as Peter makes a call, on Podesta's mobile, to another mobile:

Richardson: Allan? – Yeah, I can't really um, say much on the phone 'cause I'm using Roddo's phone . . . Li-listen. I'm just up near your place, where are you? – Oh right, I need five tickets? – Yeah – Really? – Alright – We'll come around now then – Alright. Cool – I'll just . . . I'll just run in and run out, eh? – Yep – Perfect – See ya.

Richardson [to Podesta]: There you go. Madison's.

Podesta: Oh. He's at Madison's.

Richardson: Madison's a fucking joke.

Podesta: Yeah, I'm fucking really good mates . . . and I've fucked Madison twice.

Richardson: Have ya?

Podesta: Yeah. Ages ago.

Richardson: She's a cool chick, eh?

Podesta: I used to hang . . . with Madison . . . Madison was one of the first friends I made in Bondi. You know how long I've known Madison for? From when I used to own the Piccolo Bar . . .

Richardson: Fuck.

Podesta: I was only sixteen . . . Didn't you know I used to own the Piccolo Bar?

Richardson: Bullshit . . . When was that?

Podesta: Nineteen fucking . . . was it . . . 86 to 92.

Richardson: Get fucked.

Podesta: Yeah, my uncle owned it. Opened it in 1950. Oswald Promatti . . .

Richardson: No way . . . Fat dude?

Podesta: The big fat dude. My uncle . . . Heavy in the Cross . . . The biggest heavy in the Cross.

Days after this conversation, Internal Affairs started to get nervous. Keen thought it was particularly odd that he had not heard from McDougall; that not a whisper had sounded since the secret meeting with the coroner in October. Keen was sure McDougall had been making progress because he had heard from an informant, Helen,[12] in the past few months that 'police were making inquiries in the Bondi area in relation to Constable Podesta's state of sobriety prior to the shooting incident'.[13] But even still, because of the silence, Keen sensed there was something amiss.

On 2 February, defying Brammer's order for confidentiality, Keen phoned McDougall's office and left a message. At 2.10 p.m., McDougall returned the call, and then everyone started to panic – because it became apparent there had been a massive communication bungle. Keen told McDougall, the latter reported two days later, 'the name of a female informant . . . in relation to the allegation that the police involved in the shooting of Roni Levi had been drinking alcohol in the early hours of Saturday 28 June 1997 at licensed premises . . . [and that] he believed that I was aware of the existence of the informant due to a previous . . . [secret] meeting'.[14] While McDougall knew all about the rumours that Podesta had been inebriated, this was the first time he'd been given a *source*.

McDougall went off his brain, red with rage – telling Keen he 'intended to record the lateness of the supply of information with the inquest commencing'.[15] He phoned Robinson, at the Crown Solicitor's Office, who was also alarmed, and then went to work on a formal complaint. Keen, immediately recognising the unpleasantness of it all, sprinted off to see Richmond, Brammer's deputy, to tell him what had happened, struggling to contain himself and in quite a flap. Keen told Richmond in strident terms that, despite the holding of the secret meeting and all that had been done, McDougall somehow had never been told about the Amanda allegations. Richmond, however, 'seemed to be engaged in other things. He was talking to somebody on the phone . . . he was making inquiries on his computer. He just didn't seem to comprehend . . . the information I was trying to relay to him'.[16] Frustrated at the ambivalent response, Keen went off to Martin, the legal officer, with an urgent plea for help. Something had to be done. The most serious of claims about the shooters had been ignored and shelved.

The next day, McDougall went to Internal Affairs and Martin at last told him about the Amanda allegations – what McSorley should have told him months earlier. McDougall now got to work, five months after everyone assumed he had started.

Barely hours after McDougall departed Martin's office, Dilorenzo jumped into Podesta's car, which was parked somewhere in the eastern suburbs. He had some important matters to discuss with his partner, their nerves growing more frayed at the thought of what evidence might come to light at the inquest, due in a week's time.

With the birth of his second child, a boy, Dilorenzo had necessarily been more obligated, and somewhat more stressed, than his footloose buddy. Not that his constant domestic duties were encroaching too heavily on his recreational pursuits or occasional nightclub escapades. Like Podesta, he continued to receive counselling and was using 'two different types of anti-depressants and other prescription pills to sort of try and cope with what happened'.[17]

In the initial months after the shooting, Dilorenzo had been swamped with negativity and would 'just sit around. I was doing nothing; I was pretty miserable'.[18] Then, on resuming his boxing and fitness training, pounding a bag in the back of his home in Bondi, on his own and with friends, he got temporary relief. A lot of pent-up tension seemed to ooze out with the sweat. Dilorenzo even consulted his psychiatrist on the merits of the exercise therapy 'and he told me that it was a good idea that, you know, I get back into the training and try to forget about what happened'.[19]

One of his primary motivators was TC, a regular training partner of Dilorenzo's and something of a local wizard on how to attain optimum performance. TC used and supplied a high-grade amino acid, Siyushi, which when mixed with fruit juice or water, pushed 'more oxygen through your blood and therefore allows you to train a littler bit harder when you're gasping for air'.[20] Consuming glasses of the potent powder actually helped Dilorenzo to 'relax towards training, to get back into it . . . '.[21] Dilorenzo had used his fists outside training, and in anger, at nightclubs – one occasion being at the Temple Club in the Exchange Hotel in Oxford Street. His brother, Mark Lorenzo, had been in tow.

Although Podesta and Dilorenzo had been friends before the killing, they forged a more intimate relationship in the months before court, drawn together by circumstances. They supported each other. And so it was that, at 4.29 p.m. on 2 February, the pair got together for one of their regular chats; to natter about old times and old places, like the Liberty Lunch – and about what the police, and Internal Affairs, had been doing. Perhaps not wanting to be seen together, they loitered in Podesta's car, where the bug again whirred to life:

Podesta: They've asked Stephen [Langton] . . . about us, right?
. . . He's one of my best mates . . . And then they've gone
and asked TC, who is my other best mate . . . I'm sure
they could hit us if they were looking for us.
Dilorenzo: Business at Liberty has gone downhill big time? . . .
No-one goes to Liberty anymore.
Podesta: No.

127

Dilorenzo: Nobody mate.

Podesta: Stan [Dowse]. He's blown it.

Dilorenzo: He's fucked it mate.

Podesta: No-one goes to Liberty . . .

Dilorenzo: And he fired Helena. She was beautiful, mate.

Podesta: How could they – how could you fire Helena?

Dilorenzo: Fuck. She's the best chick. She never did anything wrong.

Podesta: She was the best bar lady there. She's the only straight one.[22]

The Liberty Lunch was again the centre of activity. After just three days on the job and working on a shoestring budget, Michael Rumore had eclipsed the police shooting investigation team in several key respects. Increasingly, Rumore and McDougall's partner, Sinadinovic, would cross paths in the race to gather evidence for the inquest – material that should have already been in the bag. Sinadinovic was hunting for Robert, the man who, referred to by nickname, had been linked by Amanda to being with the shooters at the Liberty Lunch. Rumore was looking for anything, and everything. Starting from scratch, Rumore spoke to the hairdresser at Noddy's on King, who put him on to Sejuiced, at Bronte. Without the benefit that the police had of vehicle licence-plate checks, criminal record databases or intelligence holdings, the private investigator made his mark on the Bondi scene.

On 5 February, Rumore went to the Bondi Sejuiced, having already established that Andrew Ruwald (the cafe's owner) was most likely the customer to whom Katrina Rafferty had spoken. Rumore was talking with the cafe's manager, Craig Field, when Ruwald drove past, spotted them, and dropped in. They talked about the rumours and Ruwald again denied ever having had his hair cut by Rafferty, curious at the sudden renewed attention. He said he'd been contacted only the day before by Sinadinovic but had refused to be interviewed – simply because he had nothing to say. The pair talked about someone called Stephen, whose name had cropped up in conversations, and Ruwald then handed Rumore his mobile phone number, as an act of good faith. By the late evening, Rumore, moving with decisive swiftness, had spoken to Stephen Langton, having tracked down his girlfriend to a restaurant and passed on a message.

The following afternoon, 6 February, Ruwald rang up Rumore with the intriguing proposition that he wanted to give him some more information. The cafe owner suggested a meeting the next day at 8 a.m. at Sejuiced at Bondi because something had cropped up. Ruwald arrived late, cruising by in his car – at which point Rumore noticed a customised black Falcon sedan with tinted windows over the road. Moments after Ruwald appeared, 'a marked police car approached hurriedly and suddenly stopped'.[23] An inspector from Waverley police station jumped out and 'forcefully demanded to see some identification. Simultaneously, Ruwald commenced to speak loudly . . . [and] became visibly angry and we [then] . . . caused the police officer to have him stand a few paces back'.[24] Rumore calmly pulled out his wad of licences and assured the officer that he had never misrepresented himself as a policeman, as Ruwald was purporting. It was a tense scene but eventually Rumore 'respectfully suggested to the inspector that we should not be detained further'.[25]

Rumore never got to speak to TC, but he reached the Liberty's owners, to find out if they'd been aware of the rumours. Dowse, like Ruwald, was very surprised by the revived attention because, only a day earlier, he had given a statement to Sinadinovic. What was all the fuss about? he asked. It had been seven months since the shooting – why weren't questions asked then? Dowse restated his belief that Podesta and Dilorenzo were not at his place on the night before the shooting, at least not before he'd left work at about 10.30 p.m. He did concede 'that both of the police officers were regulars of the venue in their own time but he could see them perhaps three times a week for a couple of weeks running – but then he wouldn't see them for a couple of months at a time'.[26]

On the Sunday evening, 8 February, hours before the inquest was to start, Rumore typed up his final report:

> *My inquiries have fallen well short of identifying the link between the hairdresser . . . and the person with whom she allegedly had the conversation regarding . . . police activities on the night before the shooting . . . [but] from our observations of Liberty Lunch and independent casual conversations with witnesses and a formal interview with Stephen Langton, an ex-employee, certainly it is a distinct possibility that some form of private party was in progress after close of trade at midnight on Friday 27 June 1997 . . . It remains a distinct possibility . . . that the officers may have arrived after . . . Dowse's departure and kicked on at the back bar as rumoured.*[27]

On another side of town, Sinadinovic made far more conservative conclusions – having been prevailed upon to quickly investigate the Amanda allegations, the leads tossed down at the last minute from Internal Affairs. He still hadn't found Robert, the man she'd nominated as being with the officers, nor had he relocated TC, but he felt he'd done his best.

On the eve of the inquest, the most important of forums – the place to explain, uphold or condemn the circumstances of the death of a person – the nerves were fraying.

TEN

THE INQUEST

'[Dilorenza and Podesta are] two
ordinary enough looking blokes
caught up in extraordinary
circumstances. The tension they are
under is considerable and they bear
it solemnly, almost expressionless,
careful not to react.'

Philip Cornford, 'Revolvers handed over, but court tensions remain',
Sydney Morning Herald, 19 February 1998

On 8 February, the day before the inquest, the Levi family
arrived in Sydney to open a photographic exhibition, a tribute to their late son, his life and turbulent career. An eclectic
collection of framed works – brilliant shots of all types from
his unrewarding, but passionate, life behind the lens – were
hung from the Bondi Pavilion. Alongside the strip of sand
where he had fallen . . . in a building generously provided by
Waverley Council.

The exhibition was a sombre demonstration of the
dead man's commitment to art; to what he felt was his calling –
a thoughtful and reflective memorial gesture, arranged by Levi's
friends Gil Shalem, Stefan Bialoguski and Tina Dalton, and his
wife, Melinda Dundas. It was an act deeply appreciated by the
Levi family – Richard, Rebecca and their son Ilan, who had ventured to Sydney for the inquest. It would be an excruciating,
but necessary, public confronting and chronicling of their son

and brother's demise. Dundas, horrified on the inside – reeling over what she and the Newcastle lawyers felt were systemic investigative failures in the shooting, and the cavalier disregard for their concerns about the Liberty Lunch – wanted people 'to understand the richness of somebody's life . . . [because] often the whole . . . [investigation] process becomes so clinical'.[1]

On the walls were 26 of Roni Levi's images – 'portraits of famous Australians such as actors Bryan Brown and Sigrid Thornton and a photograph of a lifesaver staring out to sea from Australia's most famous beach . . . [an image] say friends . . . [that is] a poignant reminder that Roni died violently at a place he so often found peace'.[2] The Bratanoff-Firgoff image, soon to be dubbed 'Exhibit 7', was there as well, providing a disturbing counterpoint to the other work's more reverential and recreational feel. It was simply captioned: 'Never Again'. There was a brief article about Levi's life and spiritual influences which was placed at the entrance, suggesting that although the dead man's 'mind could not be stilled nor his heart quietened by the sea at Bondi on the day he died, he has found peace now'.[3]

Levi's parents were overwhelmed by their son's friends' commitment in arranging the exhibition, and as they inspected the exhibition, they sobbed, at times uncontrollably. On the verge of this major event, the emotions were raw. In the days before the inquest, police had been involved in two further controversial shootings: one involved a man armed with a knife and an iron bar; in the other, 'police shot a man . . . they believed was a burglar, and then learnt he was the son of the property's owners'.[4]

The Coroner's Office had told journalists to expect up to 100 witnesses in a hearing likely to last six weeks, a testament

THE SHOOTING A split second before his life was ended on 28 June 1997, Roni Levi, knife in his right hand, appears to be walking towards Dilorenzo (left) and Podesta (right). Away to the left, Jones keeps his revolver aimed at Levi as Seddon gets set for another baton charge. Jean Pierre Bratanoff-Firgoff, Sydney Freelance

TRUE BLUE HEROES Dilorenzo (left) and Podesta (right), in full uniform with guns and handcuffs, arrive together at Glebe Coroner's Court on 6 March 1998 for the inquest into Roni Levi's death. Dean Sewell, *Sydney Morning Herald*

CALLED TO ACCOUNT The Bondi shooters arrive for the first Police Integrity Commission hearing, on 23 February 1999, into claims that officers in Sydney's eastern suburbs were using and dealing in drugs. Toby Hillier, *Sydney Morning Herald*

THE VICTIM This picture, distributed to the media after the shooting, was the most commonly used photograph of Roni Levi in newspapers and magazines. It shows him in a typically carefree pose, well before the shooting. Melinda Dundas

THE SCEPTIC Distrustful of the police almost from the start, Roni Levi's wife, Melinda Dundas, sought help from the Newcastle Legal Centre to unravel the mismanaged inquiry. James Boddington, *Sun-Herald*

THE PARENTS Rebecca and Richard Levi, on 6 February 1998, holding a photo from their son's posthumous exhibition, which took place at Bondi Beach in the days leading up to the coronial inquest. Jon Reid, *Sun-Herald*

Left: **THE SOLICITOR** John Boersig became convinced that the Levi case should be used as a vehicle for improvements in legislation and procedure, and for changes to police culture.

Centre: **THE ADVOCATE** Robert Cavanagh, whose determined cross examination at the coronial inquest revealed serious flaws in the original police investigation.

Right: **THE ACADEMIC** Associate Professor Ray Watterson directed the campaign by his legal students to dismantle the police case and to pinpoint deficiencies in the crime scene examination and the collation of evidence. Peter Stoop

THE BONDI COMMANDER Chief Inspector Richard Baker told an impromptu media conference hours after the killing that the police conduct was totally appropriate. But he failed to tell the shooting investigation team that the shooters were the targets of a major drug inquiry. Sam Rutherford, *Sun-Herald*

THE BROTHERHOOD Police pallbearers carry the coffin from St Mary's Cathedral on 5 March 1998 after the funeral of Constable Peter Forsyth, whose stabbing in Ultimo while the Levi coronial inquest was in progress sparked sudden support for the Bondi shooters. Robert Pearce, *Sydney Morning Herald*

SPINNING THE STORY Nearing the end of the coronial inquest, on 7 March 1998, John Lorenzo, a career publicist and Dilorenzo's brother, joined with Annabelle Dilorenzo, the police officer's wife, to deplore the coroner's decision to refer the case on for possible criminal charges.
Jacky Ghossein, *Sun-Herald*

THE PENTHOUSE MAN The Liberty Lunch's owner, property developer Kieran O'Connor, his rooftop apartment on June 1999. He denied being involved in the drug scene, but the Police Integrity Commission found there was 'grave reason to doubt the accuracy' of his evidence.
on Reid, *Sun-Herald*

THE NIGHTCLUB MANAGER Easton Barrington James (also known as TC), seen here at the Police Integrity Commission inquest on 22 February 1999, was the manager of the Liberty Lunch and a friend of the shooters. He insisted that conversations between himself, Podesta and Dilorenzo, recorded secretly at his home on police bugs, related to amino acids and body building supplements rather than cocaine.
Paul Miller, *Sydney Morning Herald*

PREMATURE ELATION The shooters celebrate the decision of the director of public prosecutions, on 30 June 1998, not to proceed with murder charges over the Levi shooting. Dilorenzo is on stress leave, with Podesta only having just returned from an overseas holiday. Within months, their links with drugs and dealers would be exposed. Grant Turner, *Daily Telegraph*

to the seriousness with which the Bench viewed the encounter and the breadth and complexity of the police force's enquiries. The main issue was, undeniably, whether Levi had been 'shot by the police in their execution of their duty'.[5] Of vital, but secondary, importance was the efficacy of the overall conduct on the beach, and the appropriateness of the tactics employed to get Levi to surrender. That was obvious. But there were other questions to address, like the adequacy, or otherwise, of the police investigation into their peers, the role played by the Bondi commander in his dealings with the media, and the significance of the Bondi officers in the interviewing of witnesses in the crucial days after the death.

The Bondi shooters had all hired the same legal representative, Kenneth Madden, who had, in turn, briefed the wily and popular barrister 'Jock' Dailly to defend their interests. Madden and Dailly often worked together, and had frequently represented controversial police clients in controversial cases. They were respected and revered and, because of their familiarity, were extremely knowledgeable on the cop rule and procedure bibles.

Court One was set aside for the duration of the hearing, starting on Monday, 9 February 1998 – seven months and a week after the death. Coroner Derrick Hand presided over the case and 'the liturgical-like drone of proceedings',[6] with his counsel assisting conducting the flow of testimony at one end of the table. A feast of lawyers dined along the rest of it: Dailly and Madden, for the shooters; Greg Willis for the NSW Police Service; Robert Cavanagh, John Boersig and Ray Watterson looking after the interests of Melinda Dundas; and Ken Horler, QC and Michael Marx, the representatives for the Levi family. Their clients, and their clients' friends and families, a gaggle of journalists and other perennial court-watchers, and what seemed like a platoon of policemen, filled the remaining pews.

The Newcastle Legal Centre, 'having worked through the Christmas holidays . . . [had] carried out the most intensive research of any legal team at the bar table'.⁷ All the evidence had been forensically analysed and all statements and conclusions pulled apart and questioned – the advocates had covered all the bases. Spurned on by their students' youthful sense of outrage, and impressed with their critique, Cavanagh, Boersig and Watterson felt good about their chances in court – and hoped the coroner would heed their advice on the police's shortcomings. But 'to the high-priced Sydney lawyers and visibly cocky cops crowding the court-room, they must have looked like classic bush league outsiders . . . [having] just shared a three hour car ride from Newcastle in Cavanagh's aging sedan'.⁸

The Newcastle team's courtroom opponents might have appeared smug, but beneath the spontaneous smiles of reassurance lay a battered police case. Theirs was a brief far short of the benchmark of excellence and absoluteness that had been promised, and with possible evidence still being madly scrambled together. On the first day of the inquest, McDougall's complaint against Internal Affairs was endorsed by one of his bosses, Assistant Commissioner Clive Small – a move that immediately sparked the typical police quest to apportion blame. Urgent explanatory memorandums were being signed, and even Christopher Keen, who'd rung McDougall a week earlier with the information, had been told to submit a report, to show cause why his behaviour should not be challenged. Although intent on lambasting Internal Affairs, McDougall now had no option but to deal with the new leads and was directing important moves from the court, not certain when he might be called to give evidence.

Even as the coroner opened proceedings, asking David Cowan to outline the Crown's case and highlight its possible observations, McDougall's partner, Detective Senior Constable Sinadinovic, was patching up the holes in the police case, darting all over town looking for clues. It would not be until halfway through the first week that he would find the mysterious Robert, the subject of Amanda's claims – the man who was supposed to be at the Liberty Lunch with the shooters. And although Robert now denied the claims and refused to make a statement, he at least revealed one thing: this was the first time that he had been approached by anybody . . . five months after Amanda had first told Internal Affairs.

Before a word had been spoken, there was strife. The Bondi shooters, their identities still known only to the Newcastle legal team, Dundas, and the Levi family – but not to the pack of journalists – arrived at the court, as required, in full police uniform. With tools on their belts, and revolvers at their sides. As reported a few days later when the shooters' names were publicly known, the sight repulsed the Levi entourage: 'The . . . weapons on the hips of Senior Constable Tony Dilorenzo and Constable Rod Podesta . . . so offended . . . Mr Levi's family that they asked the police be directed not to wear them . . . Levi's widow backed the request . . . [but] it took three days to reach an agreement, with lawyers for the two police arguing that they received death threats and needed the weapons for protection.'[9]

Cowan told the court that the purpose of the hearing, and the reason for calling so many witnesses, was to explore the factors behind Levi's erratic behaviour and the legitimacy of the subsequent police conduct – and whether excessive force or illegal means had been employed in his slaying. Lessons needed to be extracted from this tragedy. Cowan described Levi, as was universally considered, 'as a polite, gentle person interested in art, painting and photography. He was a vegetarian who neither drank nor smoked'.[10] But, as the *Age* reported, 'the evidence would show that Mr Levi underwent an acute psychotic episode in the hours before his death at dawn'.[11]

Cowan then detailed the dead man's strange turn of mood in the week leading up to his death, the distant call with his family in Paris, the delusional dinner he'd had on the night before, and his admission to St Vincent's Hospital for tests and convalescence. And then the escape from hospital, the knock on the window of his flat, and the chase by Warren Brunner through Bondi's dark dawn streets. Before the pursuit by police, the dive into the ocean and the prevaricating walk up and down the sand. It was quite a story to digest. Cowan was measured, but insisted that, 'throughout these events, from the moment he entered the water, he was repeatedly asked by police to put the knife down'.[12] Dundas, who gave evidence on the first day, said she believed that these sorts of assessments were way off the mark – and that she found the idea of 'Roni lunging at police officers with a knife . . . utterly incomprehensible'.[13]

It was clear from the start that Levi's time at St Vincent's Hospital would be heavily scrutinised. How could someone needing three days of psychiatric tests be allowed to escape so easily in the middle of the night, only to be shot hours later, holding a knife, in the middle of a mental episode? Nurse Catherine Armstrong said Levi was classed as a non-urgent case when he arrived with his friends. Dr Elizabeth Meagher said he was 'one of the most co-operative patients I had that night'[14] and 'was not displaying enough signs of psychosis to warrant an urgent assessment by a psychiatrist'.[15] But while his treatment could be validated, his escape was deeply flawed. There was no evidence that Levi's family, or Brunner, had been called when his disappearance was first noticed. And Nurse Malcolm Blunt admitted at the hearing that there was no procedure for notifying police when a voluntary patient absconded.

When McDougall jumped into the witness box on the third day, Dilorenzo and Podesta were named as the shooters for the first time; their masks were finally removed. Right then, all eyes turned on the shooters, who were sitting 'side by side . . . as silent as the sphinx . . . knee-deep in words, opinions, suggestions, accusations, corrections and reminiscences . . . [but] the officers stay stoically mute, no matter how damning or supportive the evidence'.[16] McDougall's presence, as well as the pent-up anticipation of the moment, caused a change in the court's demeanour – and some alarm. Mainly due to the heated antics of Cavanagh, the bane of all witnesses, the 'lanky and slightly dishevelled . . . barrister . . . with a wild mane of greying hair'.[17] He thumped into virtually everyone who put their hands around the bible, never content with the answer. Cavanagh wrestled, painted vivid landscapes, agreed and argued and ferreted with McDougall (no stranger to the witness box after 30-plus years in the job) and at times, the banter was awkward. Watterson sat next to Cavanagh, 'hemmed in by court documents when not weighed down by them . . . [adding] fuel to Cavanagh's performance with scribbled notes, new lines of attack – somehow imbibed by the barrister in midflight during a tense cross-examination'.[18] Their tactics produced a string of revelations.

McDougall conceded that there were many flaws in the way he had supervised the investigation into the shooting (and he was not even talking about the fact that witnesses were still being hunted). Under Cavanagh's hammer, any illusion of a good police job was smashed. McDougall admitted under cross-examination that he could not guarantee there had been no collusion between officers in the preparation of their statements; and that in using workmates of the shooters to interview witnesses, the Commissioner's Instructions had been flouted. And he suggested that his superiors had not been pleased about some media releases. Cavanagh also showed, through McDougall, that 'the two officers who fired on Levi were not given the opportunity to undergo blood tests to detect the use of drugs or alcohol . . . [but] no allegation that either officer was under the influence of drugs or alcohol at the time was raised'.[19]

Cavanagh's sometimes zealous, and always irrepressible style had a devastating impact, and an overwhelming influence on the proceedings. With Watterson, they gave voice to the barely controlled anger that infused so many in the community. This was not just a normal death, a tragic passing that could be conveniently explained away; it was a killing with tremendously serious ramifications.

By the end of McDougall's evidence, at the end of a harrowing first week, the coroner was already moving to make recommendations, to ensure the tragedy was never repeated. Coroner Hand indicated his prescription was likely to 'examine whether there was a need for NSW police to be armed with disabling capsicum spray and retractable, telescopic batons'.[20]

The second week was almost exclusively devoted to eyewitness accounts, providing an expansive and divergent series of first-person memories of the day's powerful vignettes: Brunner's pursuit of his distressed friend, Levi's swim, the police stalking and the eventual shots. No one recollection was identical; as was to be expected, each witness's testimony clashed with another's. They remembered things differently and they remembered different things. Some heard particular noises, words or phrases – and saw things from varying vantage points. Some on the beach; other onlookers up close and other witnesses on the promenade. Each interpreted things differently. Indeed, opinions were often poles apart, as fractured on what had physically taken place on the beach as they were on whether the police officers' actions were appropriate.

The first civilian witness was Jean Pierre Bratanoff-Firgoff, the man whose lens was in the right place at the wrong time. His images were admitted into evidence, giving judicial credence to a sequence of shots that provided a virtual guided journey through the morning's events. Of course, the most famous of all the frames, taken 'at the exact moment he was falling down',[21] was seen as providing a critical insight into whether Levi was charging – on whether the police shooters were racing backwards toward the wall. Exhibit 7, as the shot was to become known, showed none of this expected action, and instead showed the characters to be languid, almost motionless. And the shooters seemed to have stopped in their tracks, as if they were bracing themselves for an incident.

Bratanoff-Firgoff also detailed an incident shortly after the shooting in which a policeman had told him they needed to 'cover up' the matter. He testified that the officer 'said in a panicked, shaky way: "We've got to cover this up. We've got to cover this up." I felt a lot of stress and panic in the way he was talking to me'.[22] The photographer insisted he didn't believe the officer 'meant the police had done something wrong and they were trying to hide it but that it was something that had happened, an accident, and they wished to fix it'.[23] Interestingly, Bratanoff-Firgoff said he'd mentioned the conversation in his interview with the police, a statement recorded at Bondi police station only after he had gone to the media to protest about not being contacted. But the remarks were never put in his statement. He said he told

Cavanagh about the conversation in a pre-inquest conference but had failed to mention the incident during an interview with David Cowan before the inquest – 'Mr Bratanoff-Firgoff said the reason he did not tell Mr Cowan about the matter was because "he didn't ask much." '[24] It was an evocative testimony, full of twists.

Journalist Deborah Bogle recounted how she watched the scene through her binoculars from her apartment over the road. She said Levi had never really lunged at the police, prompting his killing, but rather seemed to be 'moving quite slowly and he had his arms outstretched, holding whatever it was in his hand'.[25] Other witnesses, like Roger Cubitt, a local real estate agent, and Bondi Diggers Club worker Peter Bourke had radically different statements, believing Levi had at one stage almost been running at the police – providing a far more dramatic picture of officers in peril. Bourke said that Levi 'was in this half trot and then he lunged towards the officers . . . I was under the impression that he was trying to stab a police officer'.[26] Jogger Karen Allison said she had almost bumped into Levi, and that he had mirrored her when she tried to avoid a collision. On a repeat lap, an officer wielding a baton told her to 'fuck off' – 'Thank God he did because as he said that, it came to me that I was in the line of fire and that the police had their guns drawn.'[27]

Not all of the joggers had complimentary remarks by any means. There was a particularly aggressive letter, written to Police Commissioner Peter Ryan by David Michael, a business consultant, that was tabled in evidence, after much protest. In his letter, Michael wrote:

I wanted to express my most serious concern and absolute indignation with what can only be described as the massacre of an innocent person on Bondi Beach

. . . [and I] have come to the conclusion that the police officers in question are either incompetent, lacking in judgment or of such disposition that they should never ever be entrusted with a firearm. By legal and social definition, this shooting is the most offensive action that can happen in a civilised society. It involved the execution of an innocent person and that fact is not altered or modified by the observation Mr Levi was acting irregularly or even in a mildly threatening way.[28]

On occasions, emotions inside the courtroom reached boiling point: ' "You French bastards," one man cursed the Levis in the court vestibule. A woman mocked Ms Dundas, who had cried in court. The woman's son said: "Bitch. What a performance. It deserves a Golden Globe." '[29]

The pressure was also pounding in on Dilorenzo and Podesta, their confidence swinging back and forth with the tidal ebb and flow of the testimonies – 'two ordinary enough looking blokes caught up in extraordinary circumstances. The tension they are under is considerable and they bear it solemnly, almost expressionless, careful not to react'.[30] Luckily, others were reacting on their behalf. The talented media publicist John Lorenzo was doing his best to create a mood of empathy, to show readers and viewers the other side of the coin. Outside the court, Lorenzo told reporters that since his brother's name had been announced, Dilorenzo had 'had bricks thrown through his windows half a dozen times . . . Police had to be called and there are now protective bars installed'.[31] And, understandably, the family angle was played up: 'Tony's wife was pregnant at the time of the shooting and it was enormously traumatic for her and the family. At one stage she was in the shower and someone pounded on the window, saying "F . . . ing murderer." '[32]

The attacks on the home were retold by Annabelle Dilorenzo herself – again speaking out as her husband's PR voice, knowing he had been silenced – in a graphic Sunday newspaper item, bluntly headlined 'Life Is Hell For Policeman'. And with a front-page photograph of the family walking contemplatively along Bondi Beach – Dilorenzo clutching his daughter, Annabelle with a stroller – the imagery could not have been more slanted towards attracting the sympathy vote. It worked perfectly. An accompanying feature insisted that, although they looked 'like any young family strolling the Bondi promenade . . . life is a living hell . . . [and] the famous beach will forever be blighted by blood'.[33]

More eyewitness testimony dominated the third week. Another letter-writer, Sydney silk John Durack, SC, said he'd been trying to keep people from walking between Levi and the water when the shots rang out. He claimed the policemen had behaved aggressively in the seconds before the killing, that he 'did not hear anything conciliatory', instead he remembered 'one of the officers yelling: "Drop the knife, drop the knife you fucking deadshit", or dickhead or similar expression'.[34] Other witnesses said the police had clearly warned Levi to drop his knife or they would shoot to kill – and of police hitting Levi with a baton after he'd been floored.

Revelatory testimony came when council cleaner Leo Hamlin took the stand, to tell how Levi lunged at the officers. Hamlin told Cowan that Levi had definitely made a threatening gesture, a lunge, at the officers – and that he was endangering lives when the shots were fired. But when Cavanagh tested Hamlin in cross-examination, that version was made to look like an invention. Hamlin was shown embarrassing television footage of an interview he had given to Channel 9 only minutes after the event, where he was specifically asked if Levi had lunged at the officers. The newsclip showed him 'pause and then reply: "Well I am not too sure . . ."'[35] However, when this interview was compared with his statement to police, taken two days later – where he said Levi had definitely lunged – an obvious dilemma was displayed and Cavanagh asked for an explanation. While Hamlin insisted he'd been nervous and was upset, and had mistaken the reporter's question, he eventually conceded that watching Baker's media comments 'on the day of the shooting had put into his mind that Mr Levi had lunged'.[36]

In other words, he'd changed his story – the police had contaminated his evidence. Cavanagh had proven a direct causal link in one person's testimony but the inference the Hamlin experience raised was unforgettable: how many other witnesses had been altered in their thinking?

The paramedic, Craig Payne, gave backing to the shooters' and the McDougall version of events – that the police had retreated after an exhaustive effort to get Levi to surrender. And he introduced a previously unexplored theme: that Levi *wanted* the police to kill him. He said Levi had been 'making gestures as if to say, "Come on and shoot me" . . . making extraordinary faces to the police – as if he wanted them to shoot him, as if he didn't care'.[37] He said the shooters had been getting more anxious about their safety and 'the situation was escalating and they could not control Mr Levi . . . [and] he was getting closer to the police and closer to the public . . . they seemed not to have any other choice'.[38]

As Payne's evidence was completed, a door was shut on the third week's sessions. The prevailing sentiment still veered against the shooters. It really boiled down to waiting for Dilorenzo, Podesta and the other police evidence, or some other event, to tilt the balance. As they all walked from the courtroom at Glebe that Friday night, none could have realised how far the balance was about to be moved – in favour of the police.

It was late on Friday, 27 February when three off-duty policemen scaled the extraordinarily steep incline of William Henry Street in Ultimo, about two kilometres away from the coroner's hearing rooms and the morgue at Glebe. The officers, Constable Peter Forsyth, Constable Brian Neville and Probationary Constable Jason Semple, had just finished a few beers after playing touch football in a park with some local Aboriginal kids. Forsyth was known as a committed constable, spending time after work helping the underprivileged and unfortunate.

As Forsyth and his mates hit the top of the hill, they were approached by a gang of youths and offered drugs. The kids, from Sydney's west, had come into town for a dance party with the intention of offloading some gear. The officers produced their badges, seeking to arrest them for supplying illicit substances, surprising and alarming the would-be dealers. Then the scene flared up. One of the youths pulled a knife and Forsyth and Semple were stabbed, Forsyth being repeatedly wounded. The gang, three young men and a girl, raced off as Neville reared off madly in pursuit, his two injured mates on the ground, covered in blood.

Semple suffered wounds to the liver and other vital organs. But Forsyth, punched with the knife in the heart, died despite the effort to revive him. He was pronounced dead at 12.15 a.m. on Saturday, 28 February. Two officers had been wounded with a knife, with one dead, right in the middle of an inquest where police had shot a man who had tried to attack them with a knife. Comparisons were immediately made with the Bondi killing, and sympathy used as much for Forsyth's widow, Jackie, and her children, as it was now for the Bondi shooters.

It was immediately as if Podesta and Dilorenzo had approached Levi in Ultimo, and not on Bondi Beach; that they would have suffered the same fate if they hadn't shot their knifeman. The commissioner deplored the violence in his early-morning media statements and said it was 'a typical example of the dangers they face in the streets'.[39] The public's tune turned counter-clockwise in the blink of an eye. And so, in this most horrible of moments, in Peter Forsyth's tragic killing, Dilorenzo and Podesta had just been tossed a lifeline. They were now, before even saying a word in court or to the media, everyone's heroes. The Bondi shooters wore the same clothes and filled the same boots as their fallen Ultimo comrade.

ELEVEN
TRUE BLUE

'There's psychos out there. There
is only one thing to do to them.
It's fucking Smith and Wesson.'
Constable Rodney Podesta, bugged conversation with Easton Barrington James,
28 February 1998

Rodney Podesta was in a party mood, ready to unwind. It was
the weekend and the end of three weeks of torrid testimony,
his mind having been numbed by the procession of witnesses,
each one with a different view on what he had done. Having
to remain impassive and motionless day after day was incredibly stressful, as was the hardship of facing the dead man's
wife and distressed family. And there was the unenviable burst
of public exposure, of course.

It was the weekend of the Gay and Lesbian Mardi Gras
parade, the most decadent of affairs, with more than one million
people flooding the streets to join in the high-camp carnival
atmosphere of colourful mobile floats, outrageous garments
and musical celebration. This was the perfect opportunity for
Podesta and his girlfriend, Kylie Kummings, to escape the pressure – and get stoned. So he got up and went out looking for
cocaine, stopping first at an automatic teller machine on Bondi

Beach, near where he had slugged Levi, to whip out $500. Podesta was trying to do drug deals in the middle of an inquest that was probing his conduct as a policeman.

Podesta decided to start his hunt at TC's flat at 3 Yarranabbe Road, Darling Point. Having moved out of Podesta's premises in Bondi, TC now lived in the bottom apartment of a large divided house, set into a jagged and spectacular cliff-face that overlooked Rushcutters Bay, in a suburb that is home to some of the wealthiest people in Australia. TC was still sleeping, having been up all night, when his policeman mate got to the door at 12.14 p.m., and so the ex-Liberty employee hadn't heard anything about Peter Forsyth's knifing by a gang of youths in an Ultimo street. As their subsequent conversation would show, Podesta was delighted at the renewed support for the police that the incident would encourage, even if it was at the expense of a colleague.

Just as Podesta's car had been recently installed with a secret listening device, so TC's new abode was now bugged. The secret ears of Internal Affairs were able to listen in on the whole Podesta–TC exchange:[1]

Podesta: Oh, so you have not slept? . . . Sorry man, I didn't know. I thought you would have been up and about by lunch. What time did you get to bed?

TC: About ninish [a.m.].

Podesta: Ahhh . . . right . . . I'll let you get back to sleep then if you're tired.

TC: No worries.

Podesta: Are you going to get some today? —'Cause I wanted to get 3 g's [about $600 worth] if I could. Could you give me something like that?

TC: But it's gone already.

Podesta: Oh, has it, already?

TC: It was quite a bit. It's already gone but I should be able to . . .

Podesta: 'Cause otherwise I have to go up and see Geoff [Moore]. It's just that I . . . fucking Kylie wanted me to get it for her, 'cause she owes me heaps of fucking money, so I said . . . aahh . . . get it 'cause she's taking it to Mardi Gras or something, so she can pay me back some money. I don't really feel like going up and seeing Geoff . . . I get fucking nervous when I go up there.

TC: Not after what they said about you. Why the hell do you want to do anything?

Podesta: Mmm . . . No that's why I come to see you. What time have you organised to do this thing?

TC: Dunno. I've got to ring my mate and then . . .

Podesta: OK . . .

TC: See what we can come up with . . .

Podesta: Alright . . . like a gram.

Podesta then turned the conversation to what he wanted to do with the cocaine, if they were able to get it. He told TC he wanted to 'cut' some of his gear (adulterate it, dilute it with another powder) and then sell it to his girlfriend. Free coke courtesy of his girlfriend. This would give Podesta his own supply, and allow him to make some money out of Kylie. The policeman seemed quite unrepentant:

Podesta: I want to turn my three-and-a-half [grams] into five [grams] I put three-and-a-half . . . so one-and-a-half [grams is needed] . . . Yeah, fuck it! . . . These people are fuckwits mate. They . . . she . . . owes me heaps of money, Kylie, so it's sort of a way I can get money off her, you know.

TC: Mmm.

Podesta: Fuck her. I don't give a fuck. I don't know her friends. They'll never see me [again].

TC: I don't want to come back at this . . . [that it] come from me . . .

Podesta: Oh, no. Ah, nothing to do with you. This is from me . . . Oh, no, no, no, no, no. This is going to Kylie and she doesn't know I'm coming here. She thinks I am going to Geoff, 'cause I told her you're not doing nothing. So that's what I want to do. I'll get three-and-a-half, throw one-and-a-half in it, make it into five . . . Fucking boom! . . . Then the money I get back . . . she'll pay me back my debt. Plus that'll leave me with a few [grams] . . . so I won't have to fuckin' hassle you. Well, do you want me to, 'um, leave money with you?

It made for enlivening and robust conversation, with a noticeably confident use of drug-trade street talk and jargon. Such familiarity belied Podesta's apparent newness on the scene: he was either deeply entrenched in the culture of coke or had educated himself on the finer points of the game incredibly swiftly.

Next up was the topic of Rodney's women, in particular a Bondi babe called Sharon – 'All she is interested in is getting on the pipes [smoking cocaine], nothing else.' The conversation moved on to Podesta's drug-supplier friend in Marrickville, Zac MacKenzie, on whose voicemail the policeman left a message.

And then another matter suddenly sprung to mind. 'Last night . . . fucking last night,' Podesta stuttered, and proceeded to tell his mate about the Peter Forsyth murder, excitedly:

Podesta: Three coppers ... [were] walking to this casino. Fucking stabbed.

TC: Did they [the coppers] ...get stabbed?

Podesta: Yeah. Two of them were stabbed. One ran away, one's dead and the other one's in a critical condition.

TC: Uniform?

Podesta: No, off duty. Tried to stop a big fight and they got stabbed. Pulled their badges and they got stabbed.

TC: Well this is good for you now.

Podesta: I know.

TC: Sad about that but ...

Podesta: Fuck yeah. I know, I said that to Tony. I said it's terrible but ... It's good for us. Because it just shows that fucking ... There's psychos out there. There is only one thing to do to them. It's fucking Smith and Wesson.

The rant continued with both parties bemoaning the predicament of a police officer going about his duty. 'We're fucked, condemned,' Podesta insisted, referring to himself and Dilorenzo.

Podesta wanted no further part of the job that had taken him down to the sand that day in June: 'That's why I'm going to fuck it right off ... Get a payout and then fuck them [the police service] ... off.' Now all he wanted was for everything to end, and to get that coke – 'I can give you now,' TC later muttered, confirming that a deal could be reached, which suited Podesta:

Podesta: Thanks mate. You're a legend – Yeah I've got the money ... and that way I'll make ... that's a thousand bucks. Make myself a profit of ... she owed me a thousand bucks so at least I get a little bit back from what she owes me.

151

TC: I don't care.
Podesta: Yeah . . . It doesn't come from you. No-one knows.
No-one knows anything dude. I'm just fucked off.

Despite having had his slumber interrupted, TC was now enjoying Podesta's lively banter and so the pair continued their chinwag for another two hours, whiling away the time – and sniffing and snorting away. At 12.46 p.m., the talking turned to Robert Gould – recently dubbed by his enemies as 'the Drama Queen of Bondi' – and his shameless diluting of the cocaine he supplied. (If TC registered Podesta's hypocrisy in making this accusation, he certainly kept it to himself.) It was Gould, of course, who thought he might have used coke with Podesta on the night before the Levi shooting, and neither Podesta nor TC trusted him any longer.

Next they discussed Victor Smith,[2] a drug dealer who had told the cop they could 'go training' any night of the week, a known reference for getting some drugs. Smith appeared to have been very keen to add Podesta to his list of customers, but he and TC agreed that they would not be buying from Victor. At 2.42 p.m., Podesta left Yarranabbe Road, vowing to return later that afternoon. Police surveillance officers recorded the time in their notebooks, waiting to spring the trap.

Easton 'TC' James returned to the couch, to his desperately tired and wired world. He made a few phone calls, laid about the place, and waited for his next visitor to arrive. During this slumber, one of the most important calls he made was to a dealer, Lenin Marx Lambert, the guy whose parents, some people joked, had given him the most distinctive of names. Lambert was, quite simply, a big wheel in the drug trade. He was someone who didn't have grams, he had *ounces*, such were the quantities he carried. A teacher by day, at a TAFE college, lecturing in smash repairs, Lambert was a

drug man after hours. He lived and mined the eastern suburbs and had contacts among the police officers in the
nightclub set. Although he didn't seem to know Podesta, he
knew Dilorenzo and was particularly close to one of the sergeants who lived in the area, Peter John Murrant, a former
transit cop who operated a security business on the sly. Many
crooks kept friendly with policemen, so it seemed.

At 6.18 p.m., Lambert knocked on TC's door.
Podesta's saviour had arrived with the goodies. TC was
watching the television, but Lambert was in no such casual
mood, concerned instead about the traffic build-up due to
Mardi Gras. They got down to business immediately, the
microphone in the surveillance bug picking up vital snatches
of the particulars of the deal.[3] A cryptic, but significant, conversation had just taken place – and Internal Affairs now
waited for its lucky prize.

At 7.22 p.m., Podesta returned to TC's place for the
goodies. He kept Kylie Kummings in the car and dashed into
the flat to grab TC and get out into the party town. He was
straight in, and straight out – every movement studied by
Internal Affairs surveillance officers, hiding in the shadows.

At some stage later in the evening, on this weekend
respite from the inquest, Podesta and Kummings were pulled
over at the side of the road, down near Maroubra. The police
officers announced themselves, as required, but not for the
purpose of a routine breath test. One officer said he was from
Internal Affairs. Podesta's heart must have started pounding
through his shirt. Both he and Kummings were taken out of
the car and arrested, then frisked and manhandled, with their
car also being searched. It was the real deal. Internal Affairs
found not a skerrick of drugs, or anything vaguely incriminating, on Podesta. So he had to be let go after routine
questioning. But they didn't go completely empty-handed.

Podesta's girlfriend had something more considerable in her possession: heroin.

It was late on Saturday night when Podesta wandered away from the police station, his Mardi Gras wrecked after the closest of shaves with the law. Podesta had nearly blown everything, and he still had the coroner to deal with on Monday. The court's primary witness, the first shooter, had been arrested in the middle of the hearing, with his drug connections now exposed.

The politics of the Peter Forsyth murder were immediate and overwhelming. And they flowed into the corridors of the Coroner's Court. Everyone was touched by this most senseless of acts. The newspapers and talkback lines were full of it. The feelings of sympathy for his wife and kids, and then outrage over his killers, turned into an hysterical demand that people with knives should be stopped at all costs; the police had to be *protected*.

The government was forced to respond, with the Opposition and the police union using the stabbing to justify draconian measures. The Forsyth tragedy evoked comparisons with the horrific stabbing death a year earlier of David Carty. The young constable had been knifed repeatedly in the car park of a western Sydney tavern, with one of the killers reportedly ripping out some of his organs. Back then the pressure had been instantaneous. Premier Bob Carr had backed his police minister, Paul Whelan, in enacting legislation at the time that increased penalties for knife offences. But after Peter Forsyth, all those previous actions counted for nothing, and Carr was again under fire for being weak.

The deputy president of the Police Association, Mark Burgess, rebuked the Labor Party because the Carty legislation wasn't 'worth the paper it's written on unless the judiciary hands out the penalties the community thinks it deserves'.[4] He attacked the government for failing to protect police officers and derided the police compensation laws, claiming dramatically that Jason Semple, the officer recovering from being stabbed on the night Forsyth died, faced being ripped off: apparently Semple would only be entitled 'to be off work for 26 weeks on full pay. After that he reverts to what is called the statutory rate of pay, which is about $250 a week. Here is an officer who has put his life on the line . . . and that is basically what he is worth. That is clearly unacceptable'.[5]

Burgess, sensing the community's disquiet, said that police officers needed more power; they required the ability to search for knives and to be allowed to stop and detain people, compelling people to identify themselves and report their addresses. There were even calls 'for curfews to be imposed in certain parts of the city'.[6] Police Minister Whelan told reporters he was not even 'ruling out allowing off-duty police to go armed'.[7] The public fury was undeniable. The premier made a commitment to the Carty and Forsyth families that the laws would be made tougher.

Even the police commissioner got into the debate, backing the protests and joining the chorus – and therefore increasing the hype about Peter Forsyth, the pool of hysteria from which Podesta and Dilorenzo were drinking. Ryan told a television audience:

> *People are just getting more violent. We see road rage growing all the time . . . people are quite rude, they bump into you in the street without apologising . . . and that's just the underlying trend. Turn that a few notches up and we get personal violence. That is translating itself into confrontations with the police as well,*

where every young person, or every person the police stop to talk to, become aggressive to the police.[8]

The coronial inquest had changed course completely. As the shooters walked into the court on Monday, 2 March, terrified by Kummings's bust but comforted by the Forsyth reaction, they entered a new place, a new environment; one with a much better chance of survival.

The first policeman on the beach, Senior Constable John Jones, was the first witness of the fourth week. He was also the first of the six police witnesses to be called. He'd spoken to Brunner, Levi's flatmate, who had raced to the station for help. Jones was 'a straightforward and unshakeable witness'[9] who had most, if not all, of the answers. He presented a credible and likable face, someone who could be believed on just how bad things had been on the beach that morning.

Jones said they couldn't encircle Levi because that would've put their fellow officers in the line of fire. They didn't hurl sand in his face because they were too far away. They tried to hit him with a baton, but that didn't work. They couldn't shoot at his arm or his legs because they were trained to shoot to stop, not in shooting to disable. Jones said they had tried everything. Levi had been 'facing me, taking a couple of quick paces, holding the knife out . . . in a jabbing motion,' he said. 'When he completed that movement, the knife was inside a metre from my revolver. I took one step back and said, "Drop the knife now!" and began to squeeze the trigger.'[10] The flavour of Jones's evidence was that Podesta and Dilorenzo really had no option: 'The only reason I had my finger on the trigger is because I thought I was going to have to fire it.'[11]

Constables Christopher Goodman and Geoffrey

Smith also gave capable performances. Goodman was particularly well received because he gave voice to the 'plausible theory'[12] – discussed by Dilorenzo and Podesta within hours of the shooting and put forward by paramedic Craig Payne the previous week – that Levi had wanted to die. Levi *wanted* the police to do the killing for him. Goodman said the dead man had been making gargling noises and strange contortions with his face and that everyone had been 'continually talking to him, giving him chances . . . We gave him enough time . . . but he became more aggressive and what was done was done'.[13] Goodman said he had pulled his gun, and then noticed his colleagues had done the same; and all were pointing at Levi. The other police on the beach also gave evidence, supporting the shooters' explanation.

On Wednesday, 4 March, in a break from the proceedings, the coroner and Cowan received a briefing, in secret, on the failed Mardi Gras operation to snare Podesta, and the fact that heroin had been found on a person arrested with him. Internal Affairs arranged for the conversation to take place. Brammer, Richmond and Inspector Paul Jones (the chief investigator on Operation Borden and the officer who had stopped Podesta and Kummings), along with Hand and Cowan, met in total confidence. This was an ex parte discussion, on a matter very much at the centre of the deliberations.

Vital information was being shared, and opinions drawn, by the coroner and those charged with reaching decisions on Podesta and Dilorenzo's actions. It was the most delicate of meetings, held away from the courtroom and in the absence of the shooters' legal counsel. Indeed, the information was also denied to the lawyers representing Melinda Dundas and the Levi family. The coroner was being 'told information that was highly critical of Podesta.'[14] Brammer observed that Hand received details on 'the progress that we had made and that we fundamentally hadn't developed any evidence that would assist his inquiry'.[15] In Brammer's view, it was a relatively general discussion of topics: 'we spoke about Borden . . . the issues that we were encountering. There may have been other things . . . [but] we didn't sit there and go through every bit of evidence'.[16] Nonetheless, Hand was told that with Podesta, 'there was evidence to support drug use and possible drug supply'.[17]

On Thursday, 5 March, the Bondi shooters left the inquest to pay their respects to a murdered colleague. They journeyed into the city to join 3000 mourners at St Mary's Cathedral at the funeral of Peter Forsyth, the policeman whose death at the end of a knife had done so much to help their prospects at the hearing. The two policemen mixed with a gathering that included the premier, the police minister, the police commissioner and many other dignitaries – and lots of other police officers. There 'unfolded an extraordinary outpouring of grief', the *Sydney Morning Herald* would later report. 'A mother, a single tear glistening on her cheek, stood clutching her youngest child . . . his young mind . . . incapable of fathoming the significance of the human display.'[18] Podesta and Dilorenzo were surrounded by wellwishers. And the symbols could not have been more powerful: the dead man's son, 'three-year-old Mitchell Forsyth, was driven past in a car, waving uncomprehendingly at the sea of blue police uniforms standing to attention as his father's coffin passed. "That could have been me," Dilorenzo said'.[19]

After the funeral, John Carty, the father of David, the murdered constable, stayed to show his support for the Bondi cops. And a photograph of the occasion was taken and printed in the newspapers, like a rallying cry.

While Forsyth was being mourned, more information about the Bondi shooters came in like a bolt from the blue. Murray Dowling[20] called the Police Customer Assistance Line and told the operator, Senior Constable Anderson, 'that the two police involved in the shooting of Roni Levi on Bondi Beach had used cocaine in the Liberty Bar [sic] restaurant in Campbell Parade, Bondi, the night before the shooting'.[21] He left his name and his contact details, but asked for things to be treated sensitively.

This was information from a named person, given to the police, while the inquest was still in session – and just days after Podesta had been heard on police bugs in the middle of a cocaine deal. Dowling represented a possible witness, and he could literally have been picked up by the police and driven to the Coroner's Court. Rather than treating Dowling's information urgently, however, Anderson simply followed procedure and a file note was made and popped in the internal mail.

The next day, 6 March, in the Internal Affairs Assessment Unit, Senior Constable Hoskins, logged the intelligence report from the hotline, and put it somewhere where it was not to be seen for a further fifteen months. It disappeared, or was lost, and was not shown to any of the detectives hunting Dilorenzo and Podesta. This was yet another missed opportunity, one of the most serious transgressions in an already ham-fisted investigation. By the time Internal Affairs found the Murray Dowling note, the source of the information could not be found. He was dead.

Later on during the day of the Forsyth funeral, Dilorenzo and Podesta's records of interview were tendered into evidence. It would be their only comments. On the advice of their legal counsel, both men refused to take the stand, on the grounds they might incriminate themselves.

The shooters' statements were illuminating, if only for what they said, and didn't say, about the dead man. Levi had wanted to die, Podesta's statement colourfully recorded, and their shots had done 'his dirty work' for him.[22]

The police case over, the legal representatives – Cowan, Ken Horler, Greg Willis, Cavanagh and 'Jock' Dailly – addressed the coroner on how they felt he should weigh up the evidence; how his recommendations should be framed. David Cowan, the coroner's main instructive tool, obviously affected by the evidence, offered a litany of suggestions and improvements – as did the rest of the parties. Much of the more remarkable evidence had come not from police statements, or Cowan's questions; rather it had been extracted from the police during Cavanagh's cross-examination.

Cowan urged the coroner to look at bringing in interstate investigators to examine police shootings, in a bid to boost the impression of independence. Police officers of the rank of assistant commissioner, or above, should be called to a shooting to ensure all guidelines are being followed; and witnesses should be immediately separated and their recollections subject to 'records of interview', not statements, as had been the case with the police on Bondi Beach. Cowan insisted that only the officer in charge of the investigation should be allowed to speak to the media after police-caused fatalities, and that improved training was needed for officers in dealing with people suffering mental illness. In all circumstances, police officers should be mandatorily tested for drugs and alcohol after such incidents, to eradicate any suspicion and validate the actions of those involved. It was a comprehensive spreadsheet to consider, a reflection on the case's failings.

Horler and Cavanagh – apart from joining Cowan in urging vast improvements to police procedures – also criticised what they alleged was lackadaisical supervision at St Vincent's Hospital. The hospital authorities who first spotted Levi's chronic problems, Cavanagh claimed, were responsible for 'a series of failures' and was 'at fault for the tragic events of that morning'.[23] The two lawyers criticised the hospital's lack of a policy dealing with patients who fled their beds, and for the nonchalant manner in which they tried to reach Levi's friends and family upon his escape. Seemingly everyone who had been in contact with Levi in his final twelve hours had played a part in his demise. Dailly, for the shooters, praised his clients and played up to the court the upset that the officers continued to feel over the shooting – that they were not to blame. It was not until early afternoon on Friday, 6 March when the talking finally ended, and then the coroner indicated he had something to say.

Hand could not be overly critical of the hospital, he said, because Roni Levi, despite his agitation, had agreed to stay in bed for the tests. The coroner concluded that Levi was definitely not at the point where he had to be scheduled – or held against his wishes in a mental institution. He said general practical recommendations might be worthwhile, but avoided any particular criticism. The coroner then referred to the conduct of the police on the beach, claiming that the shooting of Levi at the hands of police officers 'was in my opinion one of the most serious events involving police that I have encountered'.[24]

Regarding the police investigation into the shooting, Hand said it was to be expected that the police would throw 'all necessary resources to properly investigate the incident in accordance with the Commissioner's Instructions', but that, sadly, this had not occurred – 'a cause for concern for myself and for the interested parties attending the inquest'.[25] This lack of resources forced McDougall to not appropriately interview four of the six officers down on the beach, but he was satisfied that this lapse had not adversely affected their recollections. 'Nevertheless, I intend to make a recommendation in regard to the interviewing of police officers who are eyewitnesses to an event such as this one . . . There is absolutely no evidence of a cover up by police officers. I am perfectly satisfied that there has been a full investigation.'[26] Hand's view, however, somewhat masked the depressing reality of the inquiry: wrecked by delay, obfuscation, incompetence and panic.

The coroner then turned to section 19 of the *Coroners Act*, which dealt with his power to halt an inquest. Specifically, if as coroner he was 'of the opinion that the evidence . . . establishes a prima facie case against any known person for an indictable offence . . . the Coroner . . . must terminate the inquest and refer the matter to the Director of Public Prosecutions'.[27] Ears started pricking up, heads began to turn. What was he saying? Coroner Hand then gave the citations of various cases to support his position, and repeated that if 'an inference of guilt may properly be drawn, the evidence is sufficient and a prima facie case has been made out . . . [I] cannot take into account any defence that may be raised'.[28] With every word, the drama intensified; and the mood soured. Hand said he had listened carefully to the shooters' legal counsel and the evidence supporting the two police officers, however, 'I cannot ignore the body of evidence which must be accepted by me . . . In my opinion, the evidence establishes a prima facie case against known persons with regard to the death of Roni Levi.'[29]

The courtroom virtually exploded. Already a hotbed of tension and terse stares, the corridors – one day after the funeral of Peter Forsyth – now overflowed with bitterness. It could not have been a more dramatic pronouncement: it meant Dilorenzo and Podesta were facing murder charges.

Floored by the announcement, the Bondi shooters careered from the court, but John Lorenzo, the publicist, couldn't help himself – saying his brother was absolutely devastated by the coroner's decision. Lorenzo said his brother had 'received citations and commendations from the service before for disarming people with knives. He's done his job and now he has become the victim of this whole circumstance.'[30] From the opposite point of view, Levi's widow praised the coroner for making a decision that, 'although it was incredibly hard to make, it was the right one. A human life was lost on Bondi beach and it was entirely preventable and avoidable'.[31]

The dead man's parents were overcome by tears, continually wiping their drenched and reddened eyes. Levi's father, Richard, said: 'My son Roni was shot down and killed . . . like a dog. There was absolutely no need to shoot him. There were many ways to contain him.'[32] His mother, Rebecca, was asked if she forgave the officers who gunned down her son:

> *Yes, I forgive them because they are young. They are like my son . . . our son Roni was a part of our heart. This part has now been broken because six young and strong policemen – six lions against a mouse – did not use their brains instead of using their guns . . . There is not a word to explain the tragedy we are still living. Since then it has been a terminal nightmare. We hardly sleep at night and still cry when we are alone.*[33]

All of these sorrowful sentiments were drowned out by the cacophony of public scorn over the decision. The police union's deputy president, Mark Burgess, whose outspoken views after the Forsyth stabbing had caused a political furore, said Coroner Hand had 'clearly got it wrong'.[34] Burgess shot straight from the hip:

> *This week we witnessed the funeral of Peter Forsyth, an officer stabbed to death in the line of duty and rightly hailed a hero. Today we witness the finding of a coroner that Constable Dilorenzo and Constable Podesta, both police officers who managed to prevent themselves, colleagues and members of the public from possibly being stabbed to death, potentially facing serious criminal charges. Do our police need to die to receive support?*[35]

So venomous was Burgess's rhetoric that officers started talking of taking industrial action if the shooters were charged.

While not countenancing such opinions, nor the attacks on the coroner, the police commissioner had virtually no alternative but to support his besieged officers, the rogues from Bondi who – unknown to a sympathetic community – were being pursued for drug dealing. Peter Ryan said all police officers faced increasing dangers and it was 'clear they have community support and the support of their commanding officers', adding on a personal note, 'I will do everything in my power to make sure this continues.'[36] This involved Ryan 'vigorously pursuing the question of effective legislation to protect them from threats to their personal safety and the consequences of unfounded and malicious complaints',[37] and, with specific reference to Dilorenzo and Podesta, 'the service will provide them with welfare and support during this difficult time to ensure that their best interests are protected until this matter is finalised'.[38] The next day, Ryan went to watch the Police Games at Narrabeen, up on Sydney's northern beaches, and so did Dilorenzo, to get away from the stress.

It took a while for the anger to subside. During the next few days, talkback radio callers only wanted to speak on one topic: more power for the police, greater respect for Dilorenzo and Podesta and for what they did. The newspapers were also awash with similar feelings. And the stabbing of a teenager, Eron Broughton, on the George Street cinema strip days after the coroner's decision – knifed nine times in a brutal attack – did not help matters. Cops, knives and police powers seemed to be the centre of everything.

In the most flagrant example of the public support the officers received, the *Daily Telegraph*, Sydney's most popular newspaper, published a front-page story and several inside commentaries on the plight of the shooters. It was bullishly headlined 'True blue', the huge type separated by photographs of the two heroes of the moment in uniform – and there were also tear-outs of some of the hundreds of letters that each had received in support of their struggle. 'It is so frustrating for Rod and I to sit and say nothing,'[39] Dilorenzo was quoted as saying in the article (apparently forgetting that his brother and wife had undertaken several recent media interviews on his behalf). 'But we are bound by the law and we are abiding by the law however long it will take. For nine months we have had to swallow everything and now we will have to continue to . . . until we get a decision from the DPP.'[40]

One of the letters to the newspaper, from Tracey Deane, urged the shooters to believe 'in your own heart that you both will get through this and that justice will prevail'.[41] Another of the pen-pals was none other than Mark Lorenzo, who claimed that Levi had been 'inflicted upon all of us', and the ruling had 'turned two of my best friends into two very disheartened young men. They were only doing their jobs;'[42] and, he advised the disgraced cops, 'stand tall, as you have done the right thing in my eyes by protecting yourselves and the community'.[43] A copy of Lorenzo's original was sent to Bondi police station, and circulated among the troops.

One of the newspaper's columnists, Miranda Devine, in an inside-page article headlined 'Message is die and let live', mirrored the well of public support for the police. She said the coroner's decision was 'a watershed in the relationship between police and the community' and that because of its timing, so soon after Forsyth's death, it reinforced the message that 'you're either with the police or you're against them'.[44]

In another newspaper's letters column, a more sober view also was taken. One correspondent, Tony Arena, from Willoughby on Sydney's north side, was grateful that, ultimately, judgment on the shooters would be left to the professionals:

> *The beauty of our legal system is that a highly trained criminal lawyer representing the people of NSW (the DPP) will determine if the police involved should go to trial. If it goes that far, a jury of citizens drawn at random from the community will decide their fate. That jury will be properly instructed to ignore matters of emotion, including any reference to other police officers put at risk in the execution of their duty, and will come to a verdict based on the evidence. How lucky we are.*[45]

On 11 March, in the midst of all this hysteria, the coroner handed down his final raft of recommendations – taking time out first to say he had sent off a copy of Burgess's comments to the attorney-general to see if they constituted a contempt of court. He was distressed that his verdict should be so violently assailed.

Hand took up almost all of Cowan's suggestions, only declining to recommend the provision of interstate investigators in shootings. The coroner condemned Chief Inspector Baker's media conference as being inappropriate behaviour, saying there was 'no doubt' that the news bulletin influenced one eyewitness report of the shooting;[46] and he also criticised the failure to check the video and audiotape interviews of the shooters – the corruption of which rendered them virtually meaningless. Importantly, the coroner also backed the automatic drug and alcohol testing of officers after shootings, although curiously, it had already been noted that the power for 'drug and alcohol testing – by way of breath, urine or hair sample analysis – of police officers, on a random or targeted basis . . . was already operative' and existed at the time of the Levi case.[47] They could have been forced to give a sample, but were never asked.

Coroner Hand later told a reporter that the inquest was 'probably the hardest from an objective viewpoint that I've ever dealt with'.[48] The police had also encountered difficulties – and the problems for Podesta and Dilorenzo were only just beginning.

TWELVE
HUNTING DILORENZO

'I should tell him: "Fucking give
me an ounce," and I'll fucking
look after him.'

Senior Constable Anthony Dilorenzo, bugged conversation with
Easton Barrington James, 1 April 1998

By the end of March 1998, barely three weeks after the coroner had referred the conduct of the Bondi shooters to the director of public prosecutions – with possible murder charges hanging over their heads – Podesta and Dilorenzo were back in the thick of things. Mixing with familiar faces, doing familiar tricks. Both were extraordinarily stressed by the prospect of facing a criminal trial and remained off work on stress leave – but since Podesta's arrest in the middle of the inquest, each was also conscious of being tailed. They were forever looking over their shoulders, fearful of being bugged or followed, and were speaking in code . . . just in case their comments were misinterpreted.

In the aftermath of the inquest, Podesta resigned from the police service, fulfilling the promise he'd made to TC, just before he had been busted. There was nothing in the job for him anymore. The cops had paid for his legal representation at

169

the Levi hearing and the police union, fuming at the mouth over the coroner's reference was backing him to the hilt. Burgess had already vowed to support him in any future court case. So, knowing he was under the hammer of Internal Affairs and no longer worried about bills for his lawyers, Podesta took the decision to jump from the police force before he was kicked, ending a lively three-year career. Now he moved slightly away from the spotlight, out of the scene, burned by his recent run-in with the law. He went overseas to get a way from everything.

Dilorenzo kept active though – and now Internal Affairs got more active in targeting him. Unlike Podesta, Dilorenzo had no intention of leaving the cops. Still on stress leave, he stayed at home mainly, with his family – punching his bags and trying to stay fit. But because he had so many idle hours up his sleeve, he was prone to take the occasional stroll. One of the places he seemed to wander to often at the start of autumn was TC's place, in Darling Point. This was a dangerous move, because the apartment was still under constant surveillance by Internal Affairs.

On April Fools' Day, Dilorenzo paid one of these visits. He wanted to see his old mate from the Liberty Lunch days, to tell him about a spectacular off-duty arrest he had just made. And the headlines that he had generated. It was 2.44 p.m. when Dilorenzo started speaking – sitting in literally the same spot Podesta had been, at the same coffee table in the same lounge room:[1]

Dilorenzo: Hey, did you see the paper yesterday?
TC: No.
Dilorenzo: I was in it again.
TC: What this time?

Dilorenzo: . . . *I was sitting at home, like this right, just sitting here talking . . . And all of a sudden I heard, I swear to God, this lady screamed like she was being raped or murdered . . . 'Aaaghh' . . . So I threw the phone down. I ran out the back courtyard and the side run there. I walked down the side and the lady next door leaned out and said: 'Quick! Quick! The guy in the white shirt.' The guy had climbed in her window when she was in the flat. She walked in the bedroom. He was there going through everything, doing a break and enter . . . She goes: 'White shirt, that way.' . . . as I got to the street out the front of my place, he already had 150, 200 foot jump on me. So I jumped in the car and drove around the corner . . . I saw him rip off his shirt, like this, and throw it on the road and kept walking like further down so it did not look suspicious . . . so I pulled up a block in front of him and got out and had my hat on like this, right? . . . Like I was coming back from the shop. I got this far away from him and . . . Bang! . . . he started fighting with me and one of the coppers with his little daughter was driving, off duty, saw me and he stopped and ran over and we both grabbed the guy.*

TC: A copper?

Dilorenzo: Yeah . . . And one of my mates. He was just driving by, by chance . . . coppers come, and arrest [the intruder] . . . I turn around and there is the fucking Daily Telegraph *. . . taking pictures. So anyway, he had broke into a house two up from where I live and broke into the house next door and I got him. And they fucking put me in the paper yesterday. And the headline was: 'Off sick but still on duty'. You know . . . and the fucking* Herald *said, 'Oh, they hailed him as a hero . . .' It was unreal.*

Dilorenzo gave an uproarious account, and TC responded with bursts of laughter. The fact that the media had been in Bondi at just the right moment was incredible, in fact there were so many incredible things about the story. It was as if the whole thing had been stage-managed. This was great publicity, the sort of stuff you can't pay to get.

The chat then moved to other things of vital importance, with the two men speaking vaguely, in code. TC had a story for Dilorenzo now, but nothing to match an off-duty arrest. This had do with Podesta, and the aftermath of their tenancy agreement:

TC: That guy . . . Rod!

Dilorenzo: What's he done?

TC: He took off and didn't sign the release form for my bond.

Dilorenzo: Oh, your bond. You're kidding?

TC: And I begged him to do that.

Dilorenzo: Oh, no . . . Well I'll get some money off Mick tonight. Well, hopefully tonight . . . If I can catch him . . . Bastard. He is so hard to get hold of . . . I think he does it on purpose, you know. But I spoke to him yesterday . . . actually this morning I spoke to him. I said: 'I have got to come over and get some money for TC.'

TC: It's hard when you give someone something way below the price and . . . and, you know . . . This . . . [other] guy doesn't give me a break . . .

Dilorenzo: Who's this . . . [other] guy? Do I know him?

TC: Who I get it from?

Dilorenzo: Who . . . Lennie?

TC: Yeah . . .

Dilorenzo: I know him. He didn't used to own the smash repairs, did he?

TC: Yeah . . .

Dilorenzo: Lennie [Marx Lambert] . . . Aaah . . . Fuck! . . .
I can't remember his last name . . . He's got blondie
sort of hair . . .
TC: Yeah . . .
Dilorenzo: Aaah . . . I should tell him: "Fucking give me an
ounce," and I'll fucking look after him. Because I'll say
I heard . . . [that there's something] coming down . . .
TC: He won't know if it's from me . . . ?
Dilorenzo: Will he? . . . He's got no back-up though . . . has
he?
TC: I don't know . . . Actually, he does.
Dilorenzo: Nothing like I can get.
TC: He's got the DEA [Drug Enforcement Agency].
Dilorenzo: Has he?
TC: Yeah . . .
Dilorenzo: Well . . . That's nothing . . . Who's that? The DEA
guy?

A burst of laughter followed and then a brief description by
Dilorenzo of how to retrieve spilled cocaine using a vacuum
cleaner and a paper towel. 'That's a good one,' huffed TC
approvingly, not realising that his every sound, even those
strange snorting noises, had again been recorded by the surveillance bug. This time he had been caught with the other shooter.

With the commentary flowing, Internal Affairs now
loomed over Dilorenzo, ready to pounce. This was a chance
to make amends for the failure to get Podesta's scalp after the
Mardi Gras parade. Internal Affairs didn't want to miss this
latest opportunity. The Borden investigators reported seeing
TC and Dilorenzo again, two days after the April Fools' Day
rendezvous, and then again on 7 April, when a much larger
team – a squad of more than a dozen officers – lay hiding in
the background.

That day, it was an interesting coincidence that, at 12.21 p.m., one of Podesta's childhood mates, David Hitchens, should arrive in the frame. Everyone seemed to know each other in this little neck of the woods. On that particular day, TC started work at Hitchens's landscaping business. Now that he was out of a legitimate job after leaving the Liberty Lunch, TC sometimes worked with Hitchens, labouring away in the plush gardens and backyards of Sydney's eastern suburbs. They shared common interests, other than Podesta, because their families had grown up in the African bush 'and we . . . got talking about animals and going to the bush and stuff like that and talking about my sister, who set up a farm in Africa.'[2]

This time, they had decided to talk about fish, about how TC could construct a spectacular sandstone fish tank for his living room, and whether Hitchens had some thick sandstone TC could use. That was the start of a quick and fateful journey back to Yarranabbe Road, apparently still with fish-tank design in mind. They could have been talking about anything of course, and Hitchens had snorted coke at TC's home and he had bought coke there in the infamous lounge room. It soon became apparent to the eager ears of the Internal Affairs investigators what the pair were discussing now, as TC appeared to have a stash of white powder bagged up and on display:[3]

Hitchens: So how much is that . . . One in . . . One point four?
TC: A [gram] . . .
Hitchens: How much in the bags . . . How much in the bag?
TC: Six point . . . point four.
Hitchens: It's on weight . . . It's perfect.
TC: It's about . . . um . . . one-and-a-half . . . almost . . .

Hitchens: How can you make a million bucks quickly like this? . . . Oh mate, I'm fucked. This fucking work like this, mate, all the time . . . It's ridiculous. I just want to make some fucking big money quickly, you know?

TC: I would love that. The person I get my shit from, he's been ringing me and hassling me. He never used to hassle me and you know it's like everyone that I get things from . . . sometimes they might be . . . a little bit slow [in paying me] . . . But now it's come through . . .

TC then offered Hitchens a taste of what he had been preparing. 'Yeah, I'd love one,' Hitchens replied. Snorts, raucous laughter and snippets of drug lingo followed as the connoisseurs passed judgment on the product. Less than an hour later, as Hitchens was about to leave – late for an appointment with his accountant – there was a knock on the door. Dilorenzo had come for a visit. Hitchens stayed around for a few minutes to catch up, and then, with a quick 'TC, I have to run mate, seriously', he was gone.

As soon as Hitchens walked out of the entrance, situated just below the level of the kerb, his plans took a turn for the worst. Out of nowhere, he got dragged to the ground and hurried out of the road. Before he had recovered his balance, Hitchens had his clothes and hair rifled through, his socks and shoes removed, and was on his way in the back of a car to Waverley police station. Back at Yarranabbe Road, Internal Affairs started to concentrate on Dilorenzo. Inside the flat, blissfully unaware that their recently departed friend had been arrested, Dilorenzo and TC carried on as normal. Talking about training and fitness, and also sniffing in long, very audible grunts.

Internal Affairs could have crashed through the front door at any time, but the officers decided against pouncing on the pair in the lounge room, even though, with the lack of escape routes, this would have been the ideal time and place. Unknown to them, Hitchens's arrest 'had caught the eye of a neighbour who, because of all the bravado, was now trembling and panicking – the maid of a former Prime Minister's wife, Margaret Whitlam . . . she feared a bomb was being planted.'[4] Shortly before Dilorenzo and TC prepared to leave the flat, she rang Rose Bay police station. Someone was meddling with a car, the woman said, and it looked as if they were planting an explosive device. 'Dilorenzo and James crossed the road,' the *Sun-Herald* later reported, '. . . a horde of Internal Affairs surveillance officers, some secreted in cars and others crouched out of sight [were] . . . each ready to pounce.'[5] The pair got into Dilorenzo's car and Dilorenzo turned on the engine and drove up toward the intersection of Yarranabbe and Darling Point roads. But in that short passage of time, officers from Rose Bay, a couple of constables, had arrived on the scene, unintentionally forcing Internal Affairs to move in more quickly than planned.

It was now 1.30 p.m. Two Internal Affairs officers in street gear, with baseball caps, walked onto the street and signalled for Dilorenzo to stop. 'One officer stood in front of the vehicle,' Inspector Monk would later state. 'The other officer approached the driver's side door of the vehicle . . . [Dilorenzo] although initially stopping, drove the vehicle forward, then stopped just short of the first officer mentioned. This caused that officer to come into contact with the front of the vehicle.'[6] The other officer quickly ripped open the driver's-side door and, before Dilorenzo could act to counter it, he had put his hands on the keys in the ignition. But 'the vehicle was again driven forward; this time with wheels spinning in acceleration'.[7] Dilorenzo was petrified, explaining that because of numerous telephone threats 'I didn't know who they were or what they were going to do. I was worried someone was going to steal my car or assault me . . . [so] I instinctively put my foot on the accelerator.'[8] One of the officers in his way flew off the bonnet of the car and his partner was 'struck by the car's open driver's-side door'[9] as Dilorenzo raced in his panic to get away from his pursuers.

When he turned left, another Internal Affairs officer ran onto the road, his police badge gripped and on display in his hand. The car was fairly flaming along, and suddenly with nowhere to turn. He nudged the car to the right of the policeman but this meant he was on the wrong side of the road. It was a bad call. The street into which he had turned so hurriedly, Marathon Road, was one-way – and Dilorenzo's big blue Commodore sedan was not pointing in the right direction.

Some of the Internal Affairs officers jumped into police cars, sirens blaring. But Dilorenzo and TC would not be caught for at least a minute, a precious minute free of police interference. Both of them were eventually arrested sitting in Dilorenzo's car in the car park of a unit block, off the street. They were searched, and so was the car. But nothing could be found. Not a sign of any drug possession. Dogs, fingerprint experts and scientific officers crawled all over TC's apartment, picking up powder traces of cocaine and Dilorenzo's fingerprints off a coffee table. An empty plastic bag with residue cocaine was found on TC's bedside table. But nothing with any weight to it was located. The search to find drugs had been a failure. And now the rest of the day would have a similarly botched feel about it.

It was decided it would be a good idea to breath-test Dilorenzo, to see if he had been driving under the influence for he'd certainly been driving recklessly. But no breath-test unit could be found. It had to be called for from Rose Bay police station, and that took time. And 'on this fateful day, the clock was ticking fast'.[10] Eventually, the breathalyser was found – and Dilorenzo proved negative.

That was not the end of it, however. Because Dilorenzo was being detained for committing a serious driving offence, police decided to exercise their legal right to compel him to give a blood sample at a hospital, a police power that expired two hours after the subject's arrest. Dilorenzo was shoved in the back of a police car and rushed to St Vincent's Hospital, about two kilometres up the road. By the time they arrived, 135 minutes had ticked over and, on the urging of his solicitor, Kenneth Madden, the man who had represented him so well in the inquest, Dilorenzo was told he didn't *have* to do it. And so Dilorenzo declined to get a needle jabbed in his arm. The cops had been beaten by the clock and the raid had ended in high farce. The paltry result was that Dilorenzo was charged, by summons, with two counts of reckless driving and negligent driving.

The next day, 8 April, the *Daily Telegraph* noted in a carefully worded four-paragraph story that Dilorenzo was fully cooperating with an Internal Affairs inquiry. It might not have seemed like much of an article but it tweaked the interest of the director of public prosecutions, Nicholas Cowdery, QC, his curiosity flowing from what was *not* said in the newspapers. After he read the item, the DPP called for one of his solicitors, Savva Persinidis, to go and see what on earth was happening. Persinidis's inquiry reached Internal Affairs – and, after some discussion, another secret meeting was held to talk about the Bondi shooters. Once again, Gary Richmond, who had been at all the previous secret meetings, convened a briefing with Persinidis. Cowdery, to keep at arm's length, did not attend. This time Richmond took along Detectives Jones and Keen, to make sure there was not another communication breakdown. The DPP's office was told that although both the shooters had been the subject of protracted drugs inquiries, there was no material that could be handed over that would help in the Levi case.

During May 1998, Internal Affairs, having arrested both of the shooters in drug raids but failing to lay heavy charges each time, held a massive review of the case, to see what further disciplinary action should, and could, be taken against Podesta and Dilorenzo – and also to find out how, and where, they had bungled so badly. Of course, the hunt for Dilorenzo and Podesta was still active. One of Keen's informants, Roger Martin,[11] had recently said that he had been 'talking to a dancer at the Men's Gallery . . . [and] the information . . . was that on the night before the shooting, Podesta was at Dancers in the Cross popping pills'.[12] Internal Affairs eventually located the dancer, Judy Hughes,[13] and although she admitted she knew Podesta, she denied ever having made the outrageous claim – and that was that.

Detective Inspector Paul Jones was particularly savage in his review. He wondered how Podesta had ever been able to get a job in the police force in the first place, considering his background and connections. The IA chief investigator had inspected the original personnel file on Podesta. It included information on his job, shortly before joining the police, as the manager of the Piccolo Bar in Roslyn Street at Kings Cross. Two years later Jones told the Police Integrity Commission: 'And from some inquiries I made of that location there are numerous events and intelligence reports which relate to drug activity at that location . . . it appeared to me . . . [to be] high risk as far as criminal activity and drug activity is concerned.'[14] Jones felt Podesta

should have been seen at some stage by police employment
officers as a high risk to recruit.

On 30 June, two days after the first anniversary of Levi's
killing, Cowdery put out a brief press release, rejecting the
prospect of any criminal charges. The DPP said he believed
that 'the prosecution could not prove beyond reasonable
doubt – as it would have to do – that the officers who shot
Mr Levi were not acting in self defence'.[15] There was no published report; or further reasoning but it was accepted that
Cowdery, acting on McDougall's brief and the transcript of
evidence from the inquest, felt that it would be difficult to
undermine Podesta and Dilorenzo's contention that their
lives had been in danger when they fired their revolvers.

Dilorenzo was at home when he got the news, and
he told the press: 'Annabelle came home . . . I was just shouting, "No trial . . . No trial." It has been a very difficult time
. . . I am just glad it is over.'[16] Podesta joined up with the
Dilorenzo family later in the night, just back from his overseas sojourn. The pair was pictured embracing, and the snap
was put in the following day's newspapers. The elation was
overwhelming, and the community reaction overwhelmingly
positive. Both must have felt that the worst of it was over,
that it couldn't sink any lower.

Levi's widow was understandably upset, saying the
failure to put the matter in the courts was a decision that
could 'only be condemned' since her husband's only crime
had been 'human frailty'.[17] Dundas said the prosecutor's decision was 'only as good as the police investigation on which it
is based'[18] – and revealed that her lawyers were looking to the
Police Integrity Commission for a fresh inquiry, to see if key
clues were missed, or glossed over. Incredibly, Dundas was

initially denied a copy of the inquest transcripts – at one stage being told by the Coroner's Office that she would have to pay an exhorbitant price to get the papers. The decision was reversed by the attorney-general, but only after a lot of huffing and puffing.

The availability of the transcripts, belatedly, made easier the Newcastle Legal Centre's research in its petition for the PIC. But, for the moment, the PIC had its eyes elsewhere – looking over the shoulders of the latest Internal Affairs investigation. For, instead of pursuing the people who were seeing TC at his place, the targets for Internal Affairs were now another crowd that TC was mixing with . . . those further up the food chain. And that, of course, involved visits to the pads of Lenin Marx Lambert, the drug dealer – the man TC complained was becoming a constant hassler, the smash-repair mechanic who Dilorenzo knew from his old Bondi days. Lambert knew plenty of cops, but he was unaware that he was being tailed and was caught up, in a roundabout way, in the hunt for the Bondi shooters.

Three days after the DPP made his announcement, Podesta was still celebrating his good fortune, unable to fathom the fact that he was off the hook. His partying comprised nothing that out of the ordinary, just the normal dose of cocaine and ecstasy with some beer and bourbon for variety, and a visit to some of the dizzy establishments along Oxford Street and in Kings Cross that had come to not only recognise his face, but also the colour of his money. No longer constrained by the responsibilities of office, having resigned months earlier as a constable, Podesta was carefree and cutting loose in a big way. But he was still seeing many of his police buddies, those who also liked to take a line, or pop a pill. Many coppers and former coppers, mainly his age and from the eastern suburbs stations, would hang around in the same clubs as he did, and sometimes they would go to the same toilet cubicles. Podesta was always bumping into familiar faces.

It was at Byblos, a popular dance venue, in the early hours of 4 July that Senior Constable Christian David Bruce, a helicopter surveillance officer met up with the shooter who had just been exonerated. Bruce was no stranger to the nightclubs. He had snorted cocaine at Byblos before with Podesta. Bruce arrived at the nightclub after an official emergency services function, an event that was well attended and well and truly watered. Now he wanted to get to that other level, beyond the inebriated state he was in. Bruce wanted it to be one of those nights.

Almost as soon as Bruce walked in, he scored drugs. For some people, it was that easy. He was offered a tab of ecstasy – 'I think I just took it – I didn't go to the toilet . . . I took it in the public area.'[19] After a little while, his heart started pumping and his hands became sweaty, with the rush. The morning had kicked off with a bang. Bruce partied on at Byblos and then went to another club, Sugar Reef, craving a new sensation. But shortly after he arrived, his girlfriend said she was tired and wanted to go home – 'So I got in a cab with her, took her home and put her to bed, so to speak. Then I caught a cab back to Sugar Reef and continued drinking.'[20] On his return, Bruce was approached by a guy he knew only vaguely, Jim Bond,[21] and the two men discussed where they could score some cocaine.

Bond was an incredible pesterer and was 'acting very excited and wasn't making much sense with his words.'[22] So, to placate him, Bruce went over to a dealer he knew in the crowd, Tony Saffron,[23] but Saffron wasn't holding. He could give them a line of coke from his own little bag, but that was all. It was too late in the morning to be trying to score. So into the toilets they went for a quick line at about 3.30 a.m. But with the heady rush gone in 30 minutes, Bond *had* to have some more and he continued to pester Bruce about scoring. Bruce, only half-reluctantly, went back to Saffron – and, after a couple of calls, the thumbs were raised. If these dudes wanted to score, they could get a $200 deal, but it would be delivered at the Black Market Cafe, the day club at Chippendale, and someone had to go and pick it up.

The deal was done and the pair partied on at Chippendale for 'between two and three hours . . . and periodically we would go to the toilet and have a line of the cocaine'.[24] They left the Black Market at 10 a.m., drugged to the eyeballs, and drove to Double Bay, where Bond picked up his car. From there, Senior Constable Bruce remembered later, 'we drove to his flat in Tamarama . . . had a shower and got changed. I . . . [even] borrowed some of his clothes.'[25]

Bruce was hoping for a quick sleep. He had to attend a birthday party for a police friend in the evening, and he needed to rest. But Bond was having none of it, intent instead on scoring some more cocaine: 'Even though there was some cocaine left over in the bag that we'd already purchased [at the Black Market Cafe] . . . Bond claimed that it wasn't as good as the cocaine that he normally got from Len.'[26]

At 10.51 a.m., Bond put in a call to one of his best friends, Lenin Lambert, a man who invariably was holding – or certainly knew how to get it. Bond was 'always harassing' Lambert for cocaine, often to Lambert's annoyance since 'he was a good friend of mine . . . [and] I didn't want him to fall into the same . . . routine that I was going through with my personal hell with that drug.'[27] Police wire-taps picked up a testy beginning to the phone call, with Lambert upset that his morning had been interrupted. He told Bond he was with his girlfriend, Lisa Troost, at her place in Woolloomooloo, in the inner city. When Bond passed the phone to Bruce, the copper, however, the conversation picked up a beat. There was talk about surf, and the big night out – but the boys were keen to know when Lambert would be getting to his place, at the beach. They wanted to kick on. Lambert said he would get down as soon as he was able.

Bruce and Bond played a game of pool as they waited, ringing Lambert on three occasions to find out how far away he was. When the thumbs-up finally came, Bond became 'out of control' with excitement – 'he actually said to me that he'd like to keep taking cocaine until he died one day, and that scared me a fair bit'.[28] To the point where Bruce was starting to have second thoughts, about going to places he had never been to before.

When they arrived at Lambert's Bondi home, and the deal was sorted, Bruce declined Bond's offer of another snort, deciding instead to head off, much to Bond's dismay. As Bruce motored home in his drugged-out state, Bond went into the toilet for a line of the premium powder he'd craved for so long. It was a dramatic snort – Bond emerging with 'blood streaming from his nose'.[29] Lambert was not pleased and complained later to a mate that Bond had 'just turned up at my place after being fucking out all night . . . comes in here . . . his nose starts bleeding, right?'[30]

This was scintillating stuff for the police wires. The net around the Bondi shooters, and the people they'd had the faintest of relationships with, was now starting to tighten. At long last.

On 17 July 1998, Internal Affairs confronted Dilorenzo with the tapes: all the snorting sounds, the mentions of measurements and even the great story about the vacuum cleaner. But

Dilorenzo, despite being told he had been seen by surveillance officers entering and leaving TC's apartment at the same times that the bug was operating, simply denied being the voice on the tape. Having botched the operation, Internal Affairs now resorted to convincing Commissioner Ryan that he could no longer have confidence in the Bondi shooter, the 'true blue' hero who had the community's confidence.

On 30 July, Magistrate Gillian Orchiston accepted Dilorenzo's guilty plea to a negligent driving charge lodged by Internal Affairs over the Yarranabbe Road incident. Orchiston noted that the Crown had decided to withdraw the more serious charge of reckless driving, and fined Dilorenzo $500 plus court costs. But not before commenting that Dilorenzo had been 'under an immense amount of stress and anxiety' since the Levi shooting and that 'With all the publicity and trauma you had been involved in, one would not doubt you would be under anxiety.'[31] The court heard no reasons for the involvement of Internal Affairs. The driving charge was made out as if it was a bit of a misunderstanding.

As Dilorenzo walked from the Downing Centre Local Court, Detective Douglass in Internal Affairs took a surprising call from a man who wished to remain anonymous. The man said there was a hooker called Samantha who had some information about the Bondi shooters – the same Samantha, of course, who had dated Podesta briefly and had been barred from the Liberty by Kieran O'Connor. The informant said Samantha had told him that she had been with one of them on the night before the shooting. Douglass told Detective Inspector Jones about the call and within days, Jones had hunted down the elusive prostitute and recorded an interview.

Although she refused to make a statement, or co-operate in any way with any court proceedings, Samantha claimed seeing Podesta at her Bondi flat on the night prior to the shooting and had 'information on him being affected by drugs . . . and the fact he was in uniform'.[32] Jones called the shooting investigator, Robert McDougall, to pass on the allegation, not wanting to be birched again for alleged tardiness, but McDougall said the inquest was over and he wanted nothing further to do with the matter. He told Jones brusquely that if Internal Affairs wanted him to do their work, then he needed a written directive. And so even with Samantha's claim, the inquiries were still at an apparent standstill, as undecisive and lethargic as ever.

On 20 August, six weeks after Jim Bond bled all over his toilet cistern, Lambert got some attention of his own. His place got raided – at least the place where he was staying. In the morning, Internal Affairs broke into Lisa Troost's flat at Woolloomooloo and went into the laundry to search the dryer. After a quick wriggle, out came a folder and the searching officer held it up to a hidden surveillance camera so the haul could be verified. Out of the folder came a pouch, and then some puffed-up bags, full of cocaine: 83.4 grams to be exact. Or, on the street, about $25 000 in undiluted powder. It was a lot of gear to find in the one place. Rather than putting the folder back into the dryer, waiting for Lambert to return, and then smashing down the door and grabbing Troost and her boyfriend with the gear, Internal Affairs preferred to take the drugs, and to listen and watch the reaction.

Troost got home first and noticed something was wrong. She then called Lambert, asking if he had been back to the apartment; Lambert remembered the conversation: 'the place was messed up . . . [and] she was quite put out. She told me there was no means of anyone breaking into the premises.'[33] Sensing the urgency of the moment, Lambert came over. On the police video, after entering, he is seen putting his fingers to his lips, for Troost to not say anything. He then goes to the laundry and has a fossick for the things he had left inside. 'Shit,' Lambert yells, thinking his stuff had been robbed by his competitors, or other coke-heads. This was no rip-off though; for Lenin Lambert, this was the end of the line.

Away from Sydney, ignorant of many of the problems that the Bondi shooters and their friends were encountering – but undistracted and able to investigate thoroughly – the Newcastle Legal Centre continued piecing together the inconsistencies in the Levi case. The team was mounting a persuasive argument for a PIC hearing. There was ample public interest, the team suggested, for an analysis of why so much had gone wrong. The lawyers, Boersig, Watterson and Cavanagh, and their students, had meticulously compiled a jigsaw of facts and leads, people and places – forensically looking at every scrap of paper and police running sheets. They posed questions, and made suggestions, never accepting the first answer, the ready explanation. In this inquisitive way, they reached the overwhelming conclusion that the Levi investigation had been mishandled virtually from the start: it was not a case of the police just making a few bad calls, the Newcastle lawyers had uncovered gaping holes throughout the investigation. It constituted grounds for an official complaint.

Just before Christmas 1998, the legal centre sent off its submission, entitled *A Very Public Death*, to the Police Integrity Commission. With indexes, a chronology and hundreds of footnotes, the case for a fresh inquiry was as compelling as it was chilling. The submission argued that, not least because the coroner had terminated the inquest (thus denying the centre opportunity to canvass a wealth of further evidence), the Levi case had never been investigated in a proper way.

The PIC announced that there would be an inquiry, partially affecting the Bondi shooters. The PIC made it clear that it would not be conducting a re-examination of the Levi shooting investigation. Nothing of the sort – Coroner Hand had already spent four weeks looking at the matter. Instead the PIC announced Operation Saigon, an inquiry into the sinewy relationship between police, former police, and drug suppliers, and the unauthorised work of officers in the private security industry. Although it was widely expected that Podesta and Dilorenzo would be witnesses, it felt for a moment as if the Newcastle Legal Centre's campaign for justice had come to nothing.

THIRTEEN

THE FIRST PHASE

'Most of the times I've taken
drugs, as I said, it was in that
period after the time my father
died and up to the coronial
inquiry and I wouldn't say my
sobriety was the best at those
times.'

Rodney Podesta, Police Integrity Commission,
Operation Saigon, 23 February 1999

The Commissioner of the Police Integrity Commission, Judge
Paul Urquhart, QC, had briefed one of the city's most
respected barristers, Patrick Barrett, to be his counsel assisting
on the Saigon hearings. Barrett's task was to ask as many prob-
ing questions as possible – and then later, if witnesses had
denied a proposition, to play back a tape or video surveillance
recording that showed how hollow their contentions had been,
to show that they had lied on oath. Even though all witnesses
were entitled to legal representation and could even take a
statutory objection – knowing that none of their answers could
be used in any future legal proceeding – it was a gaolable
offence to lie. Catching people out, confronting them with
tapes or damaging testimony, was the PIC's trademark style,
and a most powerful weapon in the fight against corruption.

It was not until the third day of the hearings, on 17 February 1999, that public allegations of wrongdoing got even remotely close to the Bondi shooters. This came when Senior Constable Bruce, Podesta's mate from the Air Wing, confessed to snorting cocaine, taking ecstasy and mixing in the wrong circles. Bruce also admitted tipping off a police mate after seeing the latter's name on a search warrant in a helicopter drugs operation. He spilled the beans on criminals and former mates, and talked of his years-long dalliance with dope, holidays in Queensland and Las Vegas, and big nights on the booze and coke with copper colleagues. Bruce actually volunteered that he had snorted coke with Podesta – at last, the shaming had started of the policemen once worshipped as heroes. The Bondi shooters were close to being defrocked, of being shown to revel not in the company of other heroes, but with rogues.

One such rogue, Lenin Lambert, told the PIC that he disagreed with all of Bruce's evidence. He conceded that he'd enjoyed cocaine with Jim Bond, but Bruce had never been to his place; Bond had never bled from the nose and nothing of the sort described by Bruce had ever taken place. Lambert repeatedly denied the allegations. He was then asked whether he had difficulty with his memory, to which he admitted 'I forget things . . . yes.'[1] A 10-minute conversation that Lambert had with Bruce and Bond was then played to the audience, the chat that had been secretly recorded after the Black Market episode. 'Were they the voices of yourself, Christian Bruce and Jim Bond?' Barrett demanded to know. 'Yes,' said Lambert, his previous denials limping alongside him. All of the tapes were then played, building up a picture of the deal that took place. Lambert couldn't recall anything specific, he said, but declared that it 'well could have happened . . . there was a number of times with Bond where I had a lot of dramas and problems.'

He was then played the video of the bag containing 83.4 grams of cocaine being found in the laundry of his girl-friend's flat. Lambert appeared on the screen in full view, just as it had happened. He said only that he recalled a break-in at Lisa Troost's apartment, but didn't 'have a great recollection of the event' and denied ever having that much cocaine. He never supplied cocaine, he claimed – he'd even given up snorting it himself – and dismissed his entire involvement with the drug as 'a phase I went through'. 'So you don't use it now?' asked Alison Stenmark, legal counsel for Police Commissioner Ryan. 'I haven't used it . . . no, not since . . . somewhere just around New Year,' Lambert replied. 'Just the last New Year, six weeks ago?' Stenmark asked. 'Yeah . . . ' faded Lambert. 'And when you did use it, where did you get it from?' counsel continued. 'Basically it's just like going to a corner shop . . . like getting a carton of milk . . . you can get it anywhere.'

This was not at all helpful so, at the end of his time, Lambert was forced to scrawl down the names of people who had given him cocaine. Lambert's girlfriend, Lisa Troost, also gave unconvincing evidence about how the huge parcel of cocaine had come to be in her dryer. When their testimony finished, both Lambert and Troost were taken away and charged with drugs offences. This was dramatic stuff and showed the PIC meant business – and it added to the heat that was about to come the way of Podesta and Dilorenzo.

TC's name had been mentioned several times during Lambert's interrogation, Lambert agreeing that he knew the former Liberty Lunch manager and had probably even been to his apartment in Darling Point – but that was all. When it came to his turn before the commission, TC said he knew Lambert and even Jim Bond, although the nosebleeder was 'not much of a good friend'.[2] Len Lambert, however, was a much better friend and did 'a bit of work for me on my cars because he's a very good panel beater'. He said he also knew the Bondi shooters and had been 'very close friends' with Podesta, his former landlord, 'but we haven't been such good friends lately – for quite a while'. Dilorenzo 'was more like a good friend because we used to work out together and go boxing together'. TC told the hearing that he had used cocaine a couple of times 'a while back' but had never wanted to get too involved with drugs because 'I've seen what it's done to quite a few of my friends'.

Barrett then asked him about the police raid at Yarranabbe Road. TC told the counsel assisting that Dilorenzo had panicked when Internal Affairs raced to his car 'because he'd been getting death threats'. When reminded that residue cocaine had been found in a bag on his bedside table during the raid, TC claimed that he had bought it two days earlier at the Regis Hotel in Bondi, simply to soothe an aching gum and help him sleep. Next, Barrett asked if he'd ever agreed to supply cocaine, to which TC replied that he hadn't but 'someone in the past may have come to me and asked if I know where they can get it. In the business I was in . . . people always have it and I might tell them: "Try that person" – but that's as far as it went'. The PIC's tape machine was started up again, replaying TC's chat with David Hitchens on the day of the Darling Point raid, just before Dilorenzo had knocked on the door. It made for an interesting exchange between Barrett and the witness:

Barrett: What were you talking about when you were refer-ring to the weight 6.9 [sic]?

TC: Well . . . a friend of mine gets me a special amino acid that I take when I go training . . . and David wanted to have some. You mix it with orange juice, not milk . . . It helps the body to absorb energy faster.

Barrett: I see . . . So it was an energy food that you were mix-
ing and referring to, was it?

TC: Yes, and you take a certain amount because too much of
it is not good.

Barrett: What did you mean when you said: 'This person I
get my shit from, he's been ringing and hassling me'?

TC: I can't recall what that was about but, I mean, the per-
son that I get that amino acid from . . . I'm not sure
where he gets it . . . Whenever I get it, he usually charges
me about $80 for about 100 grams of it . . .

Barrett: What was the reference to, 'This one's gone funny,
this bag . . . bloody nails'?

TC: Well, if you know amino acid, if you leave it in the con-
tainer and it's not closed, it can go sometimes very
hard.

At the start of the sixth day of evidence, Barrett fore-
shadowed that Podesta and Dilorenzo would soon be called
to the stand to give evidence, and that his learned friend,
Robert Cavanagh, had an application to make to the commission. Cavanagh told Judge Urquhart that he deserved a
spot at the Bar table. He wanted the right to take part in the
proceedings so he could properly represent the widow of
Roni Levi, who had been shot by the officers about to be
called. Yet not any old lawyer had the right to drop his hat
and begin cross-examining a policeman in the dock.

In order to get access to the PIC's confidential exhibits
– notes, memoranda, reports and tape transcripts – Judge
Urquhart needed to be convinced that the lawyer was representing 'an affected person' and that the hearing would have a
direct bearing on that person's reputation or standing.
Urquhart asked Barrett what he thought of Cavanagh's plea,

unconvinced at how he was related to the proceedings. 'I do not expect that there will be material before these hearings that would make the events of 28 June 1997 relevant to the hearings and the evidence that will be placed before it,' counsel assisting replied officially,[3] meaning that again Dundas was denied the opportunity to quiz, through her lawyers, the men who'd killed her husband. The Newcastle crusaders were, however, allowed by Judge Urquhart to sit at the Bar table with the other barristers, on a watching brief. Disappointed at their exclusion, Cavanagh and Watterson took their seats, eager to watch everything and ready to add to a growing inventory of facts and formulations. Urquhart's decision, despite its legal justification, took away from the PIC the opportunity to have questions hurled at Podesta and Dilorenzo from the people who knew most about the life and times of the shooters.

The hearing resumed its steady pace. The second session with TC was just as agonising as his first encounter. More excerpts from the tapes were played, making his protests of innocence sound decidedly dodgy. The witness continued to counter any insinuations that drugs were being discussed or supplied, claiming that of the many visitors he received, 'there were friends that . . . were into steroids' – perhaps that was what was being referred to on the tapes, certainly not cocaine. He was then played an altogether different tape, one that he had no inkling of: the chats he had enjoyed with Podesta before the bust on the way to the Mardi Gras. It sounded an awful lot like Podesta was scoring dope and speaking about how he was going to rip off his girlfriend. But TC said the pair could have been 'talking about anything because if someone is looking for something else, they can misinterpret what you say' and besides 'It's a long time ago and we talked about a lot of things.' It was time to get a different opinion now on the tapes that had been played, and from the other participants.

Having sat at the back of the hearing room since the start, and having heard all of the evidence, Podesta confessed to using and dealing in drugs, and ripping off his girlfriend – almost as soon as he got into the witness box. Having heard the Mardi Gras tapes, he threw up his hand almost instantly, but his hand went only so far. Podesta said he knew TC and that they used to associate with each other but 'we don't associate at all now'.[4] Although he couldn't remember saying the things he had said on the tape, 'I must have said it.' This was the first systematic stripping-down of the shooter and Podesta the drug-dealing rogue was exposed for all to see. 'Most of the times I've taken drugs,' Podesta pleaded, 'was in that period after the time my father died and up to the coronial inquiry and I wouldn't say my sobriety was the best at those times. It was usually when I'd been drinking heavily and at the same time I was on prescription drugs.' He was ambiguous throughout his testimony, with Barrett frequently feeling the need to intervene to get to the bottom of the story:

Barrett: You said you used both ecstasy and cocaine?
Podesta: Yes, I had.
Barrett: And who did you get the ecstasy from?
Podesta: I don't recall. People might have given them to me or I might have asked people in nightclubs.
Barrett: What, people just freely gave it to you?
Podesta: Possibly.
Barrett: People that you didn't know?
Podesta: Possibly.
Barrett: What do you mean, 'possibly'? You keep saying 'possibly'. I wonder what that means?
Podesta: As I say, my recollection of that period of time is not very good . . . my mental state was not very good either.

195

*Barrett: Good enough to be able to score cocaine or ecstasy
when you wanted to use it?*

*Podesta: When you're highly intoxicated and taking large
amounts of antidepressants, you don't really think
about that.*

Podesta had given up TC as a drug dealer with his evidence
– or at least that was its effect – but he did not implicate anyone else. He had gone so far as to say that he had never seen
Dilorenzo, his shooting partner, the next witness to be called,
taking drugs.

So when the series of Yarranabbe Road tapes was
played to Dilorenzo, he was under no obligation to tell anything but the truth. Dilorenzo said he didn't recognise all the
voices and that the tapes were 'pretty shabby . . . with voices
on top of voices'.[5] He said any talk at TC's apartment concerned amino acids that they drank in juice for boxing
training, and that he'd actually had a glass of it on the day of
the raid. Barrett pointed out that the tapes contained 'some
audible sniffing' at a time when he was in the apartment.
'Well, if that's correct,' Dilorenzo retorted, 'Yes, I agree to
it.' And when Internal Affairs told him that TC was supplying drugs, the officer claimed, 'I immediately stopped seeing
him and I haven't seen him since that day.' Dilorenzo denied
point-blank ever having taken cocaine or ecstasy, prompting
the following exchange.

*Barrett: Have you ever been present when any other person
has used cocaine?*

*Dilorenzo: There have been times where people have pulled it
out, either in a nightclub . . . and you've just walked
away from it because I don't want any controversy with
it.*

Barrett: What do you mean, you don't want any controversy
with it?

Dilorenzo: Being a policeman, I don't want to stand around
if somebody is going to be doing drugs.

Barrett: If someone's pulled it out and you saw it, haven't
you got an obligation to do something about it?

Dilorenzo: If I'm intoxicated and I see someone pull out a
joint of marijuana or something like that, I walk away
from it. I don't feel I've got the right, being under the
influence of alcohol, to take action that can be criti-
cised later in a court of law if I do it.

Barrett: You turn a blind eye to it, is that what you're saying?

Dilorenzo: Considering the case, if you put yourself in my
shoes, if I'm intoxicated and I go into a court of law
and it's brought up that I'm intoxicated, there is
always doubt on . . . my ability to arrest . . . so I feel
that unless I'm 100 per cent straight, I shouldn't be
doing it. It's just my sort of rules.

Dilorenzo had occasional run-ins about his attitude. At one
stage, he wanted not to answer specific questions, but to give an
explanation about what he had once told Internal Affairs –
which brought a strong rebuke from Judge Urquhart. And then
he was tripped up again by Barrett, over why he couldn't recognise his voice on the tapes that were being played repeatedly. He
even had to pause for a moment when he felt a little bit queezy:
'I'm a bit run-down from all the problems that have been going
on,' Dilorenzo told the PIC, 'and also on the antidepressants
and all that . . . it's sort of causing me a bit of problems.' Still he
continued to deny the allegations made by Barrett, that he had
been talking about drugs, and offering protection to drug dealers. The encounter had been bruising, but Dilorenzo had given
no ground, no matter how ridiculous it appeared.

Podesta was recalled to the witness box after Dilorenzo, to tidy up some matters that had been overlooked in his earlier examination. Podesta had told Barrett that he first met TC sometime in late 1997, contrary to TC's assertions to McDougall that they met when Podesta was studying to be a policeman. Alison Stenmark, the police commissioner's counsel, then asked Podesta if he was prepared to cooperate and give evidence against Easton 'TC' James?, perhaps in a criminal prosecution against him. 'Possibly . . . I'd have to consult my legal counsel for that,' Podesta replied.[6]

On the morning after Podesta's startling declaration, that he would consider giving evidence against TC in an upcoming drugs trial, the barrister who had represented the Levi family at the coronial inquest, Ken Horler, QC, got to his feet in a bid to gain leave to appear at the hearing, as Robert Cavanagh had earlier done. Horler told Judge Urquhart that 'if the evidence were to reveal that at the time of the shooting of Mr Levi . . . one or more of the police officers were under the influence of an illegal drug or alcohol or a combination of both . . . that would be a relevant matter to be dealt with by you in your findings, report and recommendations.'[7] Barrett, as counsel assisting the PIC, said he didn't 'expect that there will be any such allegations', however. Horler was therefore refused permission to be a part of the inquiry, but as with Cavanagh, Judge Urquhart allowed him to sit at the Bar table.

Like his partner, Dilorenzo was recalled as a witness. Barrett continued to ask whether he could recognise his voice on the tapes that had been recorded at Yarranabbe Road. He again reminded Dilorenzo that while the listening device was running, he had been watched by surveillance officers but, again, the stubborn shooter was evasive and hostile, and he would not budge at all from his assertion that 'some of it's my voice' but 'I cannot be 100 per cent sure, and I'm not going to say it is if it is not, and say it isn't if it is.'[8] Undeterred, Barrett kept repeating the incriminating words on the transcripts, phrases that suggested the speaker was aware of the travails of the drug trade, inside and out. It went on and on, with neither the counsel assisting nor his witness giving an inch, no matter how fanciful Dilorenzo's denials appeared.

At the end of the testimony, Stenmark got a turn to grill the policeman that her client, Police Commissioner Ryan, was in the process of sacking. She was most incisive, reminding Dilorenzo of the penalties for perjury and taking him back to his remarks that he played by his own rules and turned a blind eye to drug use after work:

Stenmark: Mr Dilorenzo, as a sworn police officer, it is not up to you to work by your sort of rules, is it?
Dilorenzo: No.
Stenmark: Your duty is to do as you have sworn to do?
Dilorenzo: Right.
Stenmark: And whether you were under the influence or not, you should have done something about it, if you've seen these other people breaking the law, shouldn't you?
Dilorenzo: Well, as I said earlier, if I'm at a party and I'm drunk and someone – I mean, people pull out joints of marijuana everywhere you go nowadays. I mean, I'd spend all my time off duty, on duty. That's all you'd be doing, walking around, locking up people 24 hours a day . . . [If] I'm at a party, I'm intoxicated with my friends, if someone smokes a joint in the corner, I just move away or I leave the party. I don't think that I should put my beer down, walk over and grab them in front of everybody and drag them down the street or

> *call the police down to the scene to arrest them.*
> *Stenmark: As you said, you turned a blind eye?*
> *Dilorenzo: Well, if I said that, well, that's what I said.*
> *Stenmark: What about if they are using other drugs?*
> *Dilorenzo: Well, that's a different story.*
> *Stenmark: Why is it a different story?*
> *Dilorenzo: I don't see people using other drugs at barbecues and that; it's usually a joint.*
> *Stenmark: Do you say still on your oath that you've never seen other people use other drugs in your presence?*
> *Dilorenzo: I've seen people go into toilets and this and that but, as I said, what's in there, I don't know what's going on.*
> *Stenmark: You turn a blind eye as well?*
> *Dilorenzo: If two people go into a toilet, I don't follow them in.*
> *Stenmark: You play by your sort of rules there as well?*
> *Dilorenzo: Well, if you say that.*
> *Stenmark: That's exactly what I am saying.*
> *Dilorenzo: That's fine.*

On 25 February 1999, the last day of the hearing, Podesta's school friend, David Hitchens, was called to the stand to give his version of what had happened at Darling Point on 7 April, the day Internal Affairs dragged him away. Hitchens threw into serious doubt TC's earlier claims that they had been talking about amino acids, saying that TC had 'a couple of bags . . . small bags . . . of cocaine' and that when offered a line – 'a little one' – he willingly accepted.[9] He snorted the cocaine in TC's bedroom before 'the doorbell went . . . [and] TC put everything away' and Dilorenzo arrived. It was a dispassion-ately given, and powerful version of events, more in keeping with what the surveillance transcript seemed to reveal, and one that also put pressure on Dilorenzo's account. However, Hitchens said he had never seen Dilorenzo taking drugs – although he conceded he had snorted cocaine with Podesta, the other shooter, on a couple of occasions.

And then the talking was over. The PIC hearing was adjourned and consideration started on whether any of the witnesses should be punished: TC, Podesta and Dilorenzo. The final witness of the hearing, however, felt he had already suffered enough: on 19 March, David Hitchens was found dead in his flat, an apparent suicide victim.

Despite the relative success of the PIC hearing – its shaming of Dilorenzo and Podesta, and the fact the shooters had been positively linked to drug dealers – the disquiet remained over the inadequacy of the shooting investigation. And the rumours over the night before refused to go away. Rather than placating the agitation over the Levi shooting, the PIC hearing only intensified the pressure for a further inquiry. It had aroused even greater suspicion, having given an insight into the type of people the Bondi shooters had called their pals. Publicly, the Newcastle Legal Centre was not giving up in its quest for another PIC inquiry, but the lawyers and students there were not expecting it. They knew it would take a lot to convince the authorities to have another crack at Dilorenzo and Podesta – and to give a serious airing of the bungling in the Levi case.

And then, just as their hopes were fading, a rough tape came to light, changing everything. Recorded by a journalist in a phone call with some of Podesta's closest friends – and passed over in strictest confidence – the tape contained allegations of the most horrific kind about Podesta. It gave the lie, seemingly, to much that the shooter had maintained.

In the late autumn of 1999, the Newcastle Legal Centre handed its second dossier to the PIC, with the secret tape attached. It was another brick-by-brick demolition of the police case, and a stirring presentation on why the Levi matter could not be left alone. Much of the same misgivings were assembled, since their importance had not faded with time. The second submission argued that, if so much illegality and bungling had been uncovered in the coronial inquest and the first PIC hearing, then more malpractice would be unearthed with a different approach and new terms of reference.

On 26 June, Dilorenzo was finally sacked by the commissioner for failing to properly explain why he was with TC at the Darling Point address – two years almost to the day since Levi's shooting. He vowed publicly to fight the decision, protesting his innocence, and he even started an appeal. This meant his dismissal papers were lodged at the Industrial Relations Commission, where they would lie virtually untended, for another twelve months. The appeal would never begin.

Although his removal allowed him to keep his superannuation benefits, accumulated over thirteen devoted years, Dilorenzo's cop life was finished. But his time in the public eye had not even begun to cease. For at the end of August, persuaded by the Newcastle Legal Centre's submission, the tape and further research, the PIC placed advertisements in newspapers to herald a new public inquiry. The terms of reference said the hearing would explore further suggestions of drug use and supply by policemen, and 'allegations of corruption or misconduct' in the investigation of the Levi shooting. But, more importantly, one term of reference would investigate allegations that Roni Levi's shooters were affected by alcohol and/or drugs at the time of the killing. The secret lives of Dilorenzo and Podesta were about to be publicly paraded.

THE SECOND PHASE

'Of course, persons in many walks of life, not just the police, may work in stressful circumstances where the use of prohibited drugs may adversely affect . . . their work. However, there is a critical additional feature which touches officers of the police . . . those officers carry firearms.'

Peter Johnson, SC, counsel assisting, Police Integrity Commission, Operation Saigon, 1 November 1999

The passing of so much time had failed to quell the expectation of closure. When the second Police Integrity Commission hearing started in November 1999 at 111 Elizabeth Street, up past the north-west end of Hyde Park, it was almost two-and-a-half years since Levi's killing. Nearly 26 months had gone by since the barrister, Robert Bromwich, had chatted with his hairdresser, Katrina Rafferty, and first given birth to the rumours that the Bondi shooters were high on drugs when they fired their revolvers. The trail of evidence, of course, had long ago turned stale, but the fervour for answers remained as fresh as ever. It was plain that the details about the night before the shooting had never been fully explored. Nothing close to a satisfactory explanation had ever been given, and the shooters themselves had not once been asked to refute the slur that had swept the Bondi promenade.

Given the appearance of the dead man's name in the

terms of reference, the Levi family's barrister, Ken Horler, again pressed Judge Urquhart on his right to appear, as did Robert Cavanagh, on behalf of Levi's widow. Both lawyers felt they stood a better chance this time of securing a spot at the Bar table. It was contended that, because the hearing would look into the behaviour of the Bondi shooters before the fatal shots, it was certainly proper, under the PIC's legislation, to give them the right to ask questions of the witnesses. Horler said he had just spoken to Levi's mother, who felt, 'with some justification, that the NSW justice system has failed them in relation to the investigation'.[1] She wanted a say at the PIC because 'the state of the evidence before the Coroner was not as it now appears to be, and in order to provide justice to the natural parents of the deceased, we say we're entitled to be here and to participate in . . . proceedings'.[2] It seemed a logical argument to follow, as did that of his learned friend, Cavanagh, who politely noted that it was the Newcastle Legal Centre that had supplied the fresh evidence to the PIC – its detailed analysis and the secret tape had helped trigger this second hearing. He ventured that his appearance, given the amount of research and knowledge that his team had accumulated, might be of assistance – and that it was only fair given that the hearing would touch on the factors leading to the death of his client's husband.

The new counsel assisting the inquiry, Peter Johnson, SC, advised Judge Urquhart that, on his reading of the statute, no such leave should be given to the dead man's representatives – even though the allegations might touch on why, and how, Levi was killed. Although Judge Urquhart deliberated for a few days, he eventually agreed with Johnson and ordered that only lawyers representing witnesses, and not those affected by the evidence, would be entitled to play an active role at the Bar table. Once again then, the people who knew the circumstances of the case backwards, but who stood outside the closed circle of official investigators – Cavanagh and the Newcastle Legal Centre – were denied a piece of the action. They could exercise a watching brief, but play no active part in the proceedings. Given Cavanagh's impressive, if unorthodox, contribution at the coronial inquest, it can only be speculated at the impact his appearance at the PIC would have had on the findings. The legal centre considered appealing to the Supreme Court, to get the right to be represented at the hearing, but the Newcastle lawyers felt it was best to stay friends with the PIC, who now held all of the cards.

Podesta was the star witness and, as if for effect, Johnson recited a long list of names: drug dealers, nightclub friends, lap-dancers and drug-taking mates. Podesta, of course, had admitted to using and supplying cocaine at the first hearing, but he had always maintained that his drug use started only after the death of his father, as if it was a coping mechanism for the grief of his passing and the mental anguish he was enduring over the shooting. Johnson's critical task, therefore, was to demonstrate somehow that Podesta's likeness for little white lines had been alive and kicking well before these two events. Johnson needed to put Podesta in places, and with people, before 28 June 1997, that were within reach of drug-taking. It was a way he could show that Podesta had either been lying, misleading, or understating his drug habits. This necessarily meant bringing up his links with the Liberty Lunch.

'How many times did you go to the Liberty Lunch in the first half of 1997?' Johnson asked. 'Probably about five times,' said Podesta,[3] belying the true extent of his association. All sorts of names were thrown about – Robert Gould,

O'Connor, TC and Stephen Langton, among many others –
and Podesta was obliged to mention when he had first met
these characters, what he'd done with them, and how close he
was to them. Early on in his testimony, Podesta was assured
and straight to the point, but when it came to Mark Lorenzo,
the clarity of his testimony suddenly appeared to grow hazy.
Initially, when Lorenzo's name had been mentioned as an
aside, Podesta had testified to meeting him in the latter part
of 1996. But when Johnson asked him about it again, a different response was elicited. Now Podesta claimed that his
association with the convicted heroin dealer only started in
mid 1997, just after the shooting, or perhaps later, in November of that year.

It was inevitable then, with Podesta minimising his
contact with Mark Lorenzo, and other identities, that the PIC
would rip out his phone accounts to see what the records stated
and to provoke some kind of reaction. Johnson recited a number of calls to Lorenzo made during a period earlier than
Podesta had conceded. 'If you were calling Mark Lorenzo as
early as 5 January 1997, what were you contacting him about?'
the counsel assisting inquired. 'I can't be sure about that, I'm
sorry. It's a very, very long time ago . . . I might have rang him
to find out where Tony is or to speak to Tony,' Podesta replied.
Johnson persisted: 'Were you contacting him to discuss the
topic of drugs?' Podesta insisted that he was not. On and on
the phone records were read out and it was indicated that, as
the months went by, so the level of contact increased. Johnson
then started to read out the times the calls were made, such as
3.43 in the morning. Podesta was asked if he had any business
with Lorenzo 'that led to late night phone calls of that sort?'.
Again the witness could offer no explanation – 'Is it a crime to
ring someone at an early hour of the morning?' he flinched,
upset at the repeated suggestions. The action was hotting up.

He now said he 'could have been' part of a crowd who 'stayed in the Liberty Lunch after it was locked up' in the first half of 1997, before the shooting:

Johnson: Was there an occasion when you walked into that . . . [Liberty Lunch] office and Easton James and Robert Gould were there having a line of cocaine?

Podesta: Not to my recollection.

Johnson: Are you sure about that?

Podesta: Yes, I am.

Johnson: And that you came in and sat down and had a line of cocaine with them? Did that occur?

Podesta: Not that I recall.

Johnson: When you say 'not that I recall', it's possible it did happen?

Podesta: If that happened, it would have happened in the late half of '97, '98.

Johnson: When do you say you first used a prohibited drug?

Podesta: After my father's death. November '97. And I continued to do so on numerous occasions up and including the time of the coronial inquest . . .

Johnson: Did you use cannabis as an adolescent?

Podesta: No, not that I recall.

Johnson: Well, did you?

Podesta: No, I can't think of an occasion. The only occasion I can think of smoking cannabis was probably ten years ago, when I was a teenager.

Johnson: Well, that's what I asked you, Mr Podesta.

Podesta: Sorry, I misunderstood your question.

Podesta's evidence was becoming more shaky the longer he stayed in the witness box. He told Johnson that before his father's death, he thought 'most people' he knew had tried ecstasy but, conversely, he believed none of his friends used cocaine. When he first snorted, therefore, Podesta agreed with the implausible suggestion that he bought the drugs 'from a club which you can't identify, from a person you can't recall'. Then he was taken back to his activities on the night before the shooting – and he told of his birthday meal on the boulevard, at Terrific Thai, overlooking Bondi Beach, and the second Asian meal at Tak's Thai on the night of the shooting. Of course, he denied, apart from having a couple of beers for his birthday, drinking any alcohol or taking drugs before his shift early the next day. Podesta said he went home to his parents' place, shared a piece of the cake, and then went to bed. To Johnson's question of whether there were occasions when, in spite of his having to work an early-morning shift on a Saturday, Podesta would party into the early hours of the morning, the ex-cop replied: 'It may have happened late '97, early '98, but prior to that it would not have happened . . . no.'

For Podesta, this was nothing like the first hearing. Unlike his encounter with Patrick Barrett – where he adequately explained that his involvement in the Mardi Gras drug deal, and his coke-snorting, was a result of the grief he felt over the death of his father – Johnson's scope of interest and range of questions was going into uncomfortable places. And Podesta at times felt physically distressed – a luncheon adjournment being taken early one day on the request of his solicitor. Despite all this inconvenience, he'd been effective and pugnacious in the witness box, up to a point, in repelling Johnson's claim he was taking drugs in the months leading up to the shooting. But Podesta's composure started to unravel when Johnson took him back to the Soho nightclub incident, to the run-in with the security guard in the toilets in May 1997, only weeks before Levi was blasted away:

Johnson: Was there an occasion when you entered the toilet cubicle . . . at the Soho Bar with another male person?

Podesta: Not that I recall.

Johnson: If it did happen, would the only possible explanation for it be for the purpose of taking drugs?

Podesta: Certainly not. Not in that time period.

Johnson: What other explanation might there be if that had occurred?

Podesta: Maybe, I might have wanted to go the toilet at the same time as the other person.

Johnson: Into a cubicle?

Podesta: I don't know . . .

Johnson: Were you in May of 1997 in a toilet cubicle with Mark Lorenzo at the Soho Bar?

Podesta: I'd say no to that.

Johnson: April 1997?

Podesta: I'd say no. I'd say no to that all the way up to . . . unless you were establishing the fact it would be November, December '97 . . . to January, February '98.

Johnson then indicated that he wanted to play some more listening-device tapes, evidence that had not been forthcoming at the previous hearing, for some reason. He took Podesta back to the week before the coronial inquest. Of particular interest was the bug that picked up Podesta arranging for certain pills to be taken to 'Kieran's place'. He agreed he 'must have been' referring to 'the Kieran from [the] Liberty' in the bugged calls – and that he was probably talking about cocaine and 'might have been referring to taking some ecstasy tablets'. Podesta agreed that he had maintained a relationship with O'Connor after the latter had sold out of the Liberty Lunch and that it was 'possibly' a friendship 'with a drug context'. Despite this admission, Podesta went on to say that, even though he snorted coke at O'Connor's apartment, he had never seen O'Connor taking drugs.

Johnson also discussed the volume of traffic that came to his mobile phone in the hours after the shooting, when he was in segregation at Bondi police station, and it was noted that the barrage of callers had all partied with him at the Liberty Lunch. This then raised another area of controversy: the police ban on the cafe. Johnson asked Podesta why he had returned to the Liberty Lunch so soon after his commander, Chief Inspector Richard Baker, had told him to stop going. A series of lame excuses followed, with Podesta being forced to concede to the counsel assisting's assertion that the cop was in fact 'in no position to judge whether circumstances had changed so that it was okay to go back'.

At the end of his gruelling full day of evidence, Podesta admitted he had sought treatment to get over his cocaine and ecstasy routine. He said he might have gone through one or two grams of cocaine at the height of his dependency and then offered a more prolific assessment of his pill-popping activity – the largest number he ever took *in one go* being 'Maybe five or six.'

On the second day of the hearings, Podesta was recalled as a witness – but for a far less bruising encounter with his interrogators. Johnson asked him about his membership of the Living Dangerously Club, and some telephone threats that he claimed to have received on the eve of his appearance. After six hours of confronting questions about his drug-taking, and his drug-taking friends, Podesta's solicitor, Kenneth Madden, got the chance to hold his client's hand, to help his client to put the most accurate spin on his version of events.

Podesta told his lawyer he had cut short by three

weeks an overseas holiday to prepare for the PIC hearings, and to 'assist the DPP and give evidence for the prosecution against a man named Easton James'. It was an interesting development, a proposition first posed to Podesta by the police commissioner's legal counsel, Alison Stenmark, in the first hearing.

Madden: The situation is you instructed me to tell the DPP that you would give evidence for the prosecution . . . against Mr James?

Podesta: I did agree to that.

Madden: And you were advised that the DPP wanted you to come home to Sydney as soon as possible.

Podesta: That's correct.

Madden: You are not suggesting, I take it, for one moment that Mr James, or someone acting on his behalf, made the [threatening] telephone call to you . . . you don't know who made the call?

Podesta: I don't know who made the call.

Madden: The fact of the matter is that since you received that call, you have decided that you won't give evidence for the DPP.

Podesta: That's correct.[4]

The next three witnesses – Terry Voto, Ronald Quin and Renee Robertshaw – were called, to examine the credence of Podesta's claim that he had been with them on the night before the shooting, specifically that Quin and Robertshaw had shared a piece of chocolate cake and a few beers over noodles at Terrific Thai on the Bondi promenade. Each gave similar renditions of the meal and their evening together: how it had been arranged, who arrived first, how long it took. In the course of this, both confessed to using cocaine and ecstasy, but declared they had never seen Podesta using drugs in the time leading up to the shooting.

Quin's flatmate, Voto, was primarily called to explain the mobile call he had received from Podesta at 9.10 p.m. on the night before the killing. Voto suggested that, as Quin used his phone so much, Podesta had not been ringing for him, but rather looking for Quin. It seemed a strange explanation, given that Podesta and Quin were supposed to have been together. Voto and Quin were asked why Podesta had rung them at 8.13 a.m. on the day of the shooting, only 40 minutes after killing Levi and less then ten minutes after he'd arrived back at the police station, sobbing uncontrollably. What had they spoken about? Johnson asked. And why was the call made so soon after the killing? After all, Podesta had phoned *them* (of all people) as soon as he had been left on his own at the police station. Yet no-one seemed to recollect the conversation, odd perhaps given its dramatic import.

Before Dilorenzo was ushered into the witness box, his wife's aunt and uncle, Nola and John Preston, testified that, as had been the longstanding practice, they had a fish dinner with the Dilorenzo family on the night before the shooting. And that one of Dilorenzo's mates, a man nicknamed Chill, had also been there.

Dilorenzo, himself, was most insistent about what he'd done on the Friday evening, right down to the minute details of what he had been wearing two-and-a-half years earlier. He'd returned from work late in the afternoon, 'had a shower . . . I always have to shower before bed . . . [then] I put on my shorts and sat down and watched TV, the football. I love the football and watch it almost every Friday night when it's in season . . . [and] I went to bed straightaway because I was on the 7 a.m. shift next morning and it was a ritual that I would always go to bed early.'[5] Dilorenzo endured a far less daunting stint than Podesta. Indeed, he was only in the box for part of an afternoon session, repeating that he was not a party person or the type to drink or take drugs:

Johnson: In the first half of 1997, on how many occasions did you go to nightclubs?

Dilorenzo: Only speculating, I'd probably say twice . . . I probably got out once in six months . . . My wife was sort of, you know, with a bit of a whip . . . [saying] 'You've got to stay home' . . . Plus I've got the kids. That's sort of my life. I've got the kids.

Johnson: What clubs did you go to?

Dilorenzo: Well, I heard you mentioned the Soho and I remember that night. That was when I arrested someone off duty for . . . snatching a female's purse, but otherwise I wouldn't remember any other nights.

Johnson: Were you out with Constable Podesta?

Dilorenzo: I'm not sure of that . . . I don't recall the incident too clearly . . .

Johnson: When you say you don't recall the incident too clearly, were you under the influence of something at the time?

Dilorenzo: No, I would have maybe had one drink. I'm not much of a drinker. That's why I declined a lot of the time to go to police do's, you know, parties or drinks, because some of them excessively drink . . .

Three more of Podesta's drug-taking friends – Robert Gould, Graeme Rooney and Mike Morrison – gave at times vague, and at other times, deeply revealing evidence, throughout the third day. Collectively, their testimony completely demolished the credibility of the Bondi shooter – routing Podesta's claim that he had been a drug virgin before the Levi killing and raising inferences that, indeed, he might have been snorting coke at the Liberty Lunch only hours before reporting for duty.

Gould, the once-constant companion of the Liberty's owner, Kieran O'Connor, was by far the most damaging witness. Giving sworn testimony with the benefit of a section 41 order – meaning none of his words could be used against him in any criminal matter – Gould dangerously recalled the high life in Bondi in early 1997, painting a florid world of excess and drugs. Gould said he first snorted lines with Podesta in the upstairs office of the Liberty with TC, and saw him using cocaine 'probably about half a dozen to a dozen times' in the months before the tragedy.[6] Gould said he snorted with 'different people coming and going . . . it varied' at Byblos and other nightclubs – and with O'Connor at the property developer's apartment in Darlinghurst. He had taken ecstasy with Podesta, but couldn't say how many times the pill-popping had occurred. Gould said he had seen Dilorenzo at the Liberty Lunch 'three or four times' before the shooting, but never in a drug context. Gould was then asked to think back to the night before the shooting:

Johnson: When had you last seen Rodney Podesta prior to learning of the fatal shooting?

Gould: It could possibly have been the evening before, or even the week before . . . at Liberty Lunch . . . [but] one Thursday, Friday, Saturday rolled into another, so I couldn't be specific.

Johnson: So what's your best recollection now as to how long it was prior to the shooting that you last saw him?

Gould: Could possibly have been the evening before.

Johnson: What time in the evening had you seen Rodney Podesta?

Gould: If it was the evening before, which I can't be specific, it was approximately 10, 10.30.

Johnson: Did you see him use any drugs on that occasion?

Gould: No.

Johnson: At the time you heard about the shooting, and heard that Rodney Podesta was involved, did any thoughts run through your mind as to his position?

Gould: I think I recollect, when I was told, I think I said: 'Oh shit, that's not good!' or something like that.

Johnson: Why did you think that?

Gould: That it's not good for anyone to shoot someone, for a start. Secondly, I thought that I possibly could have seen him the evening before, but I couldn't be specific.

Johnson: Well, given the thought processes in your mind when you heard about this, what difference would it have made to his position if you'd seen him the night before?

Gould: None, really – just that he – I was at Liberty Lunch and if he was there . . . It was just a general – basically a general comment as to his position.

Johnson: Well, did your thought process at that stage consider that he'd been doing something the night before that you thought may cause him some problem?

Gould: If I'd seen him, it was possible. But, like I say, I couldn't be specific at all. There was a general occurrence that happened. I mean, like I said, it's all a blur. I couldn't say whether it was one night or the other.

Johnson: When you say a general occurrence, what are you talking about?

Gould: My personal excess drinking and indulgence in drugs.

Johnson: What's this general occurrence, that you're talking about?

Gould: Well, that I saw him, that I possibly could have had a drink with him or a line of coke. I couldn't be specific as to the time and the place.

Johnson: I just want you to tell the commissioner your best recollection as to what you thought Rodney Podesta had been doing that caused you to think he may be in the shit, or whatever the term was you thought when you heard of this news.

Gould: Basically, as I said, there was – I can't recall, one evening being the other – but generally I would consume a lot of drugs and alcohol and sometimes I would take with Rodney and, if it had been the night before, he possibly could have done something. I couldn't be specific and, therefore, I thought, if he had been, there might be trouble but, as I said, it's all a blur. One night rolled into the other and I couldn't be specific.

Gould's performance was incredible, even if he had given his account in an unconvincingly ambiguous way. Gould said he still used cocaine but was only a 'recreational' user and not the 'everyday' regular dabbler he used to be – saying that he last had a gram, costing about $180, a few weeks earlier. At Judge Urquhart's insistence, Gould wrote down the name of the drug supplier on a piece of paper.

Graeme Rooney and Mike Morrison then joined the ever-growing circle of party types who had given evidence of taking drugs with Podesta: before he joined the police, while he was a serving policeman, and after he'd shot Levi. In fact, most of the time they'd known each other, there had been drugs. For Podesta, it was hard stuff to refute. Rooney said he was still good mates with the Bondi shooter, the target of most of his testimony, however. Rooney gave evidence of Podesta's links with Zac MacKenzie, the Marrickville dealer (and Rooney's flatmate), and of the hedonistic lifestyle they shared of drugs, booze and women. It was compelling, and damaging testimony.

The Liberty Lunch identities dominated the middle period of the hearing. TC, Kieran O'Connor, Madison Mander, Samantha, Stephen Langton, Stanley Dowse, Allan Graney and Mark Lorenzo would all be called to give their accounts of the grand old days and about the police ban.

The retired Bondi commander, Richard Baker, kicked off the inquiry's focus on the Liberty Lunch by telling of the stressful months leading up to the shooting; what it had been like to command the place bombarded by drug scandals. He spoke about the singling-out of Dilorenzo and Podesta for specific warnings – and of the Internal Affairs referral that flowed from Podesta's disobedience. But Baker was not quizzed at all on why he hadn't bothered to mention anything to McDougall about the drug inquiries on the day of the shooting, why he hadn't considered it to be relevant at the time. Nor was he asked a single question on why he had made prejudicial media comments before the Bondi shooters had been interviewed.

TC said he had taken cocaine at O'Connor's place 'once or so, or twice' and that the drug was 'always . . . there somewhere'.[7] He also conceded he had taken ecstasy – once – but it was only half a tablet. He readily accepted, however, that he worked at a restaurant where drug use and supply was prevalent. TC said that before the shooting he was good friends with Podesta and they used to 'talk about a lot of things' and that 'he likes to go out and pick up girls'; but he said he was always suspicious of the Bondi shooter – he respected Podesta 'as a police officer' but 'didn't really trust him too much'. Fending off Johnson's attempts to get the witness to elaborate on this last point, TC added nonchalantly: 'Most people never really trust a police officer. You are friends with them, but you always have to watch everything you do and say.'

217

When O'Connor was called to take the oath, he gave the immediate impression that he wanted to defuse any suggestion that he was at the heart of the Liberty Lunch's drug scene. But he didn't do a very good job. When asked by Johnson if he had ever used cocaine, O'Connor answered bluntly that he had not – only to contradict himself, foolishly, a mere eighteen questions further on in his testimony. 'Have you ever used cocaine yourself?' Johnson enquired again. 'I may have tried it at a party some time,' O'Connor fumbled. '. . . it would have been one of the fashion parties . . . one of the openings that we got invited to.'[8] But that concession aside, O'Connor denied any deeper links to cocaine or ecstasy use, refuting the conversation on the Internal Affairs tapes, recorded in Podesta's car in late January 1998, that he wanted to 'rack up' and get some little pink pills. O'Connor agreed that people had snorted cocaine at his penthouse apartment, in particular, Robert Gould, with whom he had had 'a major falling-out' as a result.

While O'Connor and TC had given illuminating alternative explanations for their apparent closeness to the drug trade, Mark Lorenzo made no attempt at such niceties. He admitted taking cocaine and ecstasy, without a problem; but overall, his evidence was given with reluctance, and barely controlled venom. Lorenzo was considered to be a pivotal player: he'd been out often with Podesta and they'd shared so many phone calls, at all sorts of hours – contacts that required an explanation that Podesta had been unable to offer. Johnson put forward the assumption, early in their duel, that he must have been close friends with Podesta, since he admitted the Bondi shooter had been to his home before the killing. 'I disagree,' Lorenzo said defiantly, 'I mean, the mailman comes to my house every day. I don't have a personal relationship with him.'[9] It was a spirited display, with Judge Urquhart needing to intervene at times. Not once in his examination could Lorenzo proffer a reason as to why he and Podesta had talked on the phone at such unusual times. It was only after being prompted by *Podesta*'s counsel, Kenneth Madden, that he finally remembered what it had all been about:

Madden: There was one thing you and Mr Podesta had in common, and that was that in the first half of 1997, Mr Podesta's father was dying of cancer.
Lorenzo: That's correct.
Madden: When had your father died?
Lorenzo: I suppose now it would have been about four-and-a-half years, five years ago, of cancer as well.
Madden: Was it the same type of cancer?
Lorenzo: I believe so. I spoke to Rod regularly, yes.
Madden: About? . . .
Lorenzo: About the cancer, and even going to the hospital, now that you remind me.

Although all of the Liberty regulars would get their time in the box, arguably the most important witnesses appeared on the fifth day of the hearing. One of Podesta's former girlfriends, Madison Mander, said she had actually wondered out loud if the policeman had been on drugs when she heard he had been involved in a shooting. Still, such a disclosure had to be drawn out of her.

The weight of evidence now supported a view that if Podesta had not been affected by drugs and booze hours before the killing, some of his closest friends thought it was a distinct possibility. That notion got a lot worse with the appearance of Samantha, the prostitute who had been barred from Liberty Lunch. Using the codename 'SA2', and giving evidence on a videolink in another room – so she wouldn't have to face the accused – she gave the most graphic descriptions of who used and supplied drugs, and the frequency with which the Bondi Beach crowd got high. The evidence matched the tense, dramatic atmosphere.

Samantha said she'd been given cocaine by TC and a manager at the restaurant called Stephen, and that she had seen O'Connor using cocaine. She recalled Dilorenzo using coke at the Sugar Reef nightclub and at Podesta's home, and of Podesta's concern that the police might soon be introducing random urine testing. She stunned the hearing room with claims that she had seen Podesta go through five grams of cocaine in one party session, and that he once had an inch-thick bag of white powder. And then came the most telling blow:[10]

Johnson: When had you last seen Rodney Podesta prior to learning of the fatal shooting?
SA2: The night prior to the shooting.
Johnson: What time that night had you seen him?
SA2: In the evening – late evening.
Johnson: Where were you at that time?
SA2: I was at home.
Johnson: How was it that Rodney Podesta came to your home that night?
SA2: He came to visit.
Johnson: How was he dressed?
SA2: In uniform.
Johnson: Did you note anything about his appearance at the time?
SA2: He was high on cocaine.
Johnson: How could you tell that?
SA2: He looked very agitated, he couldn't sit still.

Johnson: How long was he in your company that night?

SA2: About fifteen minutes to half an hour.

Johnson: Was there any prohibited drug used whilst he was at your place that night?

SA2: No, there was not.

Johnson: How long after the shooting was it that you rang him?

SA2: I think a few days after.

Johnson: Did he say anything to you about the incident when you talked to him?

SA2: He sounded very distraught. He said that he'd done something very bad.

If the PIC's case needed strengthening against Podesta and Dilorenzo, it came when Simon Duncan was brought before the hearing, to give an account of the infamous badge-pulling episode at the Soho Bar, a good month before the killing.

Although it was manifestly clear that the Bondi shooters had mixed with drug users and dealers, there was still no overwhelming material, or testimony, to implicate them in nefarious behaviour in relation to the Levi case. Nothing had undermined their accounts of innocence on the night before the shooting.

Dilorenzo's wife, Annabelle, and Podesta's mother, Charmaine, were even called up to further support the shooters. And Dilorenzo's mate from the Friday fish dinners, Angelo Astudillo (aka Chill), answered a summons to see if he could recall where he was on the fateful evening. Chill said although he ate fish and chips regularly with Dilorenzo at the end of the working week, he was not with them on the night before the shooting. Dilorenzo, of course, had earlier testified that Chill *had* been with him. There were other differences in his evidence. For one thing, he seemed to indicate that

Dilorenzo drank and partied a whole lot more than the policeman himself had ever admitted:

Johnson: When you went out to these clubs with him, did he have a drink?

Astudillo: Yeah.

Johnson: What was he drinking?

Astudillo: . . . all different sorts of stuff, ranging from beer to Jack Daniels . . .

Johnson: When you went out with him on these occasions, how much did he appear to drink? How much alcohol did he appear to drink?

Astudillo: Oh, heaps; we all did . . . just drink to get pissed, I suppose.

At the conclusion of days of damning evidence, four critical witnesses were recalled to respond to adverse allegations: O'Connor, TC and, of course, the shooters, Dilorenzo and Podesta. The key players in this tawdry jigsaw. Their denials of impropriety were repeated. O'Connor and TC refuted SA2's claims of drug use and supply – and gave insights into how Samantha had come to be barred from the Liberty Lunch.

Dilorenzo's dogged insistence of his purity also continued in his second stint at the witness box. Johnson accused Dilorenzo of understating his alcohol consumption in the months leading up to the shooting, of putting a better complexion on his lifestyle. Dilorenzo replied that Chill was wrong about not being at his place on the night before the shooting, and incorrect in his descriptions of his carousing: 'I don't drink much. I never have . . . I stayed home most of the time.'[12] Just as before, Dilorenzo didn't budge an inch, even denying he had been warned to stay away from the Liberty Lunch (despite the specific order appearing in his superior's official diary). Johnson went deeper still, showing him police reports on the Temple nightclub affair, when someone had smashed a glass into his head – trying to display that Dilorenzo, like Podesta, had been a bit of a regular on the party circuit. He denied every conceivable adverse inference raised against him.

Podesta also finished his testimony with a flourish of rebuttal. Despite the sackload of testimony that was put to him suggesting he was up to his armpits in the drug scene, Podesta either denied the accusations or shrugged his shoulders and couldn't recall. The only consistently clear recollection that he had throughout his evidence was that his cocaine tendencies started in the wake of his father's death – months after the Levi matter – and up to the time of the coronial inquest. Of that fact alone, he was certain. However, in two matters, his testimony was particularly memorable, and summed up a perplexing, and distressing, affair. The first issue related to his calls with Mark Lorenzo.

Johnson wanted to know if, in the light of Lorenzo's evidence concerning the pair's discussions about losing their fathers to cancer, Podesta could now recall what the conversations were about. Podesta ran with the lifeline his solicitor had thrown him, via Lorenzo's testimony:

Johnson: Have you had a chance to reflect further upon the possible reasons for you ringing him up at times that included frequent calls between midnight and dawn?

Podesta: Yes. As Mr Madden was speaking to him before. It was in relation to . . . problems with my father.

Johnson: What type of assistance were you looking for from Mr Lorenzo at that time of the night . . . ?

Podesta: More comforting assistance, someone I could talk to.

Johnson: How many times would you say that you rang Mark

> Lorenzo in the middle of the night to get comfort from
> him in relation to your father?

Podesta: Oh I don't know. I can't be sure of that. Sorry.

Johnson: That's something that you didn't raise last time?

Podesta: It didn't cross my mind last time.

Johnson: Wouldn't that have been a very clear reason for you
to be ringing him in the middle of the night on the
occasions I put to you then?

Podesta: No, because I've had a lot on my mind actually with
this whole inquiry.

Johnson: But the fact that you'd be ringing up someone in the
middle of the night on regular occasions would be
unusual, would you agree?

Podesta: It depends what you see as unusual . . . I don't find
ringing people at any hour of the night unusual, if
they're a friend. I still do to this day ring people up at
weird hours.

Johnson: If the reason that you're ringing up a friend in the
middle of the night on occasions is a memorable and
unfortunate one like the health of your father, that
would be something in your memory, wouldn't it?

Podesta: Yes, it would.

Johnson: But it wasn't something that you volunteered over
the two days of evidence you gave . . . was it?

Podesta: No, it wasn't.

The audience was also intrigued to hear Podesta's explanation
for the phone calls he had made, and received, from Samantha,
the witness who claimed he was high on cocaine on the night
before the shooting. He said their affair was short-lived, probably a one-night stand, and not the month-long fling she
maintained. He said when he cut off the relationship, abruptly,
Samantha had started to follow him, turning up at clubs where

he was partying. 'It wasn't a relationship,' Podesta claimed. 'She was a stalker, in my opinion.'

Johnson ended his marathon examination of Podesta with a return to the evidence that was mounting against him, but the shooter was giving nothing away:

Johnson: Would you agree that you had a circle of friends in late 1996 and the first half of 1997 that involved . . . prohibited drug users?
Podesta: I wouldn't know about that.
Johnson: Well, did you suspect that any of these persons were prohibited drug users?
Podesta: No.
Johnson: The evidence suggests that a number of the places where witnesses have said you would go from time to time – the Sugar Reef, Byblos, Liberty Lunch, Black Market – were places where there was regular prohibited drug use; do you understand that?
Podesta: I wouldn't know about that.
Johnson: Well, did you suspect it in the period up to the middle of 1997?
Podesta: No, I didn't.
Johnson: What, you didn't suspect that there was regular prohibited drug use at say, the Black Market?
Podesta: I wouldn't know, sorry. I never saw anything.

At the end of the Police Integrity Commission's second hearing, doubts still hovered over what exactly had taken place in the hours before the Bondi shooters took to the sand. Dilorenzo and Podesta had assured the inquiry they were level-headed and unaffected by drugs or alcohol. There was still unease, and uncertainty – particularly as much had been discovered about the antics of the Bondi shooters, and their friends in the lead-up to the horrible day – enough to cast the deepest of aspersions over the cops' conduct.

On 9 December 1999, Podesta appeared before Downing Centre Local Court for sentence on one charge of attempting to receive cocaine for supply. There was no evidence that Podesta had actually taken possession of the cocaine. His lawyer, Chester Porter, QC, pleaded with Magistrate Hugh Dillon for understanding of the enormous ordeal his client had suffered; and that he should not be sent to gaol. Porter claimed his client was not a drug dealer: 'This is a one-off transaction . . . Fundamentally this man is being punished for evil thoughts rather than evil actions.'[14] Magistrate Dillon was so persuaded by Porter's advocacy, that he apologised to Podesta, the man who was pleading guilty to dealing drugs:

> *The Levi shooting has been covered by the press around the world, not just in Sydney, over the last two or three years. And whatever one thinks of Mr Podesta's actions and of the other police on that day . . . as a result of that particular incident and the subsequent publicity, he has suffered a tremendous psychiatric and psychological reaction . . . Mr Podesta, if I may say personally, I am sorry to have to impose this sentence on you . . . I very much wish you the best for the future and I hope that after all this is over that things go much better for you.*[15]

And then he called on the next case. Podesta got a custodial sentence: he was ordered to spend four months in weekend detention.

FIFTEEN
END OF THE LINE

'You would reasonably expect that approximately half of the students going through the Academy would have been exposed to illicit substance use at some stage in their lives. I think that a random drug testing program would act as a deterrent to those individuals.'

Gary Jackel (manager, NSW Police Healthy Lifestyles Branch),
Police Integrity Commission, Operation Saigon, 2 March 2000

The police station at Bondi has been abandoned, with headquarters deciding in 1999 that the building had outlived its usefulness. With no occupants, and plans for sale and redevelopment stalling, the site in Wairoa Avenue became overgrown with grass and weeds, its exterior fading and paint peeling. For a long time, it looked unloved and unkempt – and forgotten, as if the structure and its memories had been purposely cut away from the police. Certainly, the tiny building – and, specifically, the action that took place inside the shaky walls on Saturday, 28 June 1997 – was an unwelcome reminder of a depressing affair. The police stayed beside the beach, though, shifting to a modern place in Gould Street, on the ground floor of a swanky apartment complex. The station was built for free by the developers in an entrepreneurial deal that would not previously have been considered – perhaps a symptom of a gradually-changing bureaucratic culture.

Indeed, change has occurred in many parts of the NSW Police Service since the shooting of Roni Levi. But much has yet to be done. Despite all the good initiatives, and all the good intentions, the police brotherhood mentality – the unwritten code that mates should be protected, no matter what the consequences – still exists in large pockets. And while the Levi investigation was not corrupt in the sense of being a cover-up, it was nonetheless a *corrupted* investigation, tainted by ineptitude and incompetence.

As a result of the coronial inquest and PIC hearings, legislative and procedural changes have been enforced, not least because of the calamities uncovered by the Newcastle Legal Centre. The government has endorsed new rules and Commissioner's Instructions to make the investigation of police shootings more independent and accountable – a reflection on the inadequacy of the Levi inquiries. It was made mandatory for all officers involved in a critical incident – like a car crash or a siege, a death in custody or a shooting – to be tested for drugs and alcohol. Capsicum spray is now being used, providing an alternative to the gun. (Ironically, the police-issue Smith and Wesson revolver was replaced in the wake of the Levi case by the more powerful nine-shot, semi-automatic Glock pistol – with its hollow-point bullets leaving no room for chance as they explode and scatter on impact.) Recruitment procedures have been tightened, with more extensive background checks conducted in a bid to weed out misfits. And officers now get training, albeit in a limited way, on how best to deal with people suffering mental illness.

All this has been welcomed by the public. But the sad reality is that great guidelines and orders have seldom been followed by police officers. The depressing thing about the Levi investigation was that specific standing instructions, issued right from the top, were ignored routinely by senior officers, almost with impunity. And it showed that the entrenched police culture, the mythical behavioural glue in the ranks, had apparently not changed in synch with rule changes at that time. The Levi case demonstrated that changes to official rules and procedures, although important, will only ever be as good as the quality of the men and women that are bound to follow them – and the authorities responsible for enforcing them.

The Levi investigation is a model of investigative failure, borne of the brotherhood. It shows how even the most ethical of brothers, when forced to investigate their own, can easily fall into the practice, however subconsciously, of looking the wrong way and asking the wrong questions (or not even asking questions at all). These errors, however manifest they appear to the outsider, are seemingly always able to be explained away – rationalised and justified. It is tempting to excuse the failings in the Levi case as innocent bungling or understandable misunderstandings. But this would be too much of a concession, it overlooks the deeper malaise. Each mistake could have been avoided. Every stuff-up served to compound another mistake: the errors were systemic and each one acted to compromise the ultimate outcome.

The problems started on the beach itself: McDougall's team got quickly swamped by the tide of enquiries and hometown detectives were used, contrary to standing instructions, to take interviews that could potentially incriminate their colleagues. In the wash-up, it was learned that of the 39 witnesses who were interviewed, only two of them had described Levi as having 'lunged' before the shots were fired – and both of those witnesses had been questioned by the *Bondi* detectives, the workmates of Dilorenzo and Podesta. Worse, McDougall's police superiors never once intervened, leaving the detective alone and isolated. They should have sensed, given that the tragedy was so huge, that more resources were needed – *independent* resources. There was the failure to segregate the officers, the 'on-the-run' decision to allow some of the police to make up their own versions of the shooting, rather than being questioned. And, of course, the media conference on the Bondi kerbside, given before Podesta and Dilorenzo had even been interviewed, allowing a police-friendly version to gain currency before any facts had been established. This all happened before lunchtime.

McDougall's efforts, however stoic, were never helped. The failure of the Bondi police commander, and Internal Affairs, to tell him that the shooters were suspects in major drugs inquiries was breathtaking. That revelation would have changed completely the nature of McDougall's enquiries. The forensic examiner, Senior Constable Clinton Nicol, sent to the beach to take measurements and identify clues that could have held the key to the shooting, omitted to put in his official statement to the coroner that the shooters had been 5.2 metres away from Levi, over two metres outside the recognised danger zone. He relegated this important fact to his notebook. It was only unearthed by the Newcastle lawyers at the inquest.

All of these breaches were significant on their own, but cumulatively they give reason aplenty to doubt the inquiry's efficacy. Every one of the unfortunate incidents and procedural breaches happened under the nose of a police inspector who had been sent from Internal Affairs specifically to ensure that the Levi case was an example of investigative excellence; to make sure all officers were following procedures.

But the Levi investigation didn't just fail on a police level. The police watchdogs, the coroner, the lawyers – and the political authorities, who made impassioned speeches at the time of the death, promising accountability – also failed. There can be no doubt that the coroner was in charge of the Levi investigation, just as he commands, technically speaking, every reportable death. However, he never *acted* as if he was fully in charge – delegating to his counsel assisting who, in turn, relied on McDougall, his police investigator. In theory, the coroner was at the helm, but in practice, the police were at the wheel. It cannot be overlooked that it took over 30 days for the Bromwich statement (the first indication that the shooters could have been affected at the time of the shooting) to be passed to McDougall by David Cowan. In such a convoluted line of reporting, these discrepancies can easily be explained, or explained away. The coroner, Derrick Hand, praised McDougall's investigation at the inquest – but then McDougall's case was, after all, under the command of the coroner.

The secret meeting with the coroner was also regrettable. It was held for two reasons: to give Hand, the official in charge of the inquiry, an update on the allegations that the Bondi shooters might have been high when they killed Levi; and to determine which squad of investigators – McDougall's team or Internal Affairs – should be responsible for investigating the allegations. The meeting, of course, turned out to be a shambles. But who to blame? Should the coroner be criticised for the fact that no-one investigated the drug allegations raised at the secret meeting? And that the problem was only learned in the week before the inquest? Should Cowan, his counsel assisting, or Stuart Robinson, the instructing solicitor from the Crown Solicitor's Office, be officially reprimanded? And Tim Sage from the Police Integrity Commission, what was his role? Why was he invited to the secret meeting? Was Sage, as watchdog, simply invited to watch – or was his presence demanded to ensure that things were done properly and above board? And shouldn't Internal Affairs' Assistant Commissioner Mal Brammer and Gary Richmond carry some of the blame for the fact that neither McDougall nor Internal Affairs investigated claims the shooters were stoned? The problem with apportioning blame is that each representative bears responsibility.

The other tragedy that emerged in the Levi investigation, however, is that each of these representatives was not called to the witness box at the Saigon hearings to account for his inaction. This dirty job of explaining a bungle was left to Brammer and McDougall, the coppers. The PIC decided to call these policemen, rather than the principal authority figures, to answer for this most incredible of miscommunications. Hand, Cowan, Robinson and Sage were considered important enough not to take the oath – and that is deserving of censure. Richmond was called out-of-session (and out of the public's gaze) to give his evidence; and when his testimony was released, it was censored. Given the enormity of the bungle, the non-appearance of the other participants is hard to fathom. It also highlights the way the PIC conducted the Saigon hearings.

It is this author's opinion that some of the witnesses got off with very light questioning, something that, it can be argued, would not have occurred if Robert Cavanagh from the Newcastle Legal Centre had been given the floor. The fact that Richard Baker, the Bondi commander at the time of the shooting, was not asked about the media conference that so tainted the Levi case is extraordinary. More seriously, he was not questioned on his failure to inform McDougall of the drugs allegations. Not one question. When the police watchdog lets such obvious questions go by unexplained, it surely leaves itself open to criticism. It can therefore be argued that the authorities – the coroner, the Crown lawyers and the PIC – were involved in the embarrassment; albeit at the end. Notwithstanding the number of police breaches in the case and their undisputed seriousness, each of these senior community figures unwittingly played a part in burying the truth.

The media played a disturbing role. In the aftermath of the Peter Forsyth stabbing, the promotion of the Bondi shooters as role models came naturally. Media commentators urged restraint from those campaigning for justice in the Levi case – pleading that their grief should not translate into venom against the shooters and that the evidence, when it was collected, should be allowed to be speak for itself. But when it came to telegraphing the community's outrage over Forsyth, and capturing the mood of the moment, the media showed no such restraint. In large part, Podesta and Dilorenzo were celebrated as heroes.

Drugs and the company young police officers tend to keep were the other issues to emerge from the Saigon hearings. Podesta and Dilorenzo were shown to have moved in a nefarious circle of friends. It begged the question: how many other police officers mixed in similar company? How deeply had the scourge of drugs infiltrated the ranks, made up increasingly of officers brought up not in a beer culture, but in one of grass, pills and powder.

In the PIC's third hearing, beginning on 21 February 2000 (which examined the serious policy implications of the Levi case), the history of police and illicit drugs, and drug testing was laid bare, like an open book.

In troubling evidence, the police's manager of the Healthy Lifestyles Branch, Gary Jackel, told how a drug-testing regime had been introduced in the months before the

Levi shooting – provoked, in large measure, by revelations at the royal commission showing young policemen and women regularly dabbling in drugs. In March 1997, at the urging of Justice Wood, Police Commissioner Peter Ryan was given the power to randomly test his ranks. The laws were cleared for use at the start of June, four weeks before Dilorenzo and Podesta fired the four fatal shots and right at the time the Bondi shooters were regularly nightclubbing and mingling with drug-taking friends. Samantha, the prostitute-cum-girlfriend of Podesta, told the PIC that Podesta was concerned by the prospect of drug-testing. When Levi was shot, the police did not compel Podesta and Dilorenzo to give urine samples and enforce the new laws, as they were entitled to.

Ryan gave drug-affected officers a chance. The commissioner's much-vaunted drugs policy started with a moratorium, allowing cops to come forward with their problems without fear of being sacked or disciplined. Officers were given lectures and drug-awareness posters were put on noticeboards – and the same policies were applied to alcohol dependency. But random breath testing for booze was far easier to operate than having to obtain urine samples in drug tests. In the beginning, 1000 officers were randomly selected to give urine samples for drugs – and only four of the officers tested positive to cannabis, with sixteen having legally obtainable opiate codeine in their system. Given that it was a one-off program held at the end of a huge publicity drive, the results were potentially illusory. However, this did not deter the police union from seizing on the statistics as being proof positive that no widespread drug problem existed – and that no random testing should be introduced.

Despite Ryan's efforts, the union won the police minister's support to constrain drug testing to a limited sphere of operation. Overshadowed by the raw data was a survey that revealed significant alcohol abuse problems, with 8.6 per cent of males and 15.6 per cent of women officers reporting an intake considered hazardous to health. Twelve per cent of officers reported using drugs, including prescription drugs, for stress-release purposes – and often while on duty. Seven per cent of officers stated they knew other officers who used illegal drugs, like anabolic steroids.

At the PIC's third hearing, Jackel said officers suspected of being drug-takers were subject to targeted tests, but that no random sampling was permitted. Of the 53 target tests conducted between November 1998 and January 2000, fifteen officers tested positive to illegal drugs. There were also 75 so-called 'critical incidents', with 223 officers being mandatorily tested. No officers had recorded an alcohol reading but one officer had cannabis in his system and another officer showed up for morphine. In March 2001, a member of the State Protection Group tested for cannabis after the fatal shooting of a man on a bush property in southern New South Wales.

Jackel said, based on intelligence and an assessment of recruiting patterns, that it was reasonable to 'expect that approximately half of the students going through the Academy would have been exposed to illicit substance use at some stage in their lives.'[1] He then went on to say, in contrast to the union's steadfast position, that 'a random drug testing program would act as a deterrent to those individuals.'[2]

In the time before the PIC delivered its official findings, some of its victims rolled through the courts. Easton 'TC' James, was convicted of supplying cocaine and sentenced to six months' home detention. This is a non-custodial system where prisoners wear electronic anklets and sleep in their own beds. TC's supplier, Lenin Lambert, pleaded guilty to one count of supplying a prohibited drug – and was placed on a fifteen-month suspended sentence. His girlfriend, Lisa Troost, saw a judge quash her indictment on cocaine charges. Levi's widow, Melinda Dundas, with the backing of the Newcastle Legal Centre, launched a civil action in late 2000 in the NSW District Court alleging negligence in the case and nervous shock. Dilorenzo and Podesta put in an application at the NSW Victim's Compensation Tribunal, looking for the maximum $50 000 payment for their suffering.

In a sympathetic interview in April 2001 in the popular women's magazine, *New Idea*, Dilorenzo revealed he had separated from Annabelle – but was engaged to be married to a new flame. Working for a gas bottle company, Dilorenzo said he was writing a book on his experiences. Podesta last got a mention on 15 June 2001 when the newspaper social columnist, Ros Reines, speculated he was on the verge of getting engaged to 'one of Sydney's most exotic women . . . Lucy, an award-winning model and pole dancer at the exclusive Men's Gallery and Dancers venue in the city'.[3]

On 15 June 2001, the Police Commission tabled its final report in the NSW Parliament. The PIC's recommendation for random drug testing persuaded Police Minister Paul Whelan, on the day of the report's release, to order its immediate introduction. But it was a belated concession. Weeks earlier, Whelan had remarked that random testing was not needed and overly expensive to justify. The PIC report detailed how Commissioner Ryan wanted to push ahead with snap drug tests in May 1999, but had been blocked by opposition from the police union and by the minister's intransigence. 'In November 1999, a submission was directed to the minister seeking a formal direction on where to go . . . There had been no response . . . by 2 March 2000,' the PIC revealed in its report.[4] 'The commission has been advised that there has been no response from the minister as at May 2001. The delay in progress in this most important area is a matter of concern. Prompt action in this issue is clearly in the public interest.'[5] Ryan said up to 600 random tests would be conducted in the first year of operation, starting in September 2001. The tests would use hair or urine samples, although consideration would be given to the PIC's preference for officers to give blood so a more accurate drug reading could be obtained.

The report criticised the evidence given by the Bondi shooters and by the Liberty Lunch principles, Kieran O'Connor and TC, Easton Barrington James, and found they all either used or supplied cocaine and, in some cases, ecstasy. It found that Podesta's testimony was unacceptable: he regularly used cocaine, ecstasy and other drugs before he became a policeman, while he served as a constable, and before and after the Levi killing. The PIC also found Dilorenzo's evidence to be chequered and lacking in credibility. It recommended Podesta and TC be considered for further drug charges.

The report condemned the shooting investigation, and the inquiries into claims the shooters were affected by drugs when they shot Levi. It found 'that no orderly or structured control was taken of the shooting immediately after it occured [and] it is clear that there was a systemic failure to comply with the then procedures, and there was a real risk that such an important investigation may have been carried out by officers who might be perceived as not being at arm's length from Podesta and Dilorenzo.'[6] The report declared that 'the allegations that both officers were affected by drugs and/or alcohol were not adequately investigated by either Internal Affairs or the shooting investigation team.'[7] It highlighted the failure of these teams to work together to share information about the shooters' behaviour 'resulting in some information not being investigated adequately and other information being effectively lost.'[8]

Judge Urquhart, in a press release, said it was troubling that Dilorenzo and Podesta, and other officers, were attending nightclubs; some of which were off-limits and that this was happening 'at the same time, and shortly after the release of the royal commission's final report. It seems the impact of the royal commission has not been felt amongst some younger officers.'[9] He went on to describe the Levi case as a 'powerful example of the necessity for an effective system of drug and alcohol testing of police officers . . . if both officers had been drug tested after the incident, there would be no doubts as to whether they were affected by drugs and alcohol at the time.'[10] Indeed, doubts still lingered. The PIC said the evidence did not support a finding that either Dilorenzo or Podesta were high when they killed Levi, but Commissioner Ryan, at a media conference to discuss the report, said he didn't want to comment about anything that happened at Bondi that morning and he could not rule out that both had been drug affected at the time of the shooting: 'I can't be confident in anything. The inquiry failed to ascertain either way. Had the officers been subject to tests we would have known one way or the other.'[11]

ENDNOTES

One: The Liberty Lunch

[1] Allan Graney, Police Integrity Commission, Operation Saigon, 11 November 1999.

[2] Robert Gould, ibid., 3 November 1999.

[3] Kieran Brian O'Connor, ibid., 4 November 1999.

[4] ibid.

[5] Graney said he used cocaine when he was 'doing the banking a couple of times . . . counting the till, making sure it balanced . . . between 12.30 and two in the morning'. Allan Graney, ibid., 11 November 1999.

[6] Graney said his customers offered him cocaine because 'they just thought it would be a nice thing. They'd be intoxicated; they would just ask me if I wanted something and I would say yes'. ibid.

[7] 'Everybody else did [it] . . . pretty much that was there.' Madison Mander, ibid., 10 November 1999.

[8] Renee Robertshaw, ibid., 2 November 1999.

[9] O'Connor said he received reports about cocaine use at the Liberty Lunch from his managers – 'and I also saw it with my own eyes, empty bags in the toilets'. He also asked TC and Stephen Langton if 'they knew of anybody that they may have thought was doing it, to try and make sure they got them out of the place' [but] 'it was endemic in most places like this'. Kieran O'Connor, ibid., 4 November 1999.

[10] TC was observing cocaine consumption 'all the time – not people doing it, but you knew it was being done . . . when you'd clean up at the end of the night, you would see bags and things on the floor'. Easton Barrington James, ibid., 4 November 1999.

[11] Kieran O'Connor, ibid., 4 November 1999.

[12] Robert Gould, ibid., 3 November 1999.

[13] Witness SA2, ibid., 10 November 1999.

[14] Anthony Stephen Dilorenzo, ibid., 2 November 1999.

[15] O'Connor also claimed that 'at least 40 officers' had sampled something on the Liberty's menu in the months prior to Roni Levi's shooting. Kieran O'Connor, ibid., 4 November 1999.

[16] Richard Raymond Baker, ibid., 4 November 1999.

[17] Michael John Cooper, ibid., 24 February 2000.

[18] Richard Baker, ibid., 4 November 1999.

[19] Michael Cooper, ibid., 24 February 2000.

[20] '[Podesta] was a close friend of everyone [in the Liberty Lunch].' Easton James, ibid., 4 November 1999.

[21] ibid.

[22] Kieran O'Connor, ibid., 4 November 1999.

[23] Rodney Joseph Walter Podesta, ibid., 2 November 1999.

[24] Mike Morrison said that he and Rodney 'may have smoked a joint together at a surf club party or maybe on the hill . . . within the fraternity, we do smoke pot, as it's commonly known and Rodney and I would smoke pot together'. Mike Morrison, ibid., 3 November 1999.

[25] As Morrison himself informed the Police Integrity Commission. ibid.

[26] Madison Mander, ibid., 10 November 1999.

[27] Ronald Quin, ibid., 2 November 1999.

[28] Patrick Eduardo Brown, ibid., 24 February 2000.

[29] Graeme Rooney, ibid., 3 November 1999.

[30] ibid.

[31] ibid.

[32] Constable Patrick Brown later credited Dilorenzo with 'running' the club and even writing the letters 'LDC' inside its members' police hats, but 'there was no list or anything'. Patrick Brown, ibid., 24 February 2000.

[33] Witness SA2, ibid., 10 November 1999.

[34] Richard Baker, ibid., 4 November 1999.

[35] Baker felt Dilorenzo's disciplinary problem was 'emotional' due to 'household type problems' such as his wife's pregnancy. ibid.

[36] Mark Lorenzo, ibid., 15 November 1999.

[37] Anthony Dilorenzo, ibid., 2 November 1999.

[38] Mark Lorenzo, ibid., 15 November 1999.

[39] Lorenzo said it wasn't too often that he'd have to buy a drink in the clubs because 'my God, hundreds of people' were shouting him. He knew a lot of people 'and they knew what hardship I had [had] and they returned, sort of, the favour in buying me a drink'. ibid.

[40] ibid.

[41] ibid.

[42] Richard Baker, ibid., 4 November 1999.

[43] Patrick Brown, ibid., 24 February 2000.

[44] Senior Constable Cooper reported that Brown was quite 'indignant that Mr Baker should make the Liberty Lunch off limits to anybody in their social time'. Michael Cooper, ibid., 24 February 2000.

[45] Baker reported that he told Podesta that 'it was unwise to be seen there off duty because of some of the concerns that the police service had in relation to their activities'. Richard Baker, ibid., 4 November 1999.

[46] Gould often bought 'from one to three grams' of coke at a time, simply 'as much as I needed'. Robert Gould, ibid., 3 November 1999.

[47] Peter Johnson, SC, counsel assisting, ibid., 3 November 1999.

[48] Robert Gould, ibid., 3 November 1999.

[49] ibid.

[50] TC recalled that Podesta wouldn't 'listen to anyone . . . it doesn't matter what you tell him when it comes to a female he hasn't been with before. There's no stopping him. He's like a train that was out of control'. Easton James, ibid., 16 November 1999.

[51] ibid.

[52] ibid.

[53] O'Connor remembered that 'Rodney certainly had a very, very high success rate with the females.' Kieran O'Connor, ibid., 4 November 1999.

[54] Known as 'Witness SA2' in evidence before Police Integrity Commission, Operation Saigon, 10 November 1999.

[55] Easton James, Police Integrity Commission, Operation Saigon, 16 November 1999.

[56] Kieran O'Connor, ibid., 16 November 1999.

[57] TC tended to 'give people a second chance'. ibid.

[58] TC told Podesta 'plain that I didn't think it was a good idea and it wouldn't be good for him to be seen with her and to be going out with her'. ibid.

[59] ibid.

[60] ibid.

[61] Witness SA2, ibid., 10 November 1999.

[62] ibid.

[63] According to Podesta's mother, her husband was 'on a walking frame and very sick' and often bedridden. Podesta's presence must have been a great help to his mother as she 'didn't really sleep at that time' since his father 'had had strontium-90 injected and he had dreadful pain in the ribs and where the tumours were'. Charmaine Julie Podesta, ibid., 12 November 1999.

[64] ibid.

Two: Living Dangerously

[1] Duncan said he looked under cubicle doors to see if 'more than one set of feet' were in each cubicle. If so, he'd make sure they left the club 'because the police may form an opinion that there are drugs being done on the premises'. Simon Duncan, Police Integrity Commission, Operation Saigon, 10 November 1999.

[2] ibid.

[3] ibid.

[4] ibid.

[5] ibid.

[6] ibid.

[7] Duncan said he probably told Dilorenzo that what his friends had just done in the toilets was 'a stupid thing to do'. ibid.

[8] Anthony Stephen Dilorenzo, ibid., 2 November 1999.

[9] Exhibit 15, ibid., 15 November 1999.

[10] Royal Commission into the New South Wales Police Service, *Final Report, Volume I: Corruption*, 1997, p.100.

[11] The beat police told Baker they were worried about 'some of the associates that Rodney Podesta was . . . [being] seen with . . . not necessarily inside the Liberty Lunch but . . . in the Bondi area' generally, while he was off duty. Some of these associates were recognised as possibly 'being involved with . . . drug activities'. Richard Raymond Baker, ibid., 4 November 1999.

[12] ibid.

[13] Allan Graney, ibid., 11 November 1999.

[14] Stanley Victor Dowse, ibid., 11 November 1999.

[15] Malcolm James Brammer, ibid., 22 February 2000.

[16] ibid.

[17] Richard Baker, ibid., 4 November 1999.

[18] ibid.

[19] ibid.

[20] ibid.

[21] Exhibit 1AC, ibid., 21 February 2000.

[22] ibid.

[23] Christopher Patrick Keen, ibid., 21 February 2000.

[24] ibid.

[25] Richard Baker, ibid., 4 November 1999.

[26] Simon Duncan, ibid., 10 November 1999.

[27] Alternatively, Duncan presumed that another doorman at the Soho must have reported the incident directly to Internal Affairs. ibid.

[28] ibid.

[29] ibid.

[30] ibid.

[31] Michael John Cooper, ibid., 24 February 2000.

[32] Patrick Edward Brown, ibid., 24 February 2000.

[33] Richard Baker, ibid., 4 November 1999.

[34] ibid.

[35] Anthony Dilorenzo, ibid., 1 March 2000.

[36] Michael Cooper, ibid., 24 February 2000.

[37] ibid.

[38] ibid.

Three: The Night Before

[1] Nick Papadopoulos, 'Standover man "was harassing" Ron Levi', *Sydney Morning Herald*, 5 July 1997.

[2] ibid.

[3] ibid.

[4] Luke Slattery, 'After death, cold reality dawns on fatal shore', *Australian*, 7 March 1998.

[5] Liz Deegan, 'After finding happiness, spiritual quest still haunted Roni', *Daily Telegraph*, 3 July 1997.

[6] Slattery, op. cit.

[7] Deegan, op. cit.

[8] Slattery, op. cit.

[9] ibid.

[10] ibid.

[11] ibid.

[12] Deegan, op. cit.

[13] According to Dilorenzo, the main guests at the Friday fish nights were 'Annabelle's girlfriend Kathy and her kids . . . and Barry, Annabelle's father. Angelo [Astudillo] used to come . . . [and] my mother. Oh, there was just a number people.' Anthony Stephen Dilorenzo, Police Integrity Commission, Operation Saigon, 2 November 1999.

[14] Rodney Joseph Walter Podesta, ibid., 30 September 1999.

[15] ibid.

[16] Renee Robertshaw, ibid., 2 November 1999.

[17] Ronald Quin, ibid., 2 November 1999.

[18] Renee Robertshaw, ibid., 2 November 1999.

[19] Witness SA2, ibid., 10 November 1999.

[20] Statement of Dr Elizabeth Meagher, Inquest into the death of Ron Levi, 1997.

[21] Statement of Dr Brennan, ibid.

[22] Statement of John Palmer, ibid.

Four: A Beautiful Day

[1] Statement of Pascal Czerwenka, Inquest into the Death of Ron Levi, 1997.

[2] Statement of Arnold Payment, ibid.

[3] ibid.

[4] Statement of Sergeant Graham Taylor, ibid.

[5] Record of interview between Detective Senior Sergeant Robert McDougall and Anthony Dilorenzo, 28 June 1997.

[6] All police radio dispatches in this chapter are from official police communications log, tabled at coronial inquest.

[7] Statement of Pascal Czerwenka, Inquest into the Death of Ron Levi, 1997.

[8] Record of Interview between Detective Sergeant Michael Fitzgerald and Rodney Podesta, 28 June 1997.

[9] Statement of Leo Hamlin, Inquest into the Death of Ron Levi, 1997.

[10] Record of Interview between Detective Sergeant Michael Fitzgerald and Rodney Podesta, 28 June 1997.

[11] ibid.

[12] ibid.

[13] ibid.

[14] Record of Interview between Detective Senior Sergeant Robert McDougall and Anthony Dilorenzo, 28 June 1997.

[15] Record of Interview between Detective Sergeant Michael Fitzgerald and Rodney Podesta, 28 June 1997.

[16] Sergeant Graham Taylor, Evidence at Coronial Inquest, February–March 1998, cross-examination (Cavanagh).

[17] Record of Interview between Detective Senior Sergeant Robert McDougall and Anthony Dilorenzo, 28 June 1997.

[18] ibid.

[19] Luke Slattery, 'After death, cold reality dawns on fatal shore', *Australian*, 7 March 1998.

[20] Record of Interview between Detective Senior Sergeant Robert McDougall and Anthony Dilorenzo, 28 June 1997.

[21] ibid.

[22] Slattery, op. cit., 7 March 1998.

[23] Constable Christopher Goodman, Evidence at Coronial Inquest, February–March 1998.

[24] Record of Interview between Detective Senior Sergeant Robert McDougall and Anthony Dilorenzo, 28 June 1997.

[25] Record of Interview between Detective Sergeant Michael Fitzgerald and Rodney Podesta, 28 June 1997.

[26] Statement of Senior Constable Grant Seddon, Inquest into the Death of Roni Levi, 28 June 1997.

[27] ibid.

[28] Record of Interview between Detective Senior Sergeant Robert McDougall and Anthony Dilorenzo, 28 June 1997.

[29] ibid.

[30] Mike Morrison, Police Integrity Commission, Operation Saigon, 3 November 1999.

Five: After the Shots

[1] Senior Constable John Jones, Inquest into the Death of Roni Levi, 1997.

[2] Statement of Sergeant Graham Taylor, Inquest into the Death of Roni Levi, 1997.

[3] Record of Interview between Detective Senior Sergeant Robert McDougall and Anthony Dilorenzo, 28 June 1997.

[4] Official police communications log, tabled at Coronial Inquest.

[5] Record of Interview between Detective Senior Sergeant Robert McDougall and Anthony Dilorenzo, 28 June 1997.

[6] ibid.

[7] ibid.

[8] John Lewis Jones, Police Integrity Commission, Operation Saigon, 29 February 2000.

[9] Statement of Dr Reginald Lord, Inquest into the Death of Roni Levi, 1997.

[10] ibid.

[11] Clinical Record on Levi admission, St Vincent's Hospital, 28 June 1997.

[12] National Nine News, 28 June 1997.

[13] ibid.

[14] Peter Thomas Fitzpatrick, Police Integrity Commission, Operation Saigon, 23 February 2000.

[15] Constable Jones recalled that 'throughout the remaining hours, we'd continually just bump into each other . . . [and say] you know, "How are you going?" . . . that sort of thing'. John Jones, ibid., 29 February 2000.

[16] Peter Thomas Fitzpatrick, ibid., 23 February 2000.

[17] Tim Barlass, 'My husband had to shoot', *The Daily Telegraph*, 3 July 1997.

[18] Renee Robertshaw, Police Integrity Commission, Operation Saigon, 2 November 1999.

[19] ibid.

[20] Robert Gould, ibid., 3 November 1999.

[21] ibid.

[22] Kieran Brian O'Connor, Police Integrity Commission, Operation Saigon, 4 November 1999.

[23] Record of Interview between Detective Senior Sergeant Robert McDougall and Easton Barrington James, 13 November 1997.

[24] Robert Norman McDougall, Police Integrity Commission, Operation Saigon, 28 February 2000.

[25] ibid.

[26] McDougall thought Sunday 'would be a time of regathering as to . . . strategies . . . [and] how we go about it' and they would begin on Monday morning with 'independent police [from areas outside Bondi police station] interviewing the witnesses'. ibid.

[27] ibid.

[28] Philip Cornford, Nick Papadopoulos, Jane Freeman & Malcolm Brown, 'Should police shoot to kill', *Sydney Morning Herald*, 1 July 1997.

[29] *Wentworth Courier*, 2 July 1997.

Six: The Remains of the Day

[1] Patrick Eduardo Brown, Police Integrity Commission, Operation Saigon, 24 February 2000.

[2] ibid.

[3] ibid.

[4] Graeme Rooney, Police Integrity Commission, Operation Saigon, 3 November 1999.

[5] Robert Norman McDougall, ibid., 28 February 2000.

[6] Stanley Victor Dowse, ibid., 11 November 1999.

[7] Clinical Records of Levi admission, St Vincent's Hospital, 28 June 1997.

[8] Report of Death to the Coroner, p79A, 28 June 1997.

[9] Record of Interview between Detective Senior Sergeant Robert McDougall and Anthony Dilorenzo, 28 June 1997.

[10] Record of Interview between Detective Sergeant Michael Fitzgerald and Rodney Podesta, 28 June 1997.

[11] Record of Interview between Detective Senior Sergeant Robert McDougall and Anthony Dilorenzo, 28 June 1997.

[12] Tim Barlass, 'My husband had to shoot', *Daily Telegraph*, 3 July 1997.

[13] Charmaine Julie Podesta, Police Integrity Commission, Operation Saigon, 12 November 1999.

[14] Record of Interview between Detective Senior Sergeant Robert McDougall and Easton Barrington James, 13 November 1997.

[15] Terry Voto, Police Integrity Commission, Operation Saigon, 2 November 1999.

[16] ibid.

[17] Angelo Osvaldo Astudillo, Police Integrity Commission, Operation Saigon, 15 November 1999.

[18] ibid.

[19] Luke Slattery, 'After death, cold reality dawns on fatal shore', *Australian*, 7 March 1998.

[20] Bronwen Gora & Sarah Harris, 'Wife identifies body after police shooting', *Sunday Telegraph*, 29 June 1997.

[21] Statement of Robert McDougall, Inquest into the Death of Roni Levi, 2 October 1997.

[22] Murray James Wilson, Police Integrity Commission, Operation Saigon, 29 February 2000.

[23] John Lewis Jones, ibid., 29 February 2000.

[24] Rodney Joseph Walter Podesta, ibid., 30 September 1999.

Seven: Wasted Time

[1] Luke Slattery, 'After death, cold reality dawns on fatal shore', *Australian*, 7 March 1998.

[2] Danny Weidler, 'Shot dead as I watch', *Sun-Herald*, 29 June 1997.

[3] ibid.

[4] Mark Jones, 'Hundreds threaten distraught officers', *Daily Telegraph*, 1 July 1997.

[5] 'Minister pledges inquiry', *Sunday Telegraph*, 29 June 1997.

[6] Patricia Le Roy, 'Letters to the Editor', *Sydney Morning Herald*, 1 July 1997.

[7] Clarissa Bye, Daniel Dasey & Heath Gilmore, 'Beach police face inquiry', *Sun-Herald*, 29 June 1997.

[8] Adam Michael Purcell, Police Integrity Commission, Operation Saigon, 29 February 2000.

[9] Philip Cornford, Nick Papadopoulos, Jane Freeman & Malcolm Brown, 'Should police shoot to kill', *Sydney Morning Herald*, 1 July 1997.

[10] Robert Norman McDougall, Police Integrity Commission, Operation Saigon, 28 February 2000.

[11] Statement of Robert McDougall, Inquest into the Death Of Roni Levi, 2 October 1997.

[12] ibid.

[13] Malcolm Thomas Brammer, Police Integrity Commission, Operation Saigon, 22 February 2000.

[14] Christopher Patrick Keen, ibid., 21 February 2000.

[15] ibid.

[16] Robert McDougall, ibid., 28 February 2000.

[17] Jeane MacIntosh, Stephen Gibbs & Shoshana Lenthan, 'Beach shooting man's last supper', *Daily Telegraph*, 1 July 1997.

[18] Dr Allan Cala, Autopsy Report on Roni Levi, 1 July 1997.

[19] ibid.

[20] ibid.

[21] Adam Purcell, Police Integrity Commission, Operation Saigon, 29 February 2000.

[22] Statement of Leo Hamlin, Inquest into the Death of Roni Levi, 30 June 1997.

[23] Jeane MacIntosh & Mark Jones, 'Why so slow', *Daily Telegraph*, 2 July 1997.

[24] Acting Police Commissioner Jeff Jarratt, ABC Radio, 1 July 1997.

[25] MacIntosh & Jones op. cit.

[26] Coroner Derrick Hand, 'Inquest into the Death of the Late Roni Levi', press release, 3 July 1997.

[27] Jeane MacIntosh, 'They didn't have to shoot him', *Daily Telegraph*, 3 July 1997.

[28] ibid.

[29] Geraldine Walsh, 'Postscript', *Sydney Morning Herald*, 7 July 1997.

[30] Leo Schofield, 'A force to reckon with', *Sydney Morning Herald*, 5 July 1997.

[31] David Landa, 'Police and the use of firearms', Letters to the Editor, *Sydney Morning Herald*, 4 July 1997.

[32] Tim Barlass, 'My husband had to shoot', *Daily Telegraph*, 3 July 1997.

[33] ibid.

[34] ibid.

[35] Letters to the Editor, *Daily Telegraph*, 3 July 1997.

[36] Miranda Devine, 'Shooting down the critics', *Daily Telegraph*, 3 July 1997.

[37] Nick Papadopoulos, 'Death at Bondi: Body flown out', *Sydney Morning Herald*, 4 July 1997.

[38] Graeme Rooney, Police Integrity Commission, Operation Saigon, 11 November 1999.

[39] ibid.

[40] TC told Podesta that he shouldn't 'sit at home because of this . . . you have to go out . . . to dinner . . . have a couple of drinks.' Record of Interview between Detective Senior Sergeant Robert McDougall and Easton Barrington James, 13 November 1997.

[41] Stanley Victor Dowse, Police Integrity Commission, Operation Saigon, 11 November 1999.

Eight: The Secret Meeting

[1] 'To whoever feels guilty, to the Sydney Bondi police, to whom it may concern', open letter from Roni Levi's brothers, *Sydney Morning Herald*, 5 July 1997.

[2] Richard Guilliat, 'The Avengers', Good Weekend, *Sydney Morning Herald*, 22 July 2000.

[3] Statement of Robert Bromwich, Inquest into the Death of Roni Levi, 8 September 1997.

[4] Stefan Bialoguski, 'Change will be justice', *Sydney Morning Herald*, 7 July 1997.

[5] Bromwich said that he wanted to call Rafferty first 'as she would be less put off by having me call'. Statement of Robert Bromwich, Inquest into the Death of Roni Levi, 8 September 1997.

[6] ibid.

[7] ibid.

[8] Bernard Roy McSorley, Police Integrity Commission, Operation Saigon, 22 February 2000.

[9] ibid.

[10] Malcolm James Brammer, ibid., 22 February 2000.

[11] 'Amanda' is a name given to a person referred to at the Police Integrity Commission's Operation Saigon as 'SA1'.

[12] Peter Johnson, SC, counsel assisting, Police Integrity Commission, Operation Saigon, 21 February 2000.

[13] Peter Thomas Fitzpatrick, ibid., 23 February 2000.

[14] Christopher Patrick Keen, ibid., 22 February 2000.

[15] ibid.

[16] Malcolm Brammer, ibid., 22 February 2000.

[17] ibid.

[18] Robert Norman McDougall, ibid., 28 February 2000.

[19] Malcolm Brammer, ibid., 22 February 2000.

[20] Private correspondence between Newcastle Legal Centre and Crown Solicitor's Office, 23 September 1997.

[21] Robert McDougall, Police Integrity Commission, Operation Saigon, 28 February 2000.

[22] Malcolm Brammer, ibid., 22 February 2000.

[23] Robert McDougall, ibid., 28 February 2000.

[24] ibid.

[25] ibid.

[26] Peter Johnson, SC, counsel assisting, ibid., 28 February 2000.

[27] Fictional name given to a person referred to as 'Witness SA5', Police Integrity Commission, Operation Saigon.

[28] Peter Johnson, SC, counsel assisting, Police Integrity Commission, Operation Saigon, 22 February 2000.

[29] Alison Stenmark, counsel for the police commissioner, ibid., 22 February 2000.

[30] Christopher Keen, ibid., 22 February 2000.

[31] Malcolm Brammer, ibid., 22 February 2000.

[32] TC told police, when asked when he first met the Bondi shooters, 'God . . . [I've known them] for so long I can't remember,' and that the Liberty Lunch was 'the local place . . . a few [police officers] . . . go down there to have dinner or have a drink'. Record of Interview between Detective Senior Sergeant Robert McDougall and Easton Barrington James, 13 November 1997.

[33] ibid.

[34] ibid.

[35] Detective Senior Constable Michael Sinadinovic, Police Running Sheet information, Death of Roni Levi, 18 November 1997.

[36] Private correspondence between Crown Solicitor's Office and Newcastle Legal Centre, 24 November 1997.

[37] Private correspondence between Newcastle Legal Centre and Crown Solicitor's Office, 12 January 1998.

[38] Private correspondence between Newcastle Legal Centre and Crown Solicitor's Office, 19 January 1998.

[39] ibid.

Nine: Panic

[1] Michael Rumore, confidential private investigator's report, Inquest into the Death of Roni Levi, 9 February 1998.

[2] Stephen Langton, Police Integrity Commission, Operation Saigon, 11 November 1999.

[3] Allan Graney, ibid., 11 November 1999.

[4] Stanley Victor Dowse, ibid., 11 November 1999.

[5] ibid.

[6] Allan Graney, ibid., 11 November 1999.

[7] ibid.

[8] Michael Rumore, confidential private investigator's report, Inquest

into the Death of Roni Levi, 9 February 1998.

[9] Rodney Joseph Walter Podesta, Police Integrity Commission, Operation Saigon, 23 February 1999.

[10] ibid.

[11] The excerpts that follow are taken from the listening device transcript of conversation on 31 January 1998, used as evidence at Police Integrity Commission, Operation Saigon, 30 September 1999.

[12] Fictional name given to informant referred to in Police Integrity Commission, Operation Saigon.

[13] Exhibit 18C (memorandum of Detective Sergeant Keen), Police Integrity Commission, Operation Saigon, 10 February 1998

[14] Report of Robert McDougall to Crime Agencies, 4 February 1998.

[15] ibid.

[16] Christopher Patrick Keen, Police Integrity Commission, Operation Saigon, 22 February 2000.

[17] Anthony Stephen Dilorenzo, ibid., 23 February 1999.

[18] ibid.

[19] ibid.

[20] ibid.

[21] ibid.

[22] Exhibit 1 (Tape of conversation on 2 February 1998 between Rodney Podesta and Anthony Dilorenzo), tabled in evidence at the Police Integrity Commission.

[23] Michael Rumore, confidential private investigator's report, 9 February 1998.

[24] ibid.

[25] ibid.

[26] ibid.

[27] ibid.

Ten: The Inquest

[1] Jennifer Foreshaw, 'Pictures frame photographer's life and death', *Australian*, 9 February 1998.

[2] Liz Hannan, 'Why did our son die?', *Sun-Herald*, 8 February 1998.

[3] Foreshaw, op. cit., 9 February 1998.

[4] Nick Papadopoulos & Les Kennedy, 'Inquest will explore police "deadly force"', *Sydney Morning Herald*, 9 February 1998.

[5] David Cowan, counsel assisting, Inquest into the Death of Roni Levi,

9 February 1998.

[6] Philip Cornford, 'Revolvers handed over, but court tensions remain', *Sydney Morning Herald*, 19 February 1998.

[7] Richard Guilliatt, 'The Avengers', Good Weekend, *Sydney Morning Herald*, 22 July 2000.

[8] ibid.

[9] Cornford, op. cit., 19 February 1998.

[10] Caroline Overington, 'Police shooting victim quit hospital, court told', *Age*, 10 February 1998.

[11] ibid.

[12] David Cowan, counsel assisting, Inquest into Death of Roni Levi, 9 February 1998.

[13] Melinda Dundas, ibid.

[14] Dr Elizabeth Meagher, ibid., 10 February 1998.

[15] Kylie Keogh, 'Shot photographer "not psychotic"', *Daily Telegraph*, 11 February 1998.

[16] Ray Chesterton, 'Bricks came flying in the weeks of trauma', *Daily Telegraph*, 18 February 1998.

[17] Guilliatt, op. cit., 22 July 2000.

[18] Luke Slattery, 'After death, cold reality dawns on fatal shore', *Australian*, 7 March 1998.

[19] Stefanie Balogh, 'Police shooting probe biased, coroner told', *Australian*, 13 February 1998.

[20] Stefanie Balogh, 'Police retreated before shooting', *Australian*, 14 February 1998.

[21] Jean Pierre Bratanoff-Firgoff, Inquest into the Death of Roni Levi, 16 February 1998.

[22] ibid.

[23] ibid.

[24] Kylie Keogh, 'It was no movie', *Daily Telegraph*, 17 February 1998.

[25] Deborah Bogle, Inquest into the Death of Roni Levi, 17 February 1998.

[26] Peter Bourke, ibid.

[27] Statement of Karen Allison, Inquest into the Death of Roni Levi, July 1997.

[28] Letter of David Michael, ibid.

[29] Cornford, op. cit., 19 February 1998.

[30] ibid.

[31] Ray Chesterton, 'Bricks came flying in the weeks of trauma', *Daily Telegraph*, 18 February 1998.

[32] ibid.

[33] Sarah Harris, 'Life is hell for policeman', *Sunday Telegraph*, 22 February 1998.

[34] Honey Webb, 'Bystander tells of officers' last words before shooting', *Sydney Morning Herald*, 24 February 1998.

[35] Jennifer Cooke, 'Witness admits changing story', *Sydney Morning Herald*, 25 February 1998.

[36] ibid.

[37] Craig Payne, Inquest into the Death of Roni Levi, 26 February 1998.

[38] ibid.

[39] Darren Goodsir, Simon Crittle & Anna Patty, 'Stabbed for showing badge', *Sun-Herald*, 1 March 1998.

Eleven: True Blue

[1] Conversation between Rodney Podesta and Easton Barrington James in this chapter is quoted from a listening device transcript of recording at James's apartment on 28 February 1998, tabled in evidence at the Police Integrity Commission.

[2] Fictional name to person referred to at the Police Integrity Commission, Operation Saigon.

[3] Conversation between Easton Barrington James and Lenin Marx Lambert in this chapter is quoted from a listening device transcript of recording at James's apartment on 28 February 1998, tabled in evidence at the Police Integrity Commission.

[4] Les Kennedy & Michael Evans, 'Stabbed officer on mend as task force track killers', *Sydney Morning Herald*, 3 March 1998.

[5] ibid.

[6] Mark Riley, 'Blood on the beat', *Sydney Morning Herald*, 7 March 1998.

[7] Kennedy & Evans, op. cit.

[8] 'Today Show', Channel 9, 3 March 1998.

[9] Ray Chesterton, 'No other option but to shoot for the heart', *Daily Telegraph*, 4 March 1998.

[10] Senior Constable John Jones, Inquest into the Death of Roni Levi, 3 March 1998.

[11] ibid.

[12] Ray Chesterton, 'Officer's version has force', *Daily Telegraph*, 5 March 1998.

[13] Constable Christopher Goodman, Inquest into the Death of Roni

Levi, 4 March 1998.

[14] Kenneth Madden, counsel representing Dilorenzo and Podesta, ibid., 21 February 2000.

[15] Malcolm Brammer, ibid., 2 March 2000.

[16] ibid.

[17] Paul Jones, ibid., 21 February 2000.

[18] Riley, op. cit.

[19] Miranda Devine, 'Message is die and let live', *Daily Telegraph*, 10 March 1998.

[20] Fictional name given to person whose name was suppressed at the Police Integrity Commission, Operation Saigon.

[21] Peter Johnson, SC, counsel assisting, Police Integrity Commission, Operation Saigon, 21 February 2000.

[22] Record of Interview between Detective Sergeant Michael Fitzgerald and Constable Rodney Podesta, 28 June 1997.

[23] Robert Cavanagh, counsel for Melinda Dundas, Inquest into the Death of Roni Levi, 5 March 1998.

[24] Coroner Derrick Hand, ibid., 6 March 1998.

[25] ibid.

[26] ibid.

[27] ibid.

[28] ibid.

[29] ibid.

[30] Anabel Dean, 'Death on Bondi Beach . . . constables may be charged', *Sydney Morning Herald*, 7 March 1998.

[31] Australian Associated Press, 6 March 1998.

[32] ibid.

[33] Dean, op. cit.

[34] ibid.

[35] Australian Associated Press, 6 March 1998.

[36] ibid.

[37] Kylie Keogh, 'Under fire', *Daily Telegraph*, 7 March 1998.

[38] Dean, op. cit.

[39] Tim Barlass, 'True blue', *Daily Telegraph*, 10 March 1998.

[40] ibid.

[41] ibid.

[42] Mark Lorenzo, Letters, *Daily Telegraph*, 9 March 1998.

[43] ibid.

[44] Devine, op. cit.

[45] Tony Arena, Letters, *Sydney Morning Herald,* 12 March 1998.
[46] Coroner Derrick Hand, Inquest into the Death of Roni Levi, 11 March 1998.
[47] Editorial, 'Guns, police and alcohol', *Sydney Morning Herald,* 14 March 1998.
[48] Marcus Casey 'The upper hand', *Daily Telegraph,* 14 March 1998.

Twelve: Hunting Dilorenzo

[1] Conversation between Anthony Dilorenzo and Easton Barrington James in this chapter is quoted from a listening device transcript of recording at James's apartment on 1 April 1998, tabled in evidence at the Police Integrity Commission.
[2] David Hitchens, Police Integrity Commission, Operation Saigon, 25 February 1999.
[3] Conversation between David Hitchens and Easton Barrington James in this chapter is quoted from a listening device transcript of recording at James's apartment on 7 April 1998, tabled in evidence at the Police Integrity Commission.
[4] Darren Goodsir, 'Stake out on Bondi death cop', *Sun Herald,* 23 August 1998.
[5] ibid.
[6] Inspector Robert Monk, Statement of facts, Prosecution of Anthony Dilorenzo, reckless driving charge, July 1998.
[7] ibid.
[8] Goodsir, op. cit.
[9] Inspector Robert Monk, op. cit.
[10] Goodsir, op. cit.
[11] Roger Martin is a fictional name for a person who was referred to as 'Witness SA8' at the Police Integrity Commission, Operation Saigon.
[12] Alison Stenmark, counsel for the police commissioner, Police Integrity Commission, Operation Saigon, 21 February 2000.
[13] Fictional name for person whose name was suppressed at the Police Integrity Commission, Operation Saigon.
[14] Detective Inspector Paul Jones, Police Integrity Commission, Operation Saigon, 21 February 2000.
[15] Director of Public Prosecutions, press release, 30 June 1998.
[16] Tim Barlass & Letitia Rowlands, 'Elated and free', *Daily Telegraph,* 1 July 1998.

[17] Andrew Clennell, 'Levi's ex wife outraged at DPP decision', *Sydney Morning Herald*, 1 July 1998.

[18] ibid.

[19] Christian David Bruce, Police Integrity Commission, Operation Saigon, 17 February 1999.

[20] ibid.

[21] Fictional name given to person whose name was suppressed at the Police Integrity Commission, Operation Saigon.

[22] Christian Bruce, Police Integrity Commission, Operation Saigon, 17 February 1999.

[23] Fictional name of person whose name was suppressed at the Police Integrity Commission, Operation Saigon.

[24] Christian Bruce, Police Integrity Commission, Operation Saigon, 17 February 1999.

[25] ibid.

[26] ibid.

[27] Lenin Marx Lambert, Police Integrity Commission, Operation Saigon, 18 February 1999.

[28] Christian Bruce, Police Integrity Commission, Operation Saigon, 17 February 1999.

[29] ibid.

[30] Bugged conversation recorded between Lenin Marx Lambert and Cameron Weston (not his real name) on 4 July 1998, Police Integrity Commission, Operation Saigon.

[31] Goodsir, op. cit.

[32] Paul Jones, Police Integrity Commission, Operation Saigon, 21 February 2000.

[33] Lenin Marx Lambert, ibid., 18 February 1999.

Thirteen: The First Phase

[1] Lenin Marx Lambert, Police Integrity Commission, Operation Saigon, 18 February 1999.

[2] Easton Barrington James, ibid., 22 February 1999.

[3] Patrick Barrett, council assisting, ibid., 22 February 1999.

[4] Rodney Joseph Walter Podesta, ibid., 23 February 1999.

[5] Anthony Stephen Dilorenzo, ibid., 23 February 1999.

[6] Rodney Joseph Walter Podesta, ibid., 23 February 1999.

[7] Ken Horler, QC, ibid., 24 February 1999.

[8] Anthony Stephen Dilorenzo, ibid., 24 February 1999.
[9] David Hitchens, ibid., 25 February 1999.

Fourteen: The Second Phase

[1] Ken Horler, QC, Police Integrity Commission, Operation Saigon, 30 September 1999.
[2] ibid., 1 November 1999.
[3] Rodney Joseph Walter Podesta, ibid., 1 November 1999.
[4] ibid.
[5] Anthony Stephen Dilorenzo, ibid., 2 November 1999.
[6] Robert Gould, ibid., 3 November 1999.
[7] Easton Barrington James, ibid., 4 November 1999.
[8] Kieran Brian O'Connor, ibid.
[9] Mark Lorenzo, ibid., 15 November 1999.
[10] Witness SA2, ibid., 10 November 1999.
[11] Angelo Osvaldo Astudillo, ibid., 15 November 1999.
[12] Anthony Dilorenzo, ibid.
[13] Rodney Joseph Walter Podesta, ibid.
[14] Stephen Gibbs, 'Magistrate "sorry" to jail Podesta', *Sydney Morning Herald*, 10 December 1999.
[15] ibid.

Fifteen: End of the Line

[1] Gary Jackel, Manager, Police Healthy Lifestyles Branch, Police Integrity Commission, Operation Saigon, 2 March 2000.
[2] ibid.
[3] Ros Reines, 'The columnist they can't silence', *Sunday Telegraph*, 25 June 2000.
[4] Police Integrity Commission, Report to Parliament, Operation Saigon, 15 June 2001, p118.
[5] ibid, p118.
[6] ibid, page iv.
[7] ibid, page iv.
[8] ibid, page iv.
[9] Press Release, 'PIC releases report on drug use in NSW Police Service', 15 June 2001.
[10] ibid.
[11] Will Temple, 'Police drug tests after Levi shooting', *Daily Telegraph*, 16 June 2001.